ISBN: 9783598215995

eISBN: 9783598215988

CONTENTS

1. Early Years and Education

Erdoğan was born in the Kasımpasa quarter of Istanbul in 26 February 1954. Erdoğan's family originates from Güneysu, Rize which is is a province of north-east Turkey, on the eastern Black Sea coast. His parents are Ahmet Erdoğan and Tenzile Erdoğan. His father Ahmet Erdoğan (1905 – 1988) was a Captain in the Turkish Coast Guard and his mother Tenzile Erdoğan (1923-2011) was a tailor. Recep Tayyip Erdoğan had a brother Mustafa (b. 1958) and a sister Vesile (b. 1965). His summer holidays were mostly spent in Güneysu, Rize.

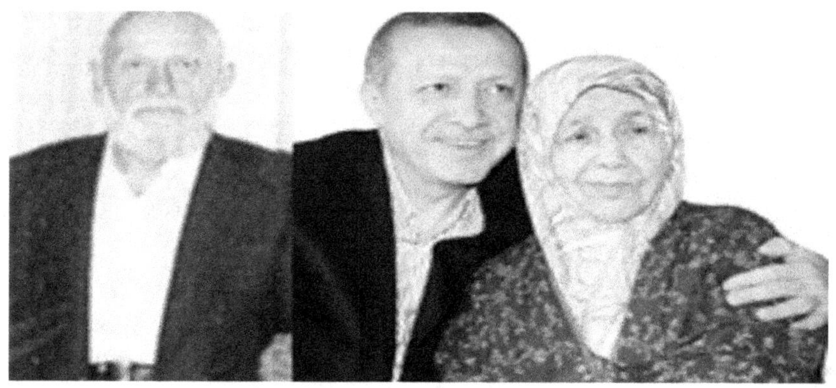

Figure 1: Ahmet Erdoğan(father), Recep Tayyip Erdoğan and Tenzile Erdoğan(mother)

Recep Tayyip Erdoğan graduated from Kasımpaşa Piyale Primary School in 1965. When he was a teenager, he sold lemonade and sesame buns (simit) on the streets of the Istanbul's rougher districts to earn extra money. He completed his high school education at Istanbul Imam Hatip School (Religious Vocational High School) in 1973. Having succeeded in the necessary examinations for additional courses, Erdoğan also received a diploma from Eyüp High School. At that time, Imam Hatip School students had to take additional courses from another high school for entering the university examination because İmam Hatip Schools' curriculum did not include some courses such as mathematics and physics. He later studied Business Administration at the Aksaray School of Economics and Commercial Sciences, today known as Marmara University's Faculty of Economics and Administrative Sciences. Erdoğan graduated from the university in 1981.

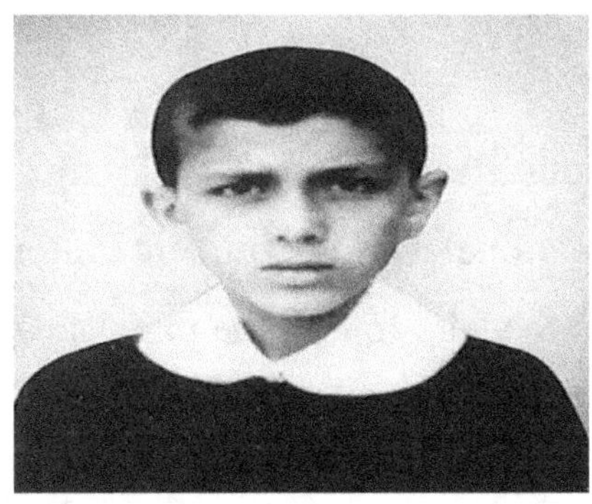

Figure 2: Erdoğan was a Primary school student in 1965

In his youth, Erdoğan played semi-professional football at some local clubs. Fenerbahçe wanted him to transfer to the club but his father prevented it.

Erdogan's adventure in football began when he was 15. He and his friends used to play with balls made out of paper in their neighborhood. While at the amateur club, Erokspor advised him to play in Camialtı, another leading amateur club in the 1970s. He played as a forward for Camialtı for seven years. He was also studying and doing youth politics at the same time.

After Camialtı, he was signed by İETT and played for seven years there. He enjoyed five titles in his seven years at İETT. It was a personal milestone for him. He was the captain there. He saw the red card once only in his career. It was because he objected the referee's decision.

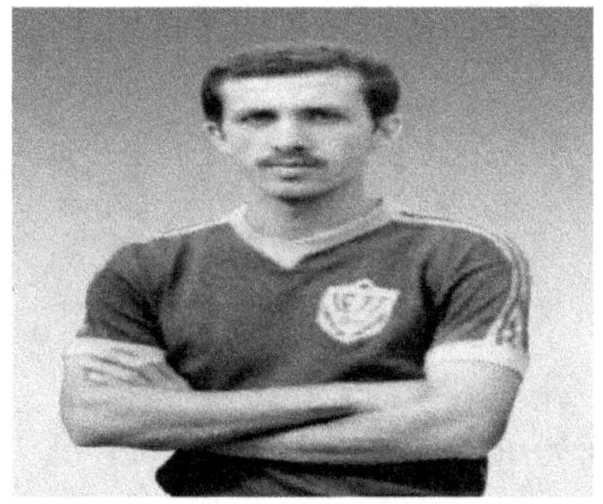

Figure 3: Erdoğan in IETT Sports Club

Speaking of how Erdogan's parents saw football as a career, Erdoğan told, "My mother never complained about it. She used to wash and iron my jersey. However, I could hardly convince my dad. My father would always say that I must study. He learned later that I was playing in a football club."

Mr. Erdoğan married Emine Gülbaran (b. 1955, Siirt) on 4 July 1978. The couple has two sons; Ahmet Burak and Necmettin Bilal, and two daughters; Esra and Sümeyye. Erdogan's father, Ahmet Erdoğan, died in 1988 and his 88-year-old mother, Tenzile Erdoğan, died in 2011.

2. Early politicial career

While he was studying business administration and playing semi-professional football, Erdoğan engaged in politics by joining the National Turkish Student Union, an anti-communist action group. In 1974, he wrote, directed and played the lead role in the play Maskomya, which presented Freemasonry, Communism and Judaism as negative concepts.

In 1976, he became the head of the Beyoğlu youth branch of the Islamist National Salvation Party (MSP), and was later promoted to chair of the Istanbul youth branch of the party. He hold this position until 1980 military coup.

The National Salvation Party was dissolved in the wake of a 1980 military coup. One year after the 12th September 1980 military coup, Erdogan earned a graduate degree from Marmara University's Faculty of Economics and Administrative Sciences in 1981. He served as consultant and senior executive in the private sector during the military coup era when the political parties were closed down.

Recep Tayyip Erdogan completed his military service as a reserve officer with the Istanbul Hasdal 77th Infantry Unit in 1982, after his training at the Tuzla Infantry School.

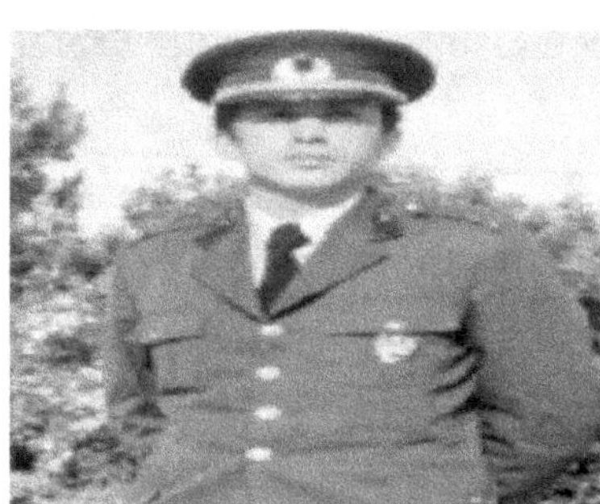

Figure 4: Erdoğan during his military service in 1982 in Tuzla, Istanbul.

Erdoğan return to political life with the Welfare Party, founded in 1983, and he was elected the Beyoğlu District Head of the Welfare Party in 1984. In 1985, he was elected the Istanbul Provincial Head of the Welfare Party and around the same time he became the member of the Central Executive Board of the Welfare Party.

Amid his incumbency as Istanbul Provincial Head, Recep Tayyip Erdoğan did ventures that went for asking the cooperation of ladies and youth in politics, hence stepping toward helping politics to be upheld and regarded among the majority.

2.1. Turkish parliamentary by-elections, 1986

The Turkish parliamentary by-elections of 1986 were held on 28 September 1986 with a specific end goal to choose 11 Members of Parliament to the Grand National Assembly of Turkey. The by-elections were held because of the vacation of 11 seats over the span of the seventeenth parliament. They took place in eleven different electoral districts, spanning ten provinces.

Erdoğan was the MP candidate for Istanbul from the Welfare Party. Welfare Party lost the by-elections and Erdoğan was not elected as an MP.

Party	Votes	%	Seats
Motherland Party	805,267	32.1	6
True Path Party	590,069	23.5	4
Social Democratic Populist Party	570,055	22.7	1
Democratic Left Party	213,168	8.5	0
Welfare Party	137,485	5.5	0
Nationalist Workers Party	55,144	2.2	0
Free Democracy Party	34,317	1.4	0
Great Nation Party	32,303	1.3	0
Citizen Party	25,814	1.0	0
Reformist Democracy Party	15,729	0.6	0
Great Anatolia Party	13,497	0.6	0
Flag Party	9,508	0.4	0
Independents	5,306	0.2	0
Invalid/blank votes	85,540	-	-
Total	**2,592,752**	**100**	**11**

Table 1: Results of the 1986 by-elections

2.2. Beyoglu local elections, 1989

Erdoğan stood up as a mayor candidate for the Beyoğlu of Istanbul. The figures presented below are the results of the 1989 Beyoğlu local elections.

Candidate	Party	Percentage	Votes	Swing
Hüseyin Aslan	Social Democratic Populist Party	29.29	27,847	
Recep Tayyip Erdoğan	**Welfare Party**	**22.83**	**21,706**	+17.71
Haluk Öztürkatalay	Motherland Party	20.60	19,579	-27.19
Doğan Yakupoğlu	True Path Party	15.26	14,502	+10.39
Osman Yılmazer	Democratic Left Party	10.83	10,295	
Niyazi Duranay	Independent	0.04	41	
	Nationalist Work Party	0.81	769	
	Reformist Democracy Party	0.34	321	
Total:		100.00	95,060	

Table 2: Beyoğlu local elections, 1989

2.3. General elections, 1991

Erdoğan became a candidate for parliament membership again and was elected in 1991 as one, after his party overcame the limit. Nevertheless, Supreme Committee of Elections dropped his parliament membership due to "preferential voting system". Rather than him, Mustafa Baş entered the parliament in that year.

2.4. Mayor of Istanbul

Erdoğan proceeded with his obligation as Istanbul Head of Province until 1994. In the local elections of 27 March 1994, Erdoğan was elected Mayor of Istanbul, with a plurality (25.19%) of the popular vote and became Metropolitan Mayor of Istanbul contradicting all estimations of media and surveys. The figures presented below are the results of the 1994 Istanbul mayoral elections.

Candidate	Party	Percentage	Votes
Recep Tayyip Erdoğan	**Welfare Party**	25.19	973,704
İlhan Kesici	Motherland Party	22.14	855.897
Zülfü Livaneli	Social Democratic Populist Party	20.30	784,693
Bedrettin Dalan	True Path Party	15.46	597,461
Necdet Özkan	Democratic Left Party	12.38	478,612
Ahmet Vefik Alp	Nationalist Movement Party	1.87	72,121
Ertuğrul Günay	Republician People's Party	1.40	54,028
	Others	1.25	48,610
Total:		100.00	3,865,126

Table 3: Istanbul mayoral elections, 1994

Amid his term in office as Mayor, he delivered remedy findings and answers for the constant issues of Istanbul, one of the world's most significant metropolitan cities through his political capacities, the significance he appended to cooperation and fruitful administration in HR and financial issues. The water issue was overwhelmed by laying several kilometers of new pipe line, the junk issue was comprehended through the foundation of the most current reusing offices and the issue of air contamination finished with the natural gas ventures created amid Erdoğan's term in office. In excess of 50 bridges, passengerways and turnpikes were built for solving traffic congestion and transportation deadlock and numerous more projects which would control alternate organizations in the city were created. Avoiding potential risk for the right effort of the city assets and to forestall defilement, Mr. Erdoğan paid a large portion of the obligations of the Istanbul Municipality which he assumed control with its 2 billion dollars obligation and he amid his residency accomplished speculations worth 4 billion dollars. Mr. Erdoğan, in this manner, achieved a leap forward in the civil history and keeping in mind that his works filled in as great models for different leaders, he won the certainty of the general population.

Erdoğan started the principal roundtable of chairmen amid the Istanbul gathering, which prompted a worldwide, sorted out development of leaders. A seven-part global jury from the United Nations consistently granted Erdoğan the UN-HABITAT grant.

2.5. Coalition Government and 1997 Military Memorandum

Welfare Party received over 19 percent of votes cast in the municipal elections of March 27, 1994. In 1994, Welfare Party captured the mayor's post in Turkey's two largest cities. (Istanbul and Ankara)

Party	Party leader	Vote	Percentage
True Path Party	Tansu Çiller	6,027,095	21.41%
Motherland Party	Mesut Yılmaz	5,937,031	21.09%
Welfare Party	Necmettin Erbakan	5,388,195	19.14%
Social Democratic Populist Party	Murat Karayalçın	3,807,921	13.53%
Democratic Left Party	Bülent Ecevit	2,463,853	8.75%
Nationalist Movement Party	Alparslan Türkeş	2,239,117	7.95%
Republican People's Party	Deniz Baykal	1,297,371	4.61%
Great Union Party	Muhsin Yazıcıoğlu	355,271	1.26%
Democratic Party	Aydın Menderes	148,719	0.53%
Nation Party	Aykut Edibali	126,118	0.45%
Rebirth Party	Hasan Celal Güzel	104,285	0.37%
Independent		96,913	0.34%
Socialist Union Party		80,714	0.29%
Workers' Party	Doğu Perinçek	79,588	0.28%
Total		28,152,191	100.00%

Table 4: 1994 local elections

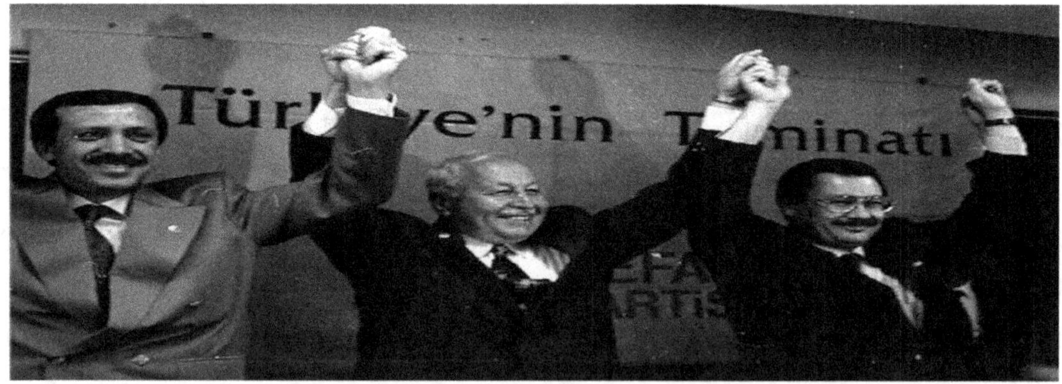

Figure 5: Erdoğan, Erbakan and Melih Gökçek, 1994 (Left to right)

The Welfare Party received over 21 percent of votes in the national elections of December 24, 1995. Despite Welfare Party captured more seats in the Turkish Grand National Assembly than any other party, it was rebuffed by other parties in its attempts to form a coalition government. After the repeated failure of centrist parties to form a viable coalition government, President Demirel offered

Prof. Dr. Necmettin Erbakan a new opportunity to create a government. After finding an unlikely coalition partner in the avowedly anti-Islamist True Path Party (Doğru Yol Partisi-DYP), Erbakan became Turkey's first Islamist prime minister in 1996.

Parties	Votes			Seats	
	No.	%	+ − %	No.	+ −
Welfare Party (*Refah Partisi - RP*)	6,012,450	21.38	+4.50	158	+96
Motherland Party (*Anavatan Partisi - ANAP*)	5,527,288	19.65	-4.36	132	+17
True Path Party (*Doğru Yol Partisi - DYP*)	5,396,009	19.18	-7.85	135	-43
Democratic Left Party (*Demokratik Sol Parti - DSP*)	4,118,025	14.64	+3.89	76	+69
Republican People's Party (*Cumhuriyet Halk Partisi - CHP*)	3,011,076	10.71	-10.04	49	-39
Nationalist Movement Party (*Milliyetçi Hareket Partisi - MHP*)	2,301,343	8.18		0	
People's Democracy Party (*Halkın Demokrasi Partisi - HADEP*)	1,171,623	4.17		0	
Independents	133,895	0.48	+0.35	0	
New Democracy Movement (*Yeni Demokrasi Hareketi - YDP*)	133.889	0.48		0	
Nation Party (*Millet Partisi - MP*)	127.630	0.45		0	
Rebirth Party (*Yeniden Doğuş Partisi - YDP*)	95.484	0.34		0	
Workers' Party (*İşçi Partisi - İP*)	61.428	0.22		0	
New Party (*Yeni Parti - YP*)	36.853	0.13		0	
No. of valid votes	28,126,993	100,00		550	0
Invalid votes	974,476				
Total votes	29,101,469				
Electorate size	34,155,981				
Voter turnout	85.5%				

Table 5: 1995 general election

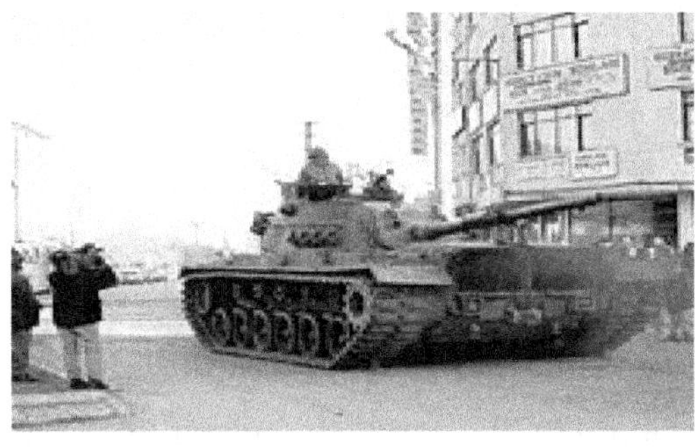

Figure 6: Tank moving on the streets of Sincan

Erbakan's early politicial activism, which included state visits to Iran and Libya, and efforts to establish an economic bloc of Muslim countries (D-8) were actively questioned were actively questioned by leaders of other politicial parties and the military establishment.

Protests were arranged by the Sincan municipality in Ankara, against alleged Israeli human rights violations that took place in guise of an "Al-Quds night" on 31 January 1997. The building in which the event took place was plastered with posters of Hezbollah and Hamas. As a reaction to the demonstration, tanks moved to the streets of Sincan on 4 February.

On 28 February 1997, the generals submitted their views on issues regarding secularism and political Islam on Turkey to the government at the National Security Council (MGK) meeting. The MGK made several decisions during this meeting, and Prime Minister Necmettin Erbakan from the Welfare Party was forced to sign the decisions, some of which were:

- Eight years of primary school education
- Shutting down many religious schools opened during his term
- Abolition of Tarikats (sectarian groups)

For several months the military continued to issue threats toward the government, mobilizing civil society and the media in an anti-Islamic drive. By June 1997 Erbakan was forced to resign, and the President called on opposition parties to form a new government. The new government, led by the center-right but secularist Motherland Party (Anavatan Partisi, ANAP), quickly showed its determination to implement the Security Council's recommendations.

In 1998, the Welfare Party was closed by the Constitutional Court for violating the constitution's separation of religion and state clause. Erbakan was banned from politics for five years, and former MP members and mayors of RP (Welfare Party) joined the successor Virtue Party. Recep Tayyip Erdoğan, Istanbul mayor from the Virtue Party, was soon afterwards given a prison sentence after he read a nationalist and Islamist poem in Siirt Province, and he was banned from politics for five years as well.

2.6. Imprisonment

In December 1997 Erdoğan recited a poem in Siirt. This poem was written by Ziya Gökalp, a pan-Turkish activist of the early 20th century. His recitation included verses translated as "The mosques are our barracks, the domes our helmets, the minarets our bayonets and the faithful our soldiers...." which are not in the original version of the poem. Erdoğan said the poem had been approved by the

Turkish National Ministry of Education to be published in textbooks. Under article 312/2 of the Turkish penal code his recitation was regarded as an incitement to violence and religious or racial hatred. He was given a ten-month prison sentence of which he served four months, from 24 March 1999 to 27 July 1999. Due to his conviction, Erdoğan was forced to give up his mayoral position. The conviction also stipulated a political ban, which prevented Erdoğan from participating in general and local elections. He had appealed for the sentence to be converted to a monetary fine, but it was reduced to 120 days instead. In 2017, this period of Erdoğan's life was made into a film titled Reis.

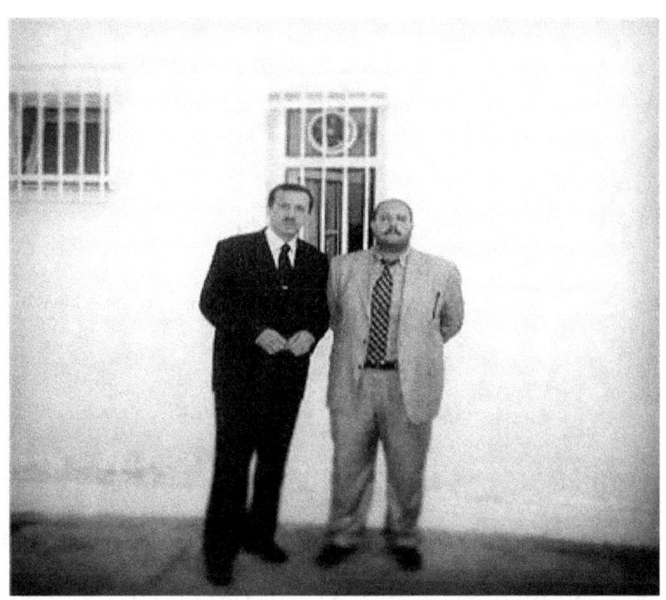

Figure 7: Erdogan in Pınarhisar Jail with his friend

2.7. Justice and Development Party

After the closure of the Welfare Party, the deputies which were left without a party joined the Virtue Party (FP) established at the end of 1997. The leader of the Virtue Party was Recai Kutan. In May 2000, when a group of reformers, led by Abdullah Gül, openly challenged Kutan for control of the party. Abdullah Gül narrowly lost a bid to replace Recai Kutan as Virtue's leader. In June 2001, the Constitutional Court closed the Virtue (Fazilet) Party, the country's largest opposition political group, for antisecular activities and expelled two of its members from Parliament.

After the closure of Virtue Party, the Virtue Party MPs founded two sections of parties: reformist Justice and Development Party (AKP) and traditionalist Felicity Party (SP). The reformist grouping had actually working for over a year on the outline for a new party. Erbakan loyalists, however, were the first to inaugurate a new party, under a new name chosen by Erbakan himself, the Felicity Party

(Saadet Patisi). Although Erbakan remained banned from politics, the party was designed as a vehicle for his re-entry and sought something of a return to the prior success of Welfare as a social and political movement. One month later, in august 2001, the reformist wing unveiled their new party, the AKP (Justice and Development Party). The AK Party, as it was sometimes known, echoed the meanings of the Turkish Word "ak" which signifies both "white" and "clean." The intended implication of such name was that the AK Party was untainted by the corruption of the past, a clean state. The AKP's logo was simply a shinig ligt-bulb with the slogan "continunal light"

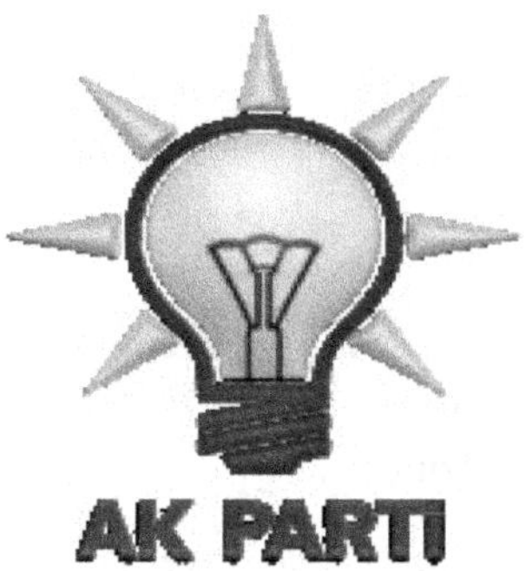

Figure 8: The AKP Logo

The AKP emerged with a formidable organization, developed through contact with former Virtue Party leaders as well as notable politicians from center-right parties. Early defections to AKP from such right-wing parties as the National Action (MHP), True Path (DYP), and Motherland (ANAP) parties served as an indication that politicians in the know were taking it seriously. The AKP did make it clear early on that it would support a market economy and push for Turkey's admission into the European Union. It pledged to respect religious belief and support moral values, but within the context of a secular state.

3. Prime Minister (2003-2014)

3.1. Elections and Referendum

3.1.1. General elections, 2002

Erdoğan established the Justice and Development Party (Adalet ve Kalkınma Partisi-AKP) in 2001. The general elections of 2002 were the first elections in which Erdoğan participated as a party leader.

After following the collapse of the DSP-MHP-ANAP coalition led by Bülent Ecevit, the 15th Turkish general election was held on 3 November 2002. All 550 members of the Grand National Assembly were up for election.

The general elections of 2002 was held during an ongoing economic crisis which followed the 2001 financial crash, which resulted in a deep resentment of coalition governments which had governed the country since the 1980 military coup. The Justice and Development Party (AKP) and Republican People's Party (CHP) made enormous gains, transitioning from the multi-party parliament under a DSP-MHP-ANAP coalition government elected in 1999 to a two-party system ruled by the AKP and CHP, with no other parties winning any seats in parliament, only nine independent MPs being elected, and the AKP and CHP combined winning 98.36% of parliament. The Justice and Development Party (AKP), which had just been formed in 2001 by Recep Tayyip Erdoğan, won the election with nearly two-thirds of the seats. The AKP won 363 seats with just 34.3% of the vote. The other party which passed the 10% threshold to gain representation was the Republican People's Party, which came second with 19.38% of the vote and 178 seats. The election results produced Turkey's first single party government since 1987 general election and the country's first two-party parliament since 1960.

Turkish stocks gave up a gain more than 7% on Monday morning. Leaders of the other parties, such as Ecevit, Bahceli, Yılmaz and Çiller, resigned. Erdoğan could not become the PM (Prime Minister) as he was still banned from politics by the judiciary for his speech in Siirt. While he was serving as the Mayor of Istanbul, Erdoğan was sentenced to a 10 month prison term in 1998 for reciting a poem in Siirt which incited racial intolerance. This prevented Erdoğan from initially seeking a seat in parliament, meaning that the AKP's co-founder Abdullah Gül became Prime Minister following their election victory. The figures presented below are the results of the 2002 general elections.

Party			Vote			Seats	
Abbreviation	Party name *in Turkish*	Leader(s)	Votes	%	swing	Elected	% of total
AKP	Justice and Development Party *Adalet ve Kalkınma Partisi*	Recep Tayyip Erdoğan	10,808,229	34.28	New	363	66.00
CHP	Republican People's Party *Cumhuriyet Halk Partisi*	Deniz Baykal	6,113,352	19.39	▲10.68	178	32.36
DYP	True Path Party *Doğru Yol Partisi*	Tansu Çiller	3,008,942	9.54	▼2.52	0	0.00
MHP	Nationalist Movement Party *Milliyetçi Hareket Partisi*	Devlet Bahçeli	2,635,787	8.36	▼9.62	0	0.00
GP	Young Party *Genç Parti*	Cem Uzan	2,285,598	7.25	New	0	0.00
DEHAP	Democratic People's	Mehmet	1,960,660	6.22	▲1.47	0	0.00

ANAP	Motherland Party *Anavatan Partisi*	Mesut Yılmaz	1,618,465	5.13	▼8.09	0	0.00
SP	Felicity Party^ *Saadet Partisi*	Recai Kutan	785,489	2.49	▼12.92	0	0.00
DSP	Democratic Left Party *Demokratik Sol Parti*	Bülent Ecevit	384,009	1.22	▼20.97	0	0.00
YTP	New Turkey Party *Yeni Türkiye Partisi*	İsmail Cem	363,869	1.15	New	0	0.00
BBP	Great Union Party *Büyük Birlik Partisi*	Muhsin Yazıcıoğlu	322,093	1.02	▼0.44	0	0.00
	Independents *Bağımsızlar*		314,251	1.00	▲0.13	9	1.64
YURT-P	Homeland Party *Yurt Partisi*	Sadettin Tantan	294,909	0.94	New	0	0.00
İP	Workers' Party *İşçi Partisi*	Doğu Perinçek	159,843	0.51	▲0.33	0	0.00
BTP	Independent Turkey Party *Bağımsız Türkiye Partisi*	Haydar Baş	150,482	0.48	New	0	0.00
ÖDP	Freedom and Solidarity Party *Özgürlük ve Dayanışma Partisi*	Ufuk Uras	106,023	0.34	▼0.46	0	0.00
LDP	Liberal Democrat Party *Liberal Demokrat Parti*	Besim Tibuk	89,331	0.28	▼0.13	0	0.00
MP	Nation Party *Millet Partisi*	Aykut Edibali	68,271	0.22	▼0.03	0	0.00
TKP	Communist Party of Turkey *Türkiye Komünist Partisi*	Aydemir Güler	59,180	0.19	New	0	0.00
Total			**31,528,783**	**100.00**		**550**	**100.00**
Valid votes			31,528,783	96.22	▲0.73		
Invalid / blank votes			1,239,378	3.78	▼0.73		
Votes cast / turnout			**32,768,161**	**79.14**	▼**7.95**		
Abstentions			8,638,866	20.86	▲7.95		
Registered voters			**41,407,027**				

Table 6: 2002 general election

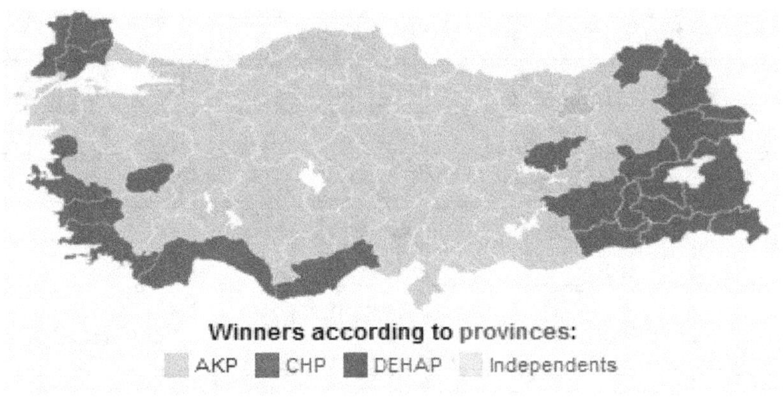

Figure 9: 2002 general election results according to provinces

The cabinet of Abdullah Gül was formed on November 19, 2002. Abdullah Gül, formed the 58th government of Turkey and he succeeded to the fifth government of previous PM Bülent Ecevit. After the legal and political problems for Erdoğan had been solved, Abdullah Gül stepped aside and became the Deputy Prime Minister and Foreign Minister of the next government while Erdoğan became Prime Minister.

The cabinet of Abdullah Gül presented below is the 58th government of Turkey.

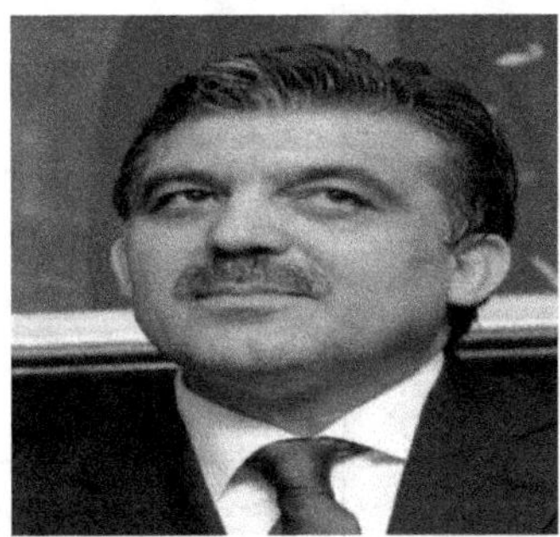

Figure 10: Prime Minister Gül, 2002

Functions		Holder	Start	End
English title	**Turkish title**			
Prime Minister	*Başbakan*	Abdullah Gül	Nov. 19, 2002	Mar. 12, 2003
Deputy Prime Minister	*Başbakan Yardımcısı*	Abdüllatif Şener	Nov. 19, 2002	Mar. 12, 2003
Deputy Prime Minister	*Başbakan Yardımcısı*	Mehmet Ali Şahin	Nov. 19, 2002	Mar. 12, 2003
Deputy Prime Minister	*Başbakan Yardımcısı*	Ertuğrul Yalçınbayır	Nov. 19, 2002	Mar. 12, 2003
Minister of State	*Devlet Bakanı*	Mehmet Aydın	Nov. 19, 2002	Mar. 12, 2003

Minister of State	Devlet Bakanı	Beşir Atalay	Nov. 19, 2002	Mar. 12, 2003
Minister of State	Devlet Bakanı	Ali Babacan	Nov. 19, 2002	Mar. 12, 2003
Minister of State	Devlet Bakanı	Kürşad Tüzmen	Nov. 19, 2002	Mar. 12, 2003
Minister of Justice	Adalet Bakanı	Cemil Çiçek	Nov. 19, 2002	Mar. 12, 2003
Minister of National Defense	Millî Savunma Bakanı	Mehmet Vecdi Gönül	Nov 19, 2002	Mar. 12, 2003
Minister of the Interior	İçişleri Bakanı	Abdülkadir Aksu	Nov. 19, 2002	Mar. 12, 2003
Minister of Foreign Affairs	Dışişleri Bakanlığı	Yaşar Yakış	Nov. 19, 2002	Mar. 12, 2003
Minister of Finance	Maliye Bakanı	Kemal Unakıtan	Nov. 19, 2002	Mar. 12, 2003
Minister of National Education	Millî Eğitim Bakanı	Erkan Mumcu	Nov. 19, 2002	Mar. 12, 2003
Minister of Public Works and Settlement	Bayındırlık ve İskân Bakanı	Zeki Ergezen	Nov. 19, 2002	Mar. 12, 2003
Minister of Health	Sağlık Bakanı	Recep Akdağ	Nov. 19, 2002	Mar. 12, 2003
Minister of Transport and Communication	Ulaştırma Bakanı	Binali Yıldırım	Nov. 19, 2002	Mar. 12, 2003
Minister of Agriculture	Tarım ve Köyişleri Bakanı	Sami Güçlü	Nov. 19, 2002	Mar. 12, 2003
Minister of Labour and Social Security	Çalışma ve Sosyal Güvenlik Bakanı	Murat Başesgioğlu	Nov. 19, 2002	Mar. 12, 2003
Minister of Industry and Commerce	Sanayi ve Ticaret Bakanı	Ali Coşkun	Nov. 19, 2002	Mar. 12, 2003
Minister of Energy and Natural Resources	Enerji ve Tabii Kaynaklar Bakanı	Mehmet Hilmi Güler	Nov. 19, 2002	Mar. 12, 2003
Minister of Culture	Kültür Bakanı	Hüseyin Çelik	Nov. 19, 2002	Mar. 12, 2003
Minister of Tourism	Turizm Bakanı	Güldal Akşit	Nov. 19, 2002	Mar. 12, 2003
Minister of Forestry	Orman Bakanı	Osman Pepe	Nov. 19, 2002	Mar. 12, 2003
Minister of Environment	Çevre Bakanı	İmdat Sütlüoğlu	Nov. 19, 2002	Mar. 12, 2003

Table 7: The cabinet of Abdullah Gül

3.1.2 Siirt Province by-election, 2003

The Supreme Election Board canceled the general election results from Siirt due to voting irregularities in December 2002 and scheduled a new election for 9 February 2003. By this time, AKP leader Erdoğan was able to run for parliament due to a legal change made possible by the opposition Republican People's Party. The AKP duly listed Erdoğan as a candidate for the rescheduled election in Siirt on 9 February 2003. Erdoğan won, becoming Prime Minister after Gül handed over the post.

The AKP won all three seats up for election with 84.82% of the votes, gaining the two other seats that had been won by the CHP and an independent candidate in November 2002 general elections. The CHP came second party with 13.79% of the vote and lost their seat despite increasing their vote share since November.

Siirt by-election, 9 March 2003				
Party	**Candidate**	**Votes**	**%**	**±**
AK Party	Recep Tayyip Erdoğan, Öner Ergenç, Öner Gülyeşil	55,203	84.82	▲67.26
CHP	*None elected*	8,972	13.79	▲4.86
İP	*None elected*	500	0.77	▲0.63
TKP	*None elected*	404	0.62	▲0.53
	Turnout	73,624	61.77	▼12.38

Table 8: Siirt by-election, 2003

The first cabinet of Prime Minister Recep Tayyip Erdoğan took office on 14 March 2003. He succeeded to the Abdullah Gul government, who was in office since 18 November 2002.

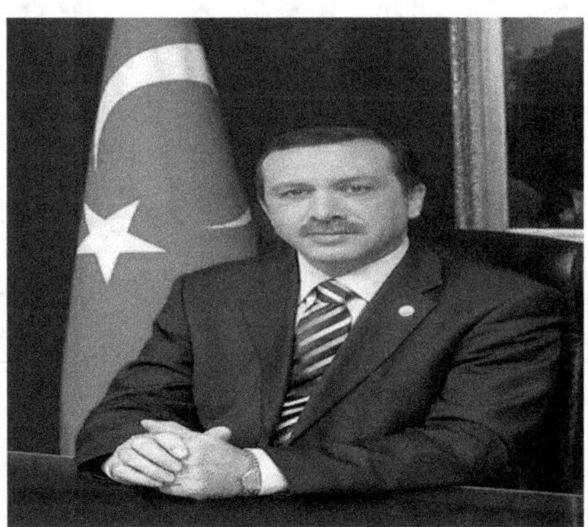

Figure 11: Prime Minister Erdoğan, 2003

Functions	Holder	Start	End
Prime Minister	R. Tayyip Erdoğan	14 March 2003	28 August 2007
Deputy Prime Minister Ministry of Foreign Affairs	Abdullah Gül	14 March 2003	28 August 2007
Deputy Prime Minister	Mehmet Ali Şahin	14 March 2003	28 August 2007
Deputy Prime Minister	Abdüllatif Şener	14 March 2003	28 August 2007
Minister of State	Ali Babacan	14 March 2003	28 August 2007
Minister of State	Nimet Çubukçu	14 March 2003	28 August 2007
Minister of State	Mehmet Aydın	14 March 2003	28 August 2007
Minister of State	Kürşad Tüzmen	14 March 2003	28 August 2007
Minister of State	Beşir Atalay	14 March 2003	28 August 2007
Ministry of Justice	Cemil Çiçek	14 March 2003	8 May 2007
Ministry of Justice	Fahri Kasırga[¶]	8 May 2007	28 August 2007
Ministry of National Defense	Mehmet Vecdi Gönül	14 March 2003	28 August 2007
Ministry of the Interior	Abdülkadir Aksu	14 March 2003	8 May 2007
Ministry of the Interior	Osman Güneş[¶]	8 May 2007	28 August 2007
Ministry of Finance	Kemal Unakıtan	14 March 2003	28 August 2007
Ministry of National Education	Hüseyin Çelik	14 March 2003	28 August 2007
Ministry of Public Works and Settlement	Faruk Nafız Özak	14 March 2003	28 August 2007
Ministry of Health	Recep Akdağ	14 March 2003	28 August 2007
Ministry of Transport and Communication	Binali Yıldırım	14 March 2003	8 May 2007
Ministry of Transport and Communication	İsmet Yılmaz[¶]	8 May 2007	28 August 2007
Ministry of Agriculture	Mehmet Mehdi Eker	14 March 2003	28 August 2007
Ministry of Labour and Social Security	Murat Başesgioğlu	14 March 2003	28 August 2007
Ministry of Industry and Commerce	Ali Coşkun	14 March 2003	28 August 2007
Ministry of Energy and Natural Resources	Mehmet Hilmi Güler	14 March 2003	28 August 2007
Ministry of Culture and Tourism	Atilla Koç	14 March 2003	28 August 2007
Ministry of Environment and Forestry	Osman Pepe	14 March 2003	28 August 2007

Table 9: Cabinet Erdoğan I

^¶ Nonpartisan minister appointed in accordance with the Article 114 of the Turkish Constitution in the wake of 2007 elections

3.1.3. Local elections, 2004

The Turkish local elections of 2004 were held on 28 March 2004 in order to elect both mayors and councillors to local government positions. All 16 metropolitan and 3,193 district municipalities were up for election, while 3,208 provincial and 34,477 municipal councillors and 50,000 neighbourhood presidents (muhtars) were also elected.

With nearly 42 percent of votes, the ruling AKP increased the 34 percent it won in the 2002 general elections by an extra 8 percent. The only opposition party with representation in Parliament, CHP, received 19 percent of the votes. The traditional parties of the Turkish establishment lost further their votes. Despite suffering a loss of 6% in their popular vote share, MHP (The Nationalist Movement Party), won above 10% of the votes.

The CHP was able to maintain a degree of support in the provincial regions on the Turkish west coast. CHP was only able to win Izmir among the four major cities. The AKP winning a majority in the cities of Istanbul, Adana and the capital city, Ankara. The AKP also took the tourist centre Antalya in local elections.

The Democratic People's Party (DEHAP), main political arm of the kurdish movement, entered these elections in a coalition with five small socialist parties. On the other hand, these parties received fewer votes (5 percent) than the DEHAP received alone in the 2002 general elections (6.1 percent).

Leader	Recep Tayyip Erdoğan	Deniz Baykal	Devlet Bahçeli
Party	AK Party	CHP	MHP
Leader since	14 August 2001	30 September 2000	6 July 1997
Last election	New party	373 mayors, 11.08%	247 mayors, 3,579 councillors, 10.45%
Mayors	1,762	469	247
Councillors	18,913	6,023	3,579
Popular vote^	13,477,287	5,882,810	3,372,249
Percentage	41.67%	18.23%	10.45%
Swing	▲41.67%	▲7.15%	▼6.72%

Table 10: Local election, 2004

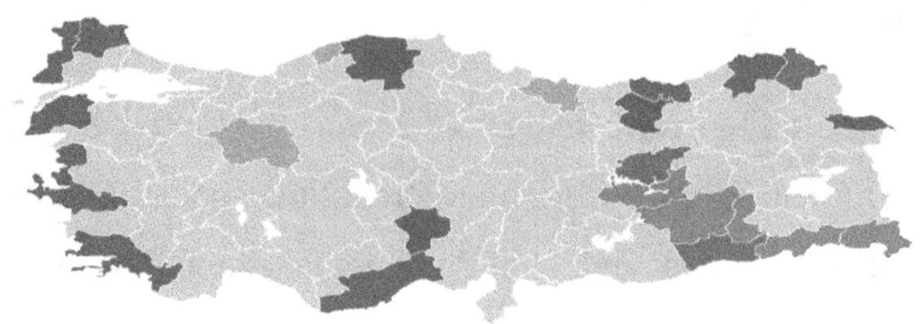

Figure 12: Results of the local elections, 2004 per province. AKP in Yellow, CHP in Red, MHP in purple, DGB (DEHAP's alliance) in Green, DSP in Blue, DYP in pink, SP in brown and Independents in Grey.

3.1.4. Presidential election, 2007

The 2007 presidential election refers to two attempts to elect the country's 11th president, to succeed president Ahmet Necdet Sezer. The most likely candidate was Abdullah Gül.

The first attempt consisted of the first rounds on 27 April 2007 and its repeat on 6 May 2007 after Constitutional Court annulled the first round on 27 April 2007. The constitutional court decided that a quorum of two-thirds (367 MPs) was necessary, which was impossible without opposition parties support. Both first rounds were almost entirely boycotted by opposition parties' MPs to disable the voting to start. Therefore, the ruling AKP was unsuccessful in electing its candidate, Foreign Affairs Minister Abdullah Gül. After that AKP, called a snap election which was held on July 22, 2007. The general elections on July 22, 2007 saw it returned to government with a larger proportion of the vote. Afterwards, Abdullah Gül was renominated and was finally elected in the third round of the second attempt of presidential election. The first round of this voting was on 20 August 2007, while a second round was on 24 August 2007 and a third round was on 28 August 2007. There was a quorum this time, since opposition party, the Nationalist Movement Party (MHP), did not boycott the election.

The presidential vote is held among MPs by secret ballot. A candidate requires a two-thirds majority to be elected in the first two rounds of election. If there is no clear winner in two rounds, the winning threshold is dropped to a simple majority (276 votes) in third round. If there is still no winner in third round, the two candidates with the most votes from the third round progress to a runoff election, where the simple majority rule still applies. In the event of no clear winner among the two, the Turkish Constitution states that a snap general election must be called to overcome the parliamentary deadlock.

Abdullah Gül's candidacy was announced by Prime Minister Erdoğan on April 24, 2007 while calling Gül as his brother. He was the official candidate of the AKP, thus making him the strongest candidate to be the 11th president of Turkey. During his campaign, Abdullah Gül met the leaders of parties represented in the Parliament, except Genç Party leader Cem Uzan. None of the party leaders said that they would vote for Gül in the elections. After the Constitutional Court's rule on the election method, Gül's chance to become the next president decreased since the support of AKP had become not enough to get elected. On May 6, 2007, Foreign Affairs Minister Abdullah Gül withdrew his candidacy after the parliament failed to achieve a quorum for a second time.

Ersönmez Yarbay was another candidate from the AKP. Yarbay announced his candidacy since he believed that there should be a second candidate in the presidential elections. By his candidacy, Ersönmez Yarbay protested the election method of the president, as he alleged that Erdoğan would decide the next president on his own. However, Yarbay withdrew his candidacy before the start of presidential voting.

On 12 April 2007, in a press conference of the Chief of the Turkish General Staff Yaşar Büyükanıt, the Armed Forces' opinion on the elections was asked. He answered the question stating that the new president should be loyal to republic principles not only by words but also by heart.

The Turkish Armed Forces issued a statement of its interests on its official website on April 27, 2007, later termed the "e-memorandum" by journalists:

"...The problem that emerged in the presidential election in 2007 process is focused on arguments over secularism. Turkish Armed Forces are concerned about the situation... the Turkish Armed Forces are a party in those arguments, and absolute defender of secularism principle..."

In response to these statements, government spokesman Mr. Cemil Çiçek made a speech. He said that government was sensitive about the secular, democratic, social, and lawful state.

The first round of voting took place on April 27, 2007, which resulted in Abdullah Gül achieving 357 votes. 361 members of the parliament were present at the elections and CHP, DYP, ANAP, SHP, HYP, GP and some independent members boycotted the voting.

The following parties were represented in the Turkish Grand National Assembly (TBMM) as of 27 April and 6 May 2007, and therefore could vote:

Presidential election:	Seats	1. round April 27	Repeated 1. round May 6
Justice and Development Party (AKP)	352	352	352
Republican People's Party (CHP)	149	1	1
Motherland Party (ANAP)	20	2	2
True Path Party (DYP)	4	2	2
Social Democratic People's Party Sosyaldemokrat Halk Partisi (SHP)	1	0	0
People's Ascent Party (HYP)	1	0	0
Young Party (GP)	1	0	0
Independents Bağımsız	13	11	
Total Seats/ Total (Yes)	541	357 (Among 361)	358(Among 358)
Total (No)		(180 boycotted)	(179 boycotted)

Please note that the distribution of seats has changed since the latest elections in 2002.

Table 11: Voting on April 27 and May 6

Votes taken by Gül was below the two-thirds of the vote needed, and so, there would be another round of voting in the following days. However, the main opposition party CHP filed a claim to the Supreme Court, seeking a declaration of nullity in relation to the first round of voting.

On May 1, 2007, the Constitutional Court ruled that if two-thirds of the votes was needed to elect the president in the first round, then it was also needed that two-thirds of the MPs were present at the parliament. If this was not the case, the first round would have to be repeated. The supreme court ruled in favour of the CHP and declared the first round annulled. Nine of the eleven members of the supreme court were in favour of annulling the voting. Therefore, there was no second round on May 2, 2007 as the first round of election had failed.

The first round was repeated on May 6, 2007. The boycotting of opposition MPS continued and the voting was not started at the parliament. The repeated round resulted in the withdrawal of Mr. Gül as the necessary amount of MPs present was not reached yet again.

The presidential elections were postponed due to the lack of a candidate after the pullout of Abdullah Gül on May 9, 2007. The following day, PM Erdoğan called for an early general election. After the general election, the newly composed parliament restarted the presidential election.

After the general election, there was some speculation about whether Abdullah Gül would be nominated again by AKP. There were hints that the PM Erdoğan might seek a consensus candidate, but ultimately Mr. Gül was renominated by his party on 13 August 2007, after opposition party MHP announced its decision not to boycott the elections. Two opposition parties have decided to field their own candidates: The Nationalist Movement Party (MHP) nominated Sabahattin Çakmakoğlu on August 17 2007, and the Democratic Left Party nominated its candidate Hüseyin Tayfun İçli. Thereafter completion of the third round, Mr. Gül was elected as president. The results are:

Candidates	Party	1st round (20 August)	2nd round (24 August)	3rd round (28 August)
Abdullah Gül	Justice and Development Party (*Adalet ve Kalkınma Partisi*)	341	337	339
Sabahattin Çakmakoğlu	Nationalist Movement Party (*Milliyetçi Hareket Partisi*)	70	71	70
Hüseyin Tayfun İçli	Democratic Left Party (*Demokratik Sol Parti*)	13	14	13
	Spoiled votes	1	0	2
	Blank votes	23	24	23
	Total MP turnout	448	446	448
Sources: Turkish Grand National Assembly online archives, newsobserver.com				

Table 12: Summary of the August 2007 Turkish presidential election candidates

3.1.5. General election, 2007

Normally due to be held in November, the general election was called early after the 2007 presidential election resulted in parliamentary deadlock. The elections were pulled forward after Turkih Parliament failed to elect a new president. The governing AKP had nominated former PM and serving Foreign Affairs Minister Mr. Gül as its presidential candidate, amid enormous opposition and concern over Gül's previous political background. The disagreement was largely caused due to the Turkish Presidency's symbolic role in safeguarding secularism. The opposition CHP subsequently boycotted the parliamentary process of electing a president, denying the government the two-thirds majority quorum of MPs necessary for Mr. Gül's election to be validated. As required by the Turkish Constitution, a snap early general election was called for 22 July 2007.

The general election was the 22nd general election to be held in the Turkish politicial history and the MPs elected formed the 23rd Parliament of the Republic of Turkey.

The result was a echoing victory for the incumbent AKP, which won 46.6% of the vote and 341 seats in parliament. The AKP's leader Erdoğan was reelected as Prime Minister of Turkey. Consequently, the opposition CHP came second with 20.9% of the vote and took 112 seats. The Nationalist

Movement Party (MHP), which had failed to surpass the 10% election threshold in the 2002 general election, re-entered Turkish Grand National Assembly with 14.3% of the vote and 71 MPs. Terrorism in Iraq, secular and religious concerns, the intervention of the military in political issues, European Union membership negotiations, the relations with United States were the main issues of general election.

In addition to the AKP, CHP and MHP, some kurdish socialist parties formed an electoral alliance named the Thousand Hope Candidates (Bin Umut Adayları) and contested the general election as Independents in order to bypass the 10% threshold. The alliance, established of the Democratic Society Party (DTP), Labour Party (EMEP), Freedom and Solidarity Party (ÖDP) and the Socialist Democracy Party (SDP), polled strongly in the south-eastern part of Turkey where there is a large kurdish population, winning 3.81% of the national vote and 22 seats in Turkish Grand National Assembly.

Election law changed before the general election. According to change, the min. age for candidates for the parliament was reduced from 30 to 25. On the other hand, laws don't take effect for one year after passage, only candidates above the age of 30 were able to be elected in 2007 general election.

Party			Vote			Seats		
Party name *in Turkish*	**Leader(s)**	**Votes**	**%**	**swing**	**Elected**	**% of total**	**± since 2002**
Justice and Development Party *Adalet ve Kalkınma Partisi*	Recep Tayyip Erdoğan	16,327,291	46.58	▲12.30	341	62.00	▼23
Republican People's Party *Cumhuriyet Halk Partisi*	Deniz Baykal	7,317,808	20.88	▲1.49	112	20.36	▼66
Nationalist Movement Party *Milliyetçi Hareket Partisi*	Devlet Bahçeli	5,001,869	14.27	▲5.91	71	12.91	▲71
Democrat Party *Demokrat Parti*	Mehmet Ağar	1,898,873	5.42	▼4.12	0	0.00	—0
Young Party *Genç Parti*	Cem Uzan	1,064,871	3.04	▼4.21	0	0.00	—0
Felicity Party *Saadet Partisi*	Recai Kutan	820,289	2.34	▼0.15	0	0.00	—0
Independent Turkey Party *Bağımsız Türkiye Partisi*	Haydar Baş	182,095	0.52	▲0.04	0	0.00	—0

Party	Leader	Votes	%	+/-	Seats	%	+/-
People's Ascent Party *Halkın Yükselişi Partisi*	Yaşar Nuri Öztürk	179,010	0.51	New	0	0.00	New
Workers' Party *İşçi Partisi*	Doğu Perinçek	128,148	0.37	▼0.14	0	0.00	—0
Bright Turkey Party *Aydınlık Türkiye Partisi*	Oktay Öztürk	100,982	0.29	New	0	0.00	New
Communist Party of Turkey *Türkiye Komünist Partisi*	Aydemir Güler	79,258	0.23	▲0.04	0	0.00	—0
Freedom and Solidarity Party *Özgürlük ve Dayanışma Partisi*	Bekir Kemal Ulusaler	52,055	0.15	▼0.19	0	0.00	—0
Liberal Democrat Party *Liberal Demokrat Parti*	Cem Toker	35,364	0.10	▼0.18	0	0.00	—0
Labour Party *Emek Partisi*	Selma Gürkan	26,292	0.08	N/A	0	0.00	N/A
Independents *Bağımsızlar*		1,835,486	5.24	▲4.24	26	4.73	▲18
Total		**35,049,691**	**100.00**		**550**	**100.00**	—**0**
Valid votes		35,049,691	97.21	▲0.99			
Invalid / blank votes		1,006,602	2.79	▼0.99			
Votes cast / turnout		**36,056,293**	**84.25**	▲**5.11**			
Abstentions		6,743,010	15.75	▼5.11			
Registered voters		**42,799,303**					

Table 13: General election, 2007

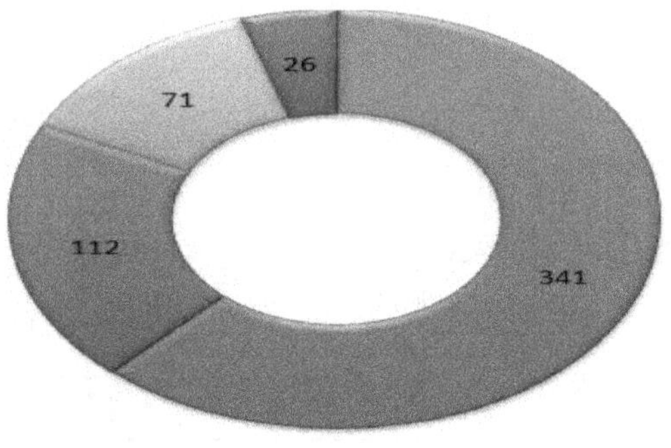

Figure 13: MP distribution:

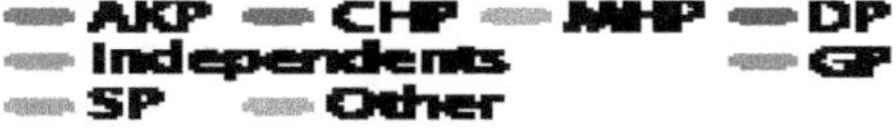

The second cabinet of Erdogan was the government of the Republic of Turkey from 29 August 2007 to 14 June 2011. This cabinet followed the first cabinet of Recep Tayyip Erdoğan. This cabinet laid down its function after the formation of the Cabinet Recep Tayyip Erdoğan III, which was formed following the 2011 general elections.

Functions	Person	Start	End
Prime Minister	R. Tayyip Erdoğan	29 Aug. 2007	14 June 2011
Deputy Prime Minister Minister of State Responsiblities: Inter-ministerial Coordination, Human Rights and Cyprus	Cemil Çiçek	29 Aug. 2007	14 June 2011
Deputy Prime Minister Minister of State Responsiblities: Foundations and TRT	Hayati Yazıcı	29 Aug. 2007	1 May 2009
	Bülent Arınç	1 May 2009	14 June 2011
Deputy Prime Minister Minister of State Responsiblities: Economy, Banking and Treasury	Nazım Ekren	29 Aug. 2007	1 May 2009
	Ali Babacan	1 May 2009	14 June 2011
Minister of State Responsiblities: Information Technology and the Alliance of Civilizations	Mehmet Aydın	29 Aug. 2007	14 June 2011
Minister of State Responsiblities: Foreign Trade	Kürşad Tüzmen	29 Aug. 2007	1 May 2009
	M. Zafer Çağlayan	1 May 2009	14 June 2011
Minister of State Responsiblities: Women and Family	Nimet Çubukçu	29 Aug. 2007	1 May 2009
	Selma Aliye Kavaf	1 May 2009	14 June 2011
Minister of State Responsiblities: The Southeastern Anatolia Project	Cevdet Yılmaz	1 May 2009	14 June 2011
Minister of State Responsiblities: Religious Affairs and the Turkish World	Mustafa Sait Yazıcıoğlu	29 Aug. 2007	1 May 2009
	Faruk Çelik	1 May 2009	14 June 2011
Minister of State Responsiblities: Youth and Sports	Murat Başesgioğlu	29 Aug. 2007	1 May 2009
	Faruk Nafız Özak	1 May 2009	14 June 2011
Minister of State Chief Negotiator with the European Union	Egemen Bağış	8 Jan. 2009	14 June 2011
Minister of State Responsiblities: Customs, Istanbul 2010 and Social Protection	Hayati Yazıcı	1 May 2009	14 June 2011
Ministry of Foreign Affairs	Ali Babacan	29 Aug. 2007	1 May 2009
	Ahmet Davutoğlu	1 May 2009	14 June 2011

Ministry of the Interior	Beşir Atalay	29 Aug. 2007	8 March 2011
	Osman Güneş¶	8 Mar. 2011	14 June 2011
Ministry of Finance	Kemal Unakıtan	29 Aug. 2007	1 May 2009
	Mehmet Şimşek	1 May 2009	14 June 2011
Ministry of Justice	Mehmet Ali Şahin	29 Aug. 2007	1 May 2009
	Sadullah Ergin	1 May 2009	8 March 2011
	Ahmet Kahraman¶	8 Mar. 2011	14 June 2011

Ministry of Energy and Natural Resources	Hilmi Güler	29 Aug. 2007	1 May 2009
	Taner Yıldız	1 May 2009	14 June 2011
Ministry of Agriculture	Mehmet Mehdi Eker	29 Aug 2007	14 June 2011
Ministry of Culture and Tourism	Ertuğrul Günay	29 Aug. 2007	14 June 2011
Ministry of Health	Recep Akdağ	29 Aug. 2007	14 June 2011
Ministry of National Education	Hüseyin Çelik	29 Aug. 2007	1 May 2009
	Nimet Çubukçu	1 May 2009	14 June 2011
Ministry of National Defense	Vecdi Gönül	29 Aug. 2007	14 June 2011
Ministry of Industry and Commerce	Mehmet Zafer Çağlayan	29 Aug. 2007	1 May 2009
	Nihat Ergün	1 May 2009	14 June 2011
Ministry of Labour and Social Security	Faruk Çelik	29 Aug. 2007	1 May 2009
	Ömer Dinçer	1 May 2009	14 June 2011
Ministry of Transport and Communication	Binali Yıldırım	29 Aug. 2007	8 Mar. 2011
	Habip Soluk¶	8 Mar.2011	14 June 2011
Ministry of Public Works and Settlement	Faruk Nafız Özak	29 Aug. 2007	1 May 2009
	Mustafa Demir	1 May 2009	14 June 2011
Ministry of Environment and Forestry	Veysel Eroğlu	29 Aug. 2007	14 June 2011

Table 14: Cabinet Erdoğan II

3.1.6. Constitutional referendum, 2007

On 21 October 2007, the constitutional referendum on electoral reform took place in Turkey. Afterwards the aborted attempt to elect the president in May 2007, the government of Erdoğan introduced substantial electoral reforms which were then passed with the votes of AKP and the opposition Motherland Party (ANAP) in parliament.

According to the 1982 Turkish Constitution, the President of Turkey, was elected by the Grand National Assembly (TBMM) of Turkey. However, the 2007 presidential election failed after the supreme court declared the first round of voting invalid, on the grounds that a quorum of two thirds in parliament was necessary. It was not reached because of the boycott of opposition parties.

The reforms proposed consisted of the following articles:

- electing the president by popular vote instead of by Turkish Grand National Assembly
- reducing the presidential term from 7 years to 5;
- allowing the president to stand for re-election for a second presidential term;

- holding parliamentary elections every 4 years instead of 5 years;

- reducing the quorum of lawmakers needed for parliamentary decisions from 367 to 184 MPs.

Parliament first passed the amendments on 11 May 2007, but president Sezer vetoed the bill over concerns that the change could pit a president with a strong popular mandate against the prime minister and cause uncertainty. AKP legislators, who currently choose the president in a parliamentary vote, voted 370 against 21 in favor of the same measure (without changing the law), which demands presidential election by the public.

Constitutional Amendment:	Seats	Votes May 11	Votes May 31
Justice and Development Party (AKP)	352		352
Republican People's Party (CHP)	149		0
Motherland Party (ANAP)	20		2
Democrat Party(DP)	- 24		-
True Path Party (DYP)	4		0
Social Democratic People's Party (SHP)	1		0
People's Ascent Party (HYP)	1		0
Young Party (GP)	1		0
Independents Bağımsız	13		11
Total Seats/ Total (Yes)	541	376	370
Total (No)		(165 boycotted)	21 - (150 boycotted)

Table 15: Constitutional Amendment, 2007

According to constitution, the President of Turkey is unable to veto a bill a second time, but the president could refer it to a referendum for decision. Opposition lawmakers also said they could seek a cancellation of the vote by the Supreme Court on the grounds of procedural flaws on 4 June 2007.

The president Sezer referred it for a referendum on 15 June 2007. However, at the same time Sezer stated he would ask the Supreme Court to invalidate the parliamentary vote due to procedural errors. President Sezer's rigid opposition reportedly comes from fears that a president with a strong popular mandate might produce a deadlock when in disagreement with the prime minister. The Constitutional court ruled in early July that the reforms were indeed valid, so the constitutional referendum took place as planned.

Moreover, president Sezer vetoed another law, which would have made it possible to hold the constitutional referendum on 22 July 2007 instead of in October 2007, making the constitutional reform increasingly unlikely to take place before the election.

Prime Minister Erdoğan claimed that the position of president is political and it should be elected by the public not by the MPs. "How could those who see the election of the president by popular vote as a problem for the regime ask votes from the citizens?" asked Mr. Erdoğan.

The CHP accused PM Erdoğan of acting with "a sense of vengeance" for having failed first to secure his then Abdullah Gül's election to this position and now at the expense of creating a "degenerated parliamentary system", he tries to secure a new way to reach his goal. The CHP leader Deniz Baykal said it would mount a legal challenge to this ideology. Mr. Baykal claimed that position of president is a non-partisan, over political concerns and designed as an oversight. President's job description and powers demands that the policies originated from this position should reflect a balance, which all the parties in parliament could trust president. Because of this balancing act, according to him, it was very important to create the neutral point of the president and prevent domination of a one party (which might generate Prime Minister and President at the same time) and control the every mechanism of the political system in Turkey.

60 % of all voters participated in the referendum. Almost 70 % percent of the participants supported the constitutional changes.

Turkish constitutional referendum, 2007		
Choice	**Votes**	**%**
✓ Yes	19,403,987	68.95
No	8,738,794	31.05
Valid votes	28,142,781	97.74
Invalid or blank votes	651,435	2.26
Total votes	**28,794,216**	**100.00**
Registered voters and turnout	42,665,149	67.49

Table 16: Results of the Constitutional Referendum, 2007

3.1.7. Local election, 2009

Local elections held on 29 March 2009. The overall winner was the ruling party AKP, although the party saw a decline in its vote rate relative to the 2007 general election. The leading opposition party, the CHP, increased its vote rate, as did a number of smaller parties including the SP, DTP and BBP, whose party leader Muhsin Yazıcıoğlu had died in a helicopter crash four days before the local election. The third largest party, the MHP (Nationalist Movement Party), enjoyed a more modest vote surge. The local election was not contested by Cem Uzan's GP (Young Party). The AKP failed to take some provinces it had publicly targeted, such as Diyarbakır, İzmir and Urfa, and did not achieve its aim of exceeding 47% of the overall vote share. There was localized election-related fighting in southeastern part of Turkey, in which five people were reported to have been killed and nearly a hundred injured.

Leader	Recep Tayyip Erdoğan	Deniz Baykal	Devlet Bahçeli
Party	AK Party	CHP	MHP
Leader since	14 August 2001	30 September 2000	6 July 1997
Last election	1,762 mayors, 18,913 councillors, 41.67%	469 mayors, 6,023 councillors, 18.23%	247 mayors, 3,579 councillors, 10.45%
Mayors	1,452	506	484
Councillors	16,621	6,737	6,419
Popular vote^	15,353,553	9,229,936	6,386,279
Percentage	38.39%	23.08%	15.97%
Swing	▼3.28%	▲4.85%	▲5.52%

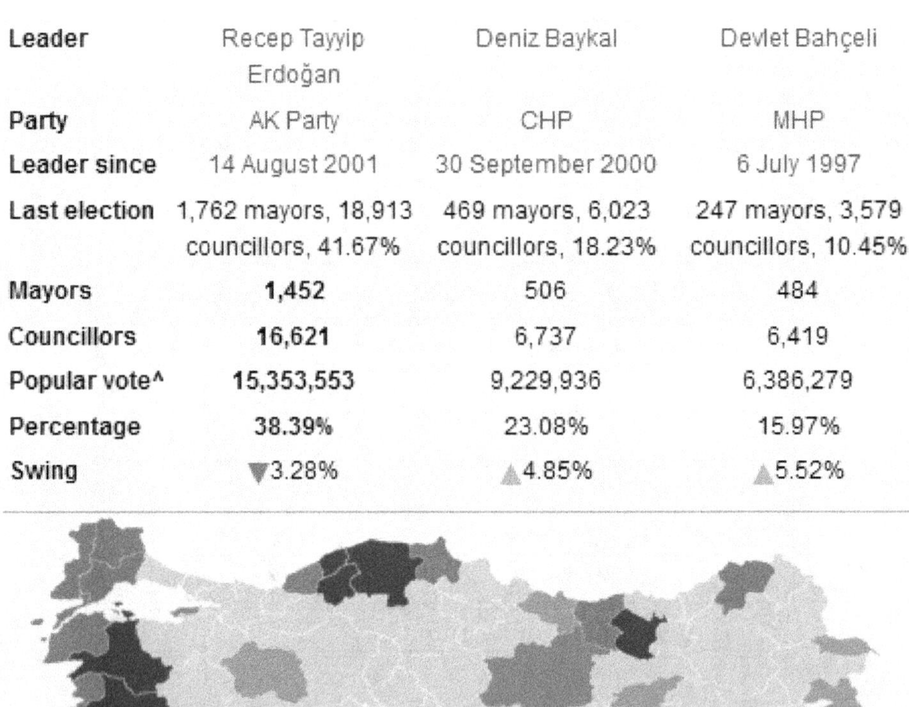

Figure 14: Results of the local election, 2009 per province.

3.1.8. Constitutional referendum, 2010

On 12 September 2010, a constitutional referendum on a number of changes to the Turkish Constitution was held in Turkey The results of the referendum demonstrated the majority supported the constitutional changes with 58% in favour and 42% against. The changes were aimed at bringing the Turkish Constitution into compliance with European Union principles. Supporters of Turkish EU membership hope this reform will ease the membership process.

Peace and Democracy Party (BDP) stated that they would boycott the vote, because it is not mentioned in the constitution that kurdish people exist in Turkey.

Afterwards the military coup of 12 September 1980, a new constitution was prepared in 1982 by the military junta that came to power. 28 years later, a constitutional referendum was held regarding a number of amendments to that constitution.

In 2010, the Turkish Grand National Assembly adopted a series of constitutional amendments. The amendments did not reach the required two-thirds majority (67%) for immediately implementing the changes. However, a majority of 330 votes (60%) was reached and enough to present the amendments to the electorate in a referendum. A constitutional change, to make it more difficult for the Constitutional Court to dissolve parties, failed to pass.

The reform package was accepted in parliament on 7 May 2010, starting the referendum process. The referendum was expected to be held 60 (sixty) days after the publication of the reform package in the Official Gazette, but the Supreme Election Board (YSK) announced that referendum would be held 120 days later, on 12 September 2010. The changes by article of the constitution are presented below.

- Measures ensuring equality between men and women, and protecting children, the elderly, disabled people, widows and orphans of martyrs as well as for invalid and veterans would not be considered a violation of the principle of equality. (Revises Article 10)

- The protection of personal data and privacy would be revised, and everyone would be entitled to the protection of privacy. Access to data about personal information would be included within the new protection measures. (Revises Article 20)

- Travel bans would be relaxed. Trips abroad would be restricted only if a person is subject to a criminal investigation or a legal case. (Revises Article 23)

- Additional protections would be granted regarding family and children's rights. All children would expressly have the right to have direct communication with their mother and father and continue relations with them. (Revises Article 41)

- Public servants would be allowed to be members of more than one union. Civil servants would also have the right to collective bargaining with a body for conciliation to be established in the event of disagreement. (Revises Article 53)

- The ban on general strikes would be lifted. The measure would also include strikes held for political or solidarity purposes, as well as slowdown strikes. (Revises Article 54)

- An ombudsman system to deal with problems that may arise between state institutions and citizens would be established. Every citizen would be granted the right to request information and apply to the ombudsman. (Revises Article 74)

- Deputies would remain in their posts until their elected term ends, even if their parties are closed. (Revises Article 84)

- The tenure of deputies elected for Parliament's presidential board would be modified. (Revises Article 94)

- Decisions by the Supreme Military Council (YAŞ), that result in the expulsion of military officers from the Turkish Armed Forces, or TSK, would be allowed to be appealed in court. The amendment, however, has excluded YAŞ decisions that force military personnel to retire due to promotion procedures and the absence of tenure. Under current law, YAŞ decisions to expel military officers from the armed forces cannot be taken to court. (Revises Article 125)

- Public servants would be granted the right to collective bargaining with regard to their financial and social rights. (Revises Article 128)

- Public servants would be provided the right to apply to courts over censure or warning punishments they face in their workplaces. (Revises Article 129)

- Justice services and the supervision of prosecutors with regard to their administrative duties would be performed by Justice Ministry inspectors. (Revises Article 144)

- Civilian courts would be permitted to try military personnel, and military courts would not be permitted to try civilians other than during times of war. (Revises Article 145)

- The size and membership of the Constitutional Court would be restructured. The number of members of the country's top court would be raised to 17 from 11, and Parliament and the president would elect and appoint members. Currently only the president can appoint members to the Constitutional Court. (Revises Article 146)

- New court members would be selected for terms of 12 years or until they reach the age of 65. The current article does not set a term limit but stipulates that members retire upon reaching the age of 65. (Revises Article 147)

- Citizens would be allowed the right to make personal applications to the Constitutional Court. The article would also pave the way for the court to act as the Supreme Council and acquire the authority to judge the chief of General Staff, force commanders and the Parliament speaker in the event of abuses of power. It also allows for the appeal of decisions made while the court acts as the Supreme Council. (Revises Article 148)

- A quorum would be established for the Constitutional Court to convene and the minimum number of votes required to close a political party or annul constitutional amendments would be changed to two-thirds from three-fifths. (Revises Article 149)

- The organization and function of the military Supreme Court of Appeals would be restructured. (Revises Article 156)

- The function of the Supreme Military Administrative Court would be based on the principle of the freedom of the courts rather than the "necessity of military duty." (Revises Article 157)

- The HSYK would be restructured to consist of 22 regular and 12 substitute members. Nineteen members would be appointed, four by the president. The court would also function in three separate departments and would have the power to launch investigations against judges and prosecutors. (Revises Article 159)

- The Economic and Social Council would be established as a constitutional institution. The council provides consultation to the government in creating economic and social policies. (Revises Article 166)

- An article banning the prosecution of the 1980 coup leaders would be annulled. (Annuls temporary Article 15)

On 30 March 2010, Turkey's ruling party AKP submitted its package of constitutional amendments to the parliament. The constitutional amendments were passed in parliament in late April and early May 2010 with over 330 votes, below the two-thirds majority of 367 votes needed to pass constitutional amendments directly, but enough to send constitutional amendments to a referendum within 60 days after President Mr. Gül signs the law. President Abdullah Gül signed the reform package on 13 May 2010.

The composition of the parliament (550 seats) during the voting process was as follows: AKP: 336, CHP: 97, MHP: 69, BDP: 20, Independent MPs: 12, DSP: 6, DP: 1, TP: 1. The ruling AKP has 336 seats, but deputy M. Ali Şahin could not vote as he is the parliament speaker. CHP and BDP decided to boycott the voting. The MHP voted against the articles in parliament.

Each article required more than 330 MPs' votes in order to pass. The amendment for Article 69, which would have limited the ability of the Constitutional Court to dissolve political parties, did not meet this 330 threshold in the 2nd round and was therefore dropped from the reform package.

The Constitution	Issue[9]	First round				Second round				Results
		MP turnout	Yes	No	Other	MP turnout	Yes	No	Other	
Article 10	Equality before the Law	407	336	70	1	408	332	75	1	✓
Article 20	Privacy protection	405	337	68	0	408	334	72	2	✓
Article 23	Prohibition to leave the country	408	337	71	0	407	335	71	1	✓
Article 41	Family law and children's rights	408	336	69	3	408	338	69	1	✓
Article 51	More than 1 union membership	405	333	70	2	409	335	70	4	✓
Article 53	Collective bargaining	408	336	70	2	409	338	71	0	✓
Article 54	Strike and lockout	408	335	69	4	409	337	71	1	✓
Article 69	Political party closure	414	337	72	5	410	327	76	7	✗
Article 74	Ombudsman	406	334	70	2	409	340	69	0	✓
Article 84	Membership in parliament	408	335	70	3	409	335	73	1	✓
Article 94	Parliament's presidential board	409	338	70	1	408	336	70	2	✓
Article 125	Recourse to judicial review	408	336	70	2	409	338	69	2	✓
Article 128	The right to collective bargaining	408	338	70	0	409	339	70	0	✓
Article 129	The right to apply to courts	408	336	71	1	408	339	69	0	✓
Article 144	Judicial oversight	407	335	71	1	409	338	70	1	✓
Article 145	Military Justice	407	337	70	0	410	336	72	2	✓
Article 146	Organisation of Constitutional Court	407	331	72	4	410	337	69	4	✓
Article 147	Term of office and membership	406	335	70	1	408	337	71	0	✓
Article 148	Functions and powers	407	337	69	1	408	337	70	1	✓
Article 149	Functioning and trial procedure	408	338	70	0	408	336	71	1	✓
Article 156	Military Court of Cassation	408	338	70	0	407	336	71	0	✓
Article 157	High Military Administrative Court	407	335	70	2	408	337	71	0	✓
Article 159	Organisation of the HSYK	409	336	72	1	409	334	73	2	✓

Table 17: Voting of referendum, 2010 in Parliament

The main opposition party CHP not only argues that the constitutional reform package includes unconstitutional reforms, but also that package was passed through procedural violations. It wants the Supreme Court to review the proposal process. The legal advisers of CHP also argued that the changes the package makes to the structures of the Supreme Court and the Supreme Board of Judges and Prosecutors (HSYK) are in violation of the constitutional principle in terms of separation of powers. With this assertion, the CHP alleges that the AKP is trying to change one of Turkey's constitutional articles that cannot be amended. So in addition to a review of the package on procedural principles, the CHP also demands a review of the content of the reform package. The CHP also requested a stay of the referendum results, bringing the total of the party's demands to three.

On 7 July 2010, the Turkish Supreme Court delivered its final verdict on a reform package of constitutional amendments, which is to be subject to a referendum on 12 September 2010. The Supreme Court has ruled in favour of the vast majority of the AKP government's proposed reforms to the constitution. The court did not annul the entire package. Judges annulled some parts of two articles, but rejected the demands of the opposition party CHP to scrap the whole package on technical grounds. The partially annulled articles belong to the structure of the Constitutional Court and the Supreme Board of Judges and Prosecutors (HSYK). They were moot due to the changes envisioned in the member appointment processes.

Both the government and the opposition partys expressed disappointment with the SupremeCourt's decision.

The results of the Turkish constitutional referendum are presented below:

Turkish constitutional referendum, 2010		
Choice	Votes	%
✓Yes	21,788,272	57.88
No	15,855,041	42.12
Valid votes	37,643,313	98.11
Invalid or blank votes	725,852	1.89
Total votes	38,369,165	100.00
Registered voters and turnout	52,051,828	73.71

Table 18: The results of the Turkish constitutional referendum

3.1.9. General election, 2011

17th general election of Turkey was held on 12 June 2011 to elect 550 new members of Turkish Grand National Assembly (TBMM). In accordance to the result of the constitutional referendum held in October 2007, the election was held four years after the previous one instead of five years.

The result was a third sequential victory for the incumbent AKP, with its leader Mr. Erdoğan being re-elected as Prime Minister for a third term with 49.8% vote rate and 327 MPs. This result indicated an rise of 3.2% since the 2007 general election and an 11.4% increase since the 2009 local elections. The success was related to the strong continuous economic recovery after the 2008 global economic crisis as well as the completion of many projects such as the İzmir commuter railway, inter-city high speed rail lines and airports in Amasya, Gökçeada and Antalya.

The CHP also saw a rise in its popular vote share, taking 26.0% and 135 MPs. The MHP received 13.0% and 53 MPs, representing a small loss of support since 2007. The election was the first general election to be competed by the CHP's new leader Kemal Kılıçdaroğlu, who replaced Deniz Baykal as party leader in 2010.

Encouraged by the 2010 constitutional referendum, AKP leaders said they would create a new constitution after the 2011 general elections.

In accordance with a law approved by Parliament in 2010 that made changes to Turkey's election laws, Turkish citizens encountered some new rules and reforms during the general election of 2011. These changes sought to bring election campaign rules and regulations up to EU standards.

- The age for parliamentary eligibility was reduced from thirty to twenty five.
- Wooden ballot boxes were replaced by hard plastic ballot boxes that were transparent, shatterproof, and resistant to heat.
- Voting booths were replaced by a stronger, safer, and more portable model.
- Voting envelopes were made bigger and had dissimilar colors for each matter that was being voted upon.
- Campaigning was allowed until 2 hours after sunset. In the previous law, campaigning after sundown was forbidden.
- Voters were able to vote without official identification as long as they could provide their ID number.
- Anyone who prevented a voter from casting their vote would receive 3 to 5 years in prison.

Turkish voters living in foreign countries needed to cast their votes at customs gates.

The results of the general elections, 2011 are presented below.

Leader	Recep Tayyip Erdoğan	Kemal Kılıçdaroğlu	Devlet Bahçeli
Party	AK Party	CHP	MHP
Leader since	14 August 2001	22 May 2010	6 July 1997
Leader's seat	İstanbul (I)	İstanbul (II)	Osmaniye
Last election	341 seats, 46.58%	112 seats, 20.88%	71 seats, 14.27%
Seats before	331	102	72
Seats won	327	135	53
Seat change	▼ 4	▲ 33	▼ 19
Popular vote	21,399,082	11,155,972	5,585,513
Percentage	49.83%	25.98%	13.01%
Swing	▲ 3.25 pp	▲ 5.10 pp	▼ 1.26 pp

Table 19: The results of the general election, 2011

The 3rd cabinet of Prime Minister Erdogan is the government of Turkey from 2011 to 2014, during the 24th parliamentary term of the Turkish parliament.

Functions	Holder	Start	End
Prime Minister	Recep Tayyip Erdoğan	6 July 2011	28 Aug. 2014
Deputy Prime Minister Responsible for Foundations and TRT	Bülent Arınç	6 July 2011	29 Aug. 2014
Deputy Prime Minister Resp. for Religious Affairs and the Turkish World	Bekir Bozdağ	6 July 2011	25 Dec. 2013
	Emrullah İşler	25 Dec. 2013	29 Aug. 2014
Deputy Prime Minister Resp. for the Economy, Banking and Treasury	Ali Babacan	6 July 2011	29 Aug. 2014
Deputy Prime Minister Resp. for Counter-terrorism, Human Rights and Cyprus	Beşir Atalay	6 July 2011	29 Aug. 2014
Ministry of Foreign Affairs	Ahmet Davutoğlu	6 July 2011	29 Aug. 2014
Ministry of the Interior	İdris Naim Şahin	6 July 2011	24 Jan. 2013
	Muammer Güler	24 Jan. 2013	25 Dec. 2013
	Efkan Ala	25 Dec. 2013	29 Aug. 2014
Ministry of Finance	Mehmet Şimşek	6 July 2011	29 Aug. 2014
Ministry of Justice	Sadullah Ergin	6 July 2011	25 Dec. 2013
	Bekir Bozdağ	25 Dec. 2013	29 Aug. 2014
Ministry of Energy and Natural Resources	Taner Yıldız	6 July 2011	29 Aug. 2014
Ministry of Food, Agriculture and Livestock	Mehmet Mehdi Eker	6 July 2011	29 Aug. 2014

Ministry	Name	Start	End
Ministry of Culture and Tourism	Ertuğrul Günay	6 July 2011	24 Jan. 2013
	Ömer Çelik	24 Jan. 2013	29 Aug. 2014
Ministry of Health	Recep Akdağ	6 July 2011	24 Jan. 2013
	Mehmet Müezzinoğlu	24 Jan. 2013	29 Aug. 2014
Ministry of National Education	Ömer Dinçer	6 July 2011	24 Jan. 2013
	Nabi Avcı	24 Jan. 2013	29 Aug. 2014
Ministry of National Defence	İsmet Yılmaz	6 July 2011	29 Aug. 2014
Ministry of Science, Industry and Tech.	Nihat Ergün	6 July 2011	25 Dec. 2013
	Fikri Işık	25 Dec. 2013	29 Aug. 2014
Ministry of Labour and Social Security	Faruk Çelik	6 July 2011	29 Aug. 2014
Ministry of Transport, Maritime and Comm.	Binali Yıldırım	6 July 2011	25 Dec. 2013
	Lütfi Elvan	25 Dec. 2013	29 Aug. 2014
Ministry of Family and Social Policy	Fatma Şahin	6 July 2011	25 Dec. 2013
	Ayşenur İslam	25 Dec. 2013	29 Aug. 2014
Ministry of European Union Affairs	Egemen Bağış	6 July 2011	25 December 2013
	Mevlüt Çavuşoğlu	25 Dec. 2013	29 Aug. 2014
Ministry of Economy	Zafer Çağlayan	6 July 2011	25 Dec. 2013
	Nihat Zeybekçi	25 December 2013	29 August 2014
Ministry of Youth and Sports	Suat Kılıç	6 July 2011	25 Dec. 2013
	Akif Çağatay Kılıç	25 Dec. 2013	29 Aug. 2014
Ministry of Development	Cevdet Yılmaz	6 July 2011	29 Aug. 2014
Ministry of Customs and Trade	Hayati Yazıcı	6 July 2011	29 Aug. 2014
Ministry of Envir. and Urban Planning	Erdoğan Bayraktar	6 July 2011	25 Dec. 2013
	İdris Güllüce	25 Dec. 2013	29 Aug. 2014
Ministry of Forest and Water Management	Veysel Eroğlu	6 July 2011	29 Aug. 2014

Table 20: Cabinet Erdogan III

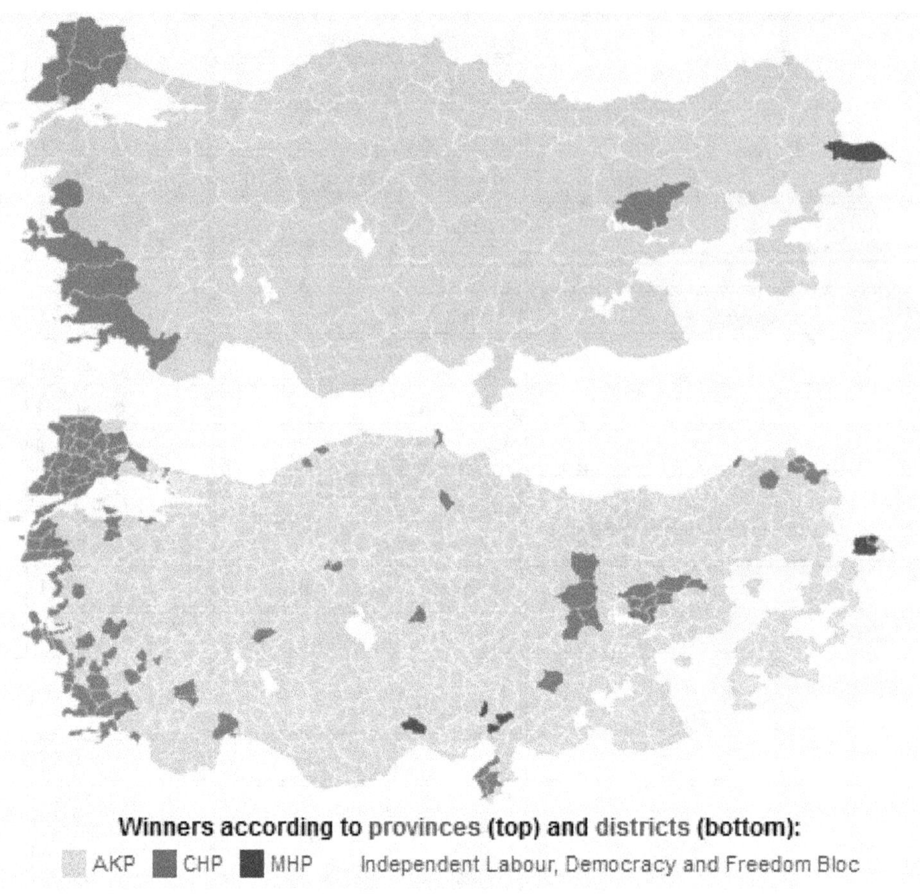

Figure 15: Results of the general election, 2011 per province.

3.1.10. Local elections, 2014

Local elections were held on 30 March 2014, with repeated for some districts on 1 June 2014. Metropolitan and district mayors as well as their municipal council members in cprovinces, and muhtars were elected. Nearly 50 million people were eligible to vote.

A local government reform took place before the election, decreasing the total number of elected officials from 38,592 to 23,132. Nearly 1,500 small municipal towns had their municipalities abolished, meaning that a significantly fewer number of mayors were elected compared to the previous local elections. Many provinces no longer elect any provincial councillors. On the other hand, the number of metropolitan municipalities increased from 16 to 30.

The ruling AKP announced its victory in the early hours of 31 March, receiving 42.89% of the vote, 818 municipalities and 11,309 councillors. The opposition party CHP came second party with 26.34%, 232 municipalities and 4,320 councillors, declared that it would be filing complaints against alleged electoral manipulation. Several municipalities changed mayors following recounts on 4 April

2014. Gradual post-election revelations of alleged widespread irregularities in some cities sparked pro-democracy protests after provisional results were announced, while the Supreme Electoral Council declared results in some areas null and void. A repeat of the elections in these areas took place on 1 June 2014. These most notably occurred in Yalova and Ağrı cities, in which the ruling AKP had lost by a small margin to the CHP and BDP respectively on 30 March 2014. In a first of a series of trials relating to electoral fraud claims in local elections, a returning officer was sentenced to 5 years in prison in June 2015 after being found delinquent of transferring CHP votes to the AKP.

The table below shows the numbers of metropolitan and district municipalities, also provincial and municipal councillors elected in 2009 and in 2014. Municipal mayors and councillors are the only partisan officials elected in local elections.

Office	2009 election	2014 election	Change
Number of Metropolitan municipalities	16	30	▲14
Number of District municipalities	2,903	1,351	▼1,552
Number of Provincial councillors	3,281	1,251	▼2,030
Number of Municipal councillors	32,392	20,500	▼11,892
Total Number	38,592	23,132	▼15,460

Table 21: The numbers of metropolitan and district municipalities

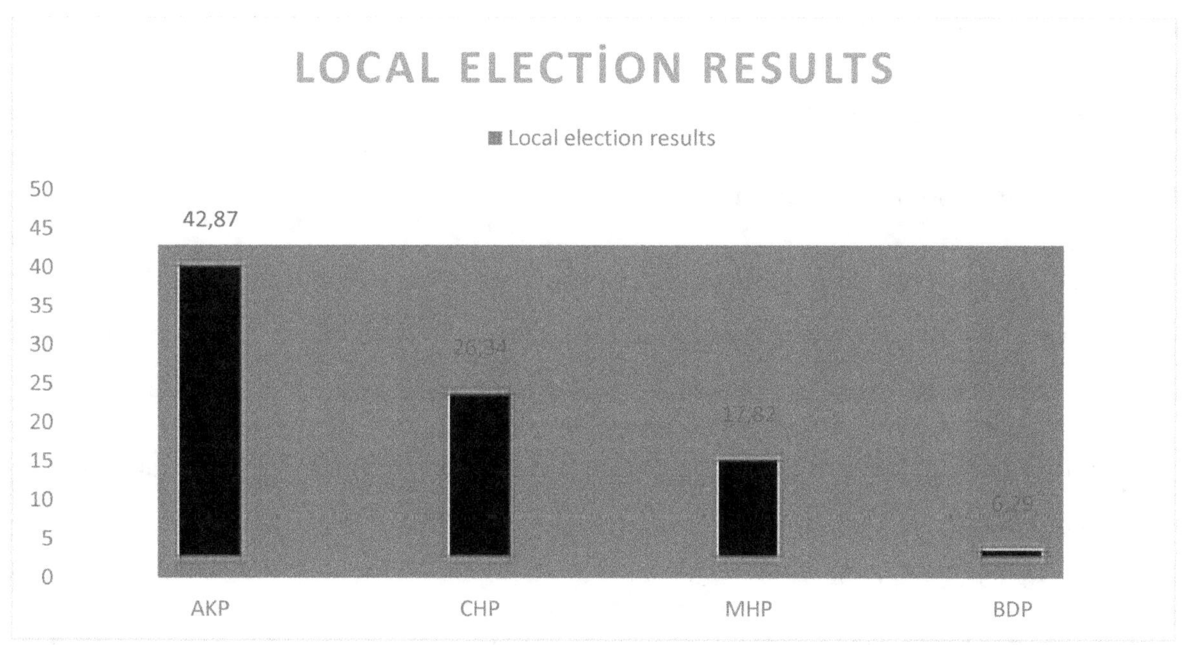

Figure 16: The resulst of the local elections, 2014

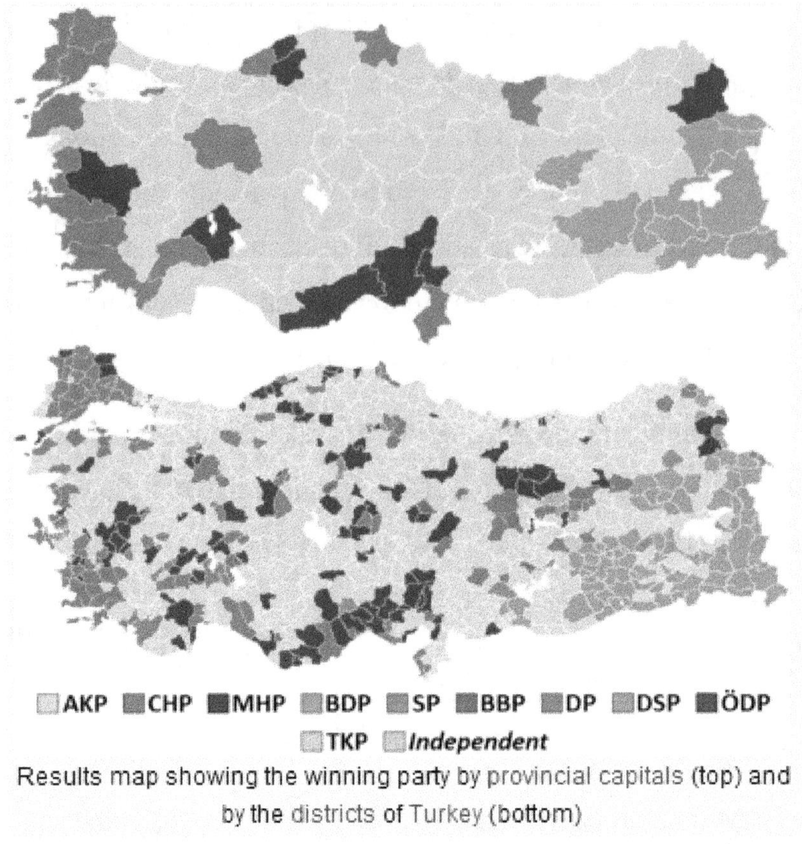

Figure 17: Results of the local elections, 2014 per province.

4. Presidency (2014- present)

4.1. Elections and Referendums

4.1.1. Presidential election, 2014

Presidential elections were held on 10 August 2014 in Turkey for electing the 12th President of Turkey. PM Recep Tayyip Erdoğan was elected outright with an absolute majority of the vote in the first round, making a scheduled second round for 24 August unnecessary.

The election took place under reforms arising from the 2007 constitutional referendum, which introduced a direct popular vote, rather than election by MPs. Over 55 million citizens were eligible to vote, both within Turkey and abroad.

Mr. Erdoğan, first elected Prime Minister in 2003, won with 51.79% of the vote presidential election. Previous Organisation of Islamic Cooperation General Secretary Ekmeleddin İhsanoğlu, who ran as the joint candidate of thirteen opposition parties including the CHP and MHP, came second with 38.44%. The leader of the HDP, Selahattin Demirtaş who ran the joint candidate of 8 left-wing parties, came third with 9.76% in election.

Erdoğan took over as president from Mr. Gül on 28 August, while Mr. Davutoğlu, who was elected leader of the AK Party (AKP), succeeded Mr. Erdoğan as PM on the same date. It has been speculated that Mr. Erdoğan will continue to pursue his political agenda as president while Ahmet Davutoğlu takes a docile approach as PM, breaking away from the neutral and ceremonial functions of the presidency and potentially pursuing constitutional changes to turn Turkey's system into a presidential system or semi-presidential system.

Despite praising the authorities for safeguarding the right to assembly as well as the peaceful electoral conduct, the Organization for Security and Cooperation in Europe (OSCE) stressed concerns over the unequal distribution of campaign resources and media intimidation.The historic 12-year low turnout of 74.13% in the election, attributed to the fact that the presidential election was held in summer while many people were on holiday, was seen by most of the politicians such as MHP leader Devlet Bahçeli as an important factor in affecting the outcome. The election loss for the opposition party CHP resulted in its leader Mr. Kılıçdaroğlu taking the decision to hold a party convention with a leadership election in response to growing dissatisfaction against his electoral failure.

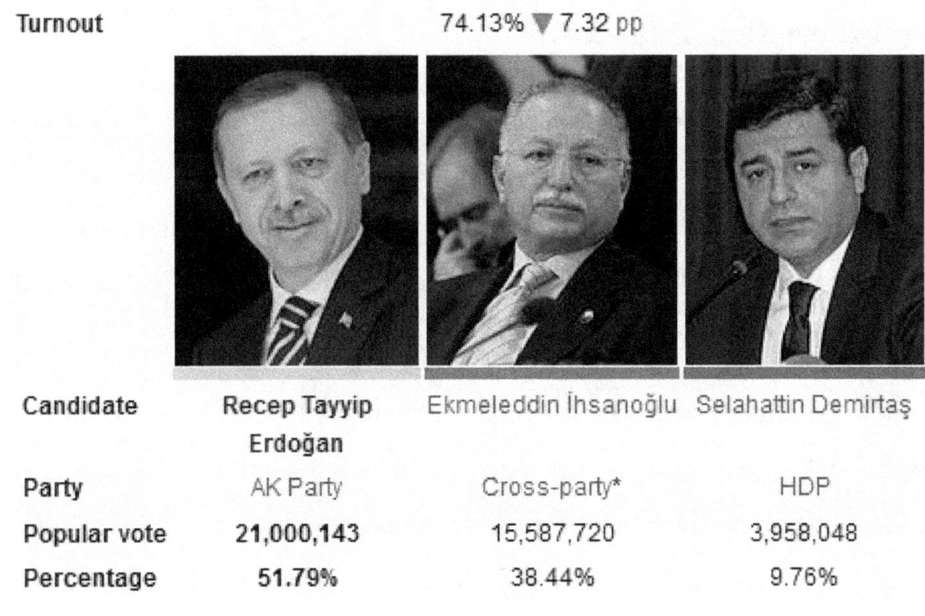

Figure 18: The results of the presidential election, 2014

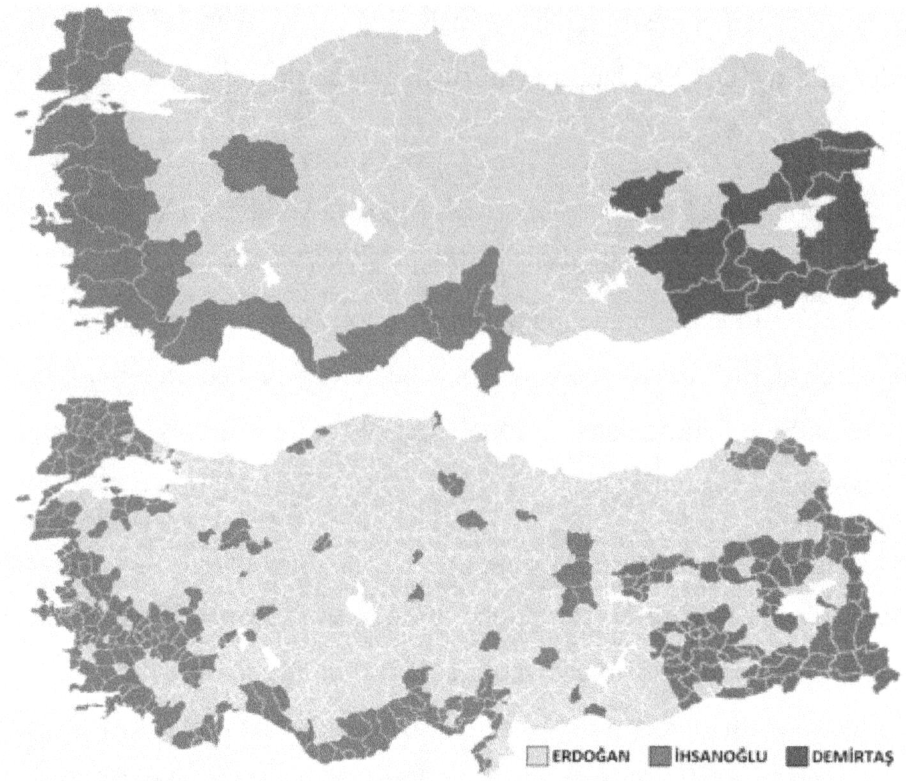

Maps showing the winners by province (top) and by district (bottom). Yellow denotes those won by Recep Tayyip Erdoğan, red denotes those won by Ekmeleddin İhsanoğlu, purple denotes those won by Selahattin Demirtaş.

Figure 19: Results of the presidential election, 2014 per province.

4.1.2. General election, June 2015

The general election took place on 7 June 2015 in all 85 electoral districts of Turkey to elect 550 members to the parliament. This was the 24th general election in the Turkish politicial history, electing the Turkeys 25th Parliament. The result of the election was the first hung parliament since the 1999 general election. Unsuccessful attempts to form a coalition government resulted in a snap general election were held on November 2015.

The AKP, which had governed the Republic of Turkey since 2002, lost its parliamentary majority and won 258 seats with 40.9% vote rate. The main opposition party CHP also fared worse than its 2011 result, and won 132 seats with 25.0% vote rate. The other opposition party MHP had been projected to win over many disaffected ctizens from the AKP. MHP's vote rate increased, and the MHP won 80 seats with 16.3% share of vote. The Peoples' Democratic Party (HDP) decided to contest the general election as a party rather than fielding candidates as independents, despite some concerns about HDP could have fallen below the 10% election threshold and lose its all representation in parliament. The

HDP fared better than expectations: HDP won 13.1% of the vote and took 80 seats in parliament, the same as the MHP. The potential for a hung parliament had been throughly considered and predicted before the general election so the citizens and politicians were better prepared for the constitutional change process that would follow such a result.

Campaigning before the election focused primarily on a faltering economy, the political conflict between the AKP government and the Gülen Movement, and country's involvement in the Syrian Civil War. Growing claims of AKP government's corruption and authoritarianism, mainly originating from the 17-25 December 2013 corruption scandal and the 2013 Gezi Park protests respectively, were also part of the issues raised during the opposition parties' campaigns.

The general election was largely praised by the Organisation for Security and Cooperation in Europe for being very well-organised and was declared free and fair by the EU Parliament.

On 11 June 2015, the AKP appeared to backtrack on its support for an executive presidency, with party leader Mr. Davutoğlu stating that he was not against the current parliamentary system. Mr. Davutoğlu also claimed that the AKP did not have any non-negotiable preconditions for a coalition goverment despite earlier contradictory reports.

Party		24th Parliament (28 June 2011 – 23 June 2015)			25th Parliament (23 June 2015 –)
		2011 vote %	Elected	At dissolution	Elected
AKP	Justice and Development Party	49.83	327 / 550	311 / 550	258 / 550
CHP	Republican People's Party	25.98	135 / 550	125 / 550	132 / 550
MHP	Nationalist Movement Party	13.01	53 / 550	52 / 550	80 / 550
	Independents	6.57	35 / 550	13 / 550	0 / 550
HDP	Peoples' Democratic Party	New Party		29 / 550	80 / 550
DBP	Democratic Regions Party*	Contested as independents		1 / 550	Did not contest
ANAPAR	Anatolia Party	New Party		1 / 550	0 / 550
eP	Electronic Democracy Party	New Party		1 / 550	Did not contest
MEP	Centre Party	New Party		1 / 550	0 / 550
Total		95.39	550	535^	550

Table 22: Parliamentary composition, 2015

President Erdoğan formally tasked Mr. Davutoğlu with forming a new government on 9 July, with the Turkish Constitution granting Davutoğlu 45 days (until 23 August 2015) to form a new government. The first round of coalition talks involved discussions between the AKP with the opposition parties CHP, MHP and HDP. Afterwards the AKP announced that it would no longer pursue any negotiations with the HDP. The second round of coalition talks mainly focused on the CHP, while the MHP declared its support for a snap election and closed its doors on any form of deal soon after. Talks between the AKP and CHP continued into August, enduring collectively over 35 hours. The CHP unveiled fourteen principles upon which a coalition government involving them would stick to, involving many of its manifesto pledges. The MHP later backtracked on its support for a snap election and supported the formation of an AKP-CHP coalition government. The leaders of the AKP and CHP met finally in a meeting that had been perceived to be where a final decision would be made on whether to form a coalition government on 13 August 2015. The meeting ended after the AKP proposed a three-month interim government followed by snap elections, despite the CHP's insistence that the coalition government should last four years.

The breakdown of coalition talks between the AKP and the CHP, as well as the MHP's scepticism of forming a government resulted in Mr. Davutoğlu stating that a snap election was the only option, though he requested a final meeting with MHP leader Mr. Bahçeli. With a spate of terrorist attacks by the PKK and the Islamic State of Iraq and the Syria (ISIS) on Turkish soil in response to the government's Operation Martyr Yalçın, Bahçeli ended his support for a snap election claiming that it was not possible during such circumstances. He set out four new unconditional terms for a coalition government, which were the complete end to discussions over changing the first 4 articles of the Turkish Constitution, the ending of the kurdish issue solution process, a limit on Mr. Erdoğan's powers within a parliamentary system with checks and balances restored as well as the re-opening of the suppressed corruption investigations into 4 former AKP government ministers. The coalition negotiations, held on 17 August, broke down, effectively ending all probabilities for a coalition government. Davutoğlu stated that he would subsequently gave up the task of forming a new government.

It has been widely reported during the coalition talks that the AKP heavily favours going into a snap election, with President Mr. Erdoğan also being reported to have been heavily suspicious of a coalition government. Proponents of a snap election also included the leader of the AKP coalition negotiation team Mr. Çelik, whom Davutoğlu allegedly tried to remove from his role in the coalition negotiations but he failed due to Çelik's close relations with President Mr. Erdoğan. The snap election were held on 1 November 2015.

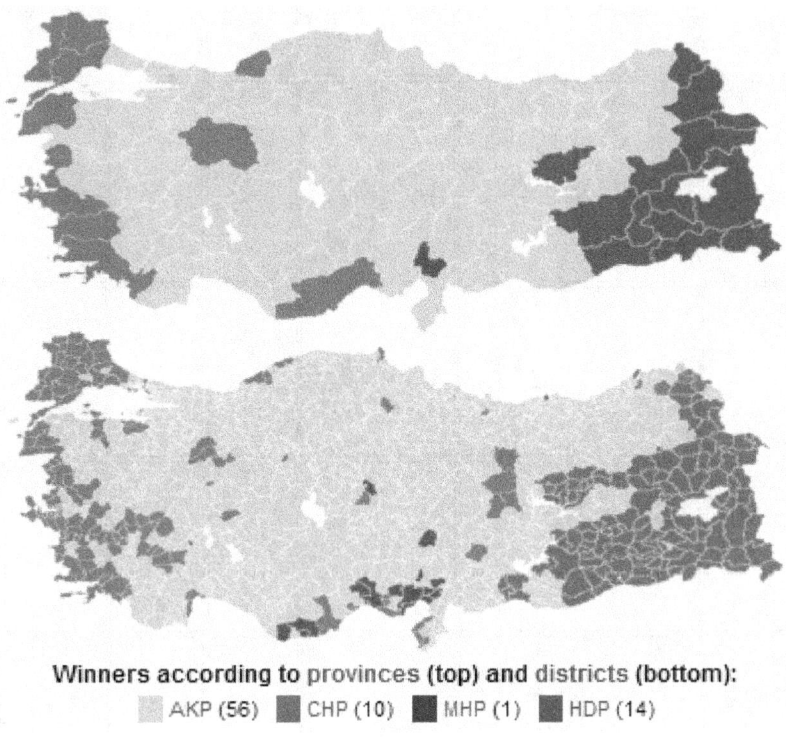

Figure 20: Results of the general election, June 2015 per province.

Party			Vote			Seats			
Abbr.	Party name *in Turkish*	Leader(s)	Votes	%	swing (pp)	Elected	% of total	± since 6 June	± since 2011
AKP	Justice and Development Party *Adalet ve Kalkınma Partisi*	Ahmet Davutoğlu	18,867,411	40.87	▼8.96	258	46.91	▼53	▼69
CHP	Republican People's Party *Cumhuriyet Halk Partisi*	Kemal Kılıçdaroğlu	11,518,139	24.95	▼1.03	132	24.00	▲7	▼3
MHP	Nationalist Movement Party *Milliyetçi Hareket Partisi*	Devlet Bahçeli	7,520,006	16.29	▲3.28	80	14.55	▲28	▲27
HDP	Peoples' Democratic Party *Halkların Demokratik Partisi*	Selahattin Demirtaş Figen Yüksekdağ	6,058,489	13.12	▲7.45	80	14.55	▲51	▲80
SAADET	Felicity Party *Saadet Partisi*	Mustafa Kamalak	949,178	2.06	▲0.79	0	0.00	—0	—0
	Independents *Bağımsızlar*		488,226	1.06	▲0.16	0	0.00	▼15	▼35

Table 23: The results of the general election, June 2015

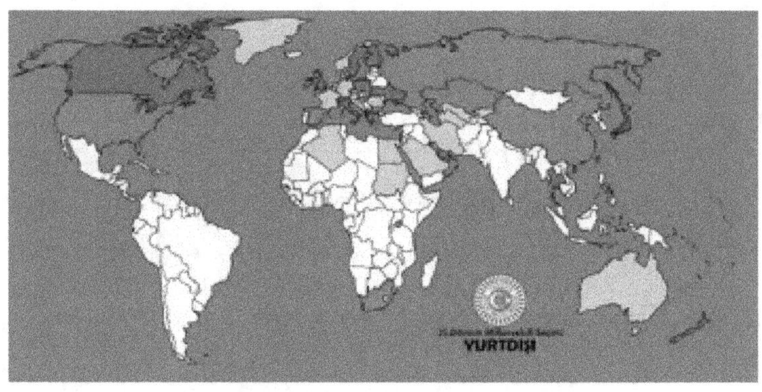

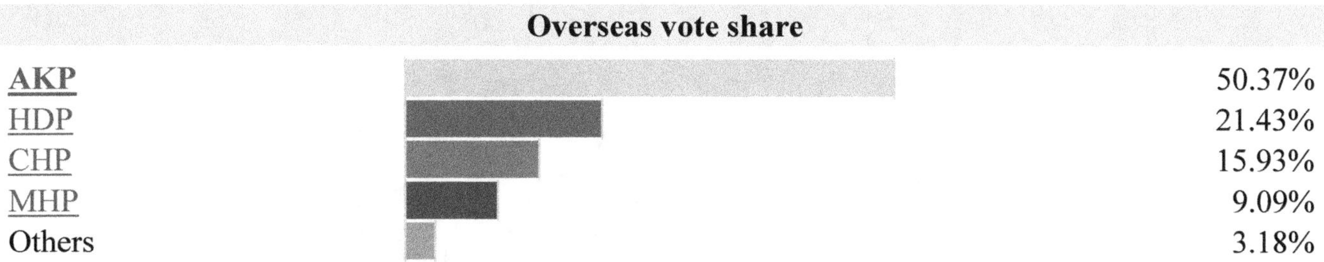

Figure 21: Overseas results of the general election, June 2015

4.1.3. General election, November 2015

The general election was held on 1 November 2015 throughout the 85 electoral districts of Turkey to elect 550 members to the parliament. It was the 25th general election in Turkish history and elected the Turkey's 26th parliament. The election resulted in the AKP regaining a parliamentary majority following a 'shock' triumph, having lost it 5 months earlier in the June 2015 general election.

The early election was called by President Erdoğan on 24 August 2015 after the June 2015 general election resulted in a hung parliament and coalition government negotiations broke down. Although the general election, dubbed as a 're-run' of the inconclusive June election by Mr. Erdoğan, was the 7th snap election in the history of Turkish politics, it was the first to be overseen by an temporary election government. The general election rendered the 25th parliament of Turkey, elected in June 2015, the shortest in the Turkish Grand National Assembly's history, lasting for just 5 months and being in session for a total of 33 hours.

Amid speculation that the general election would likely result in a 2nd hung parliament, pollsters and commentators were found to have strongly underestimated the AKP vote, which bore resemblance to its record 2011 general election victory. With 49.5% of the vote and 317 seats, the AKP won a comfortable majority in parliament, while the CHP retained its main opposition status with 134 seats and 25.4% vote rate. These results were widely seen as a 'shock' victory for the AKP and was hailed as a huge personal victory for President Erdoğan. The MHP and the HDP both saw decreases in their support, with both hovering dangerously close to the 10% election threshold needed to win seats in parliament. The MHP, which was seen to have been punished for its perceivably unconstructive stance since June 2015, halved its parliamentary representation from 80 MPs to 40 MPs and gain 11.9% of the vote, while the HDP came 3rd in terms of seats with 59 MPs despite coming 4th in terms of votes with 10.7%. The general election was broadly regarded as free and fair.

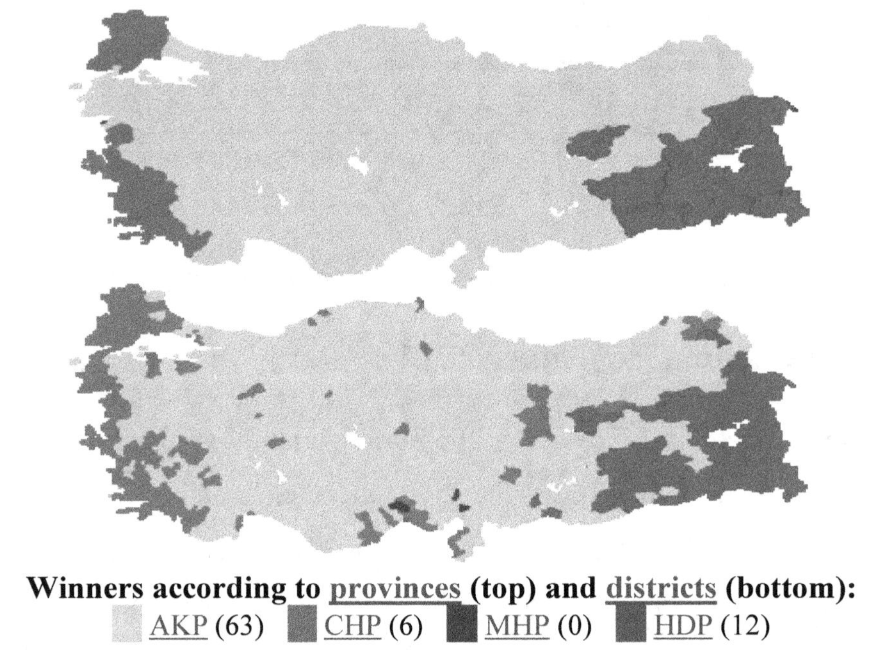

Figure 22: Results of the general election, November 2015 per province.

Party		Vote			Seats			
Party name *in Turkish*	**Leader(s)**	**Number**	**%**	**swing**	**Elected**	**% of total**	**± since 31 Oct**	**± since Jun 2015**
Justice and Development Party *Adalet ve Kalkınma Partisi*	Ahmet Davutoğlu	23,681,926	49.50	▲ 8.63	317	57.64	▲58	▲59
Republican People's Party *Cumhuriyet Halk Partisi*	Kemal Kılıçdaroğlu	12,111,812	25.32	▲0.37	134	24.36	▲3	▲2
Nationalist Movement Party *Milliyetçi Hareket Partisi*	Devlet Bahçeli	5,694,136	11.90	▼4.39	40	7.27	▼39	▼40
Peoples' Democratic Party *Halkların Demokratik Partisi*	Selahattin Demirtaş Figen Yüksekdağ	5,148,085	10.76	▼2.36	59	10.73	▼21	▼21
Felicity Party *Saadet Partisi*	Mustafa Kamalak	325,978	0.68	▼1.38	0	0.00	—0	—0
Great Union Party *Büyük Birlik Partisi*	Mustafa Destici	253,204	0.53	N/A	0	0.00	N/A	N/A
Patriotic Party *Vatan Partisi*	Doğu Perinçek	118,803	0.25	▼0.10	0	0.00	—0	—0

Table 24: The results of the general election, November 2015

4.1.4. Constitutional Referendum, 2017

A constitutional referendum took place on 16 April 2017 on whether to approve 18 proposed amendments to the Turkish Constitution that were brought forward by the ruling AKP and the MHP. If amendments approved, the office of the Prime Minister would be removed and the existing parliamentary system of government would be altered with an executive presidency and a presidential system. The number of seats in Grand National Assembly was proposed to be raised from 550 to 600 while the Turkish President was proposed to be given more control over appointments to the Supreme Board of Judges and Prosecutors (HSYK). The referendum was held under a state of emergency that was declared following a failed military coup attempt on 15th July 2016.

Early results exuded a 51–49% lead for the "Yes" vote. In an unprecedented move, the Supreme Electoral Council (YSK) allowed non-stamped ballots to be accepted as valid ballots. The opposition parties decried this move to be illegal, claiming that nearly 1.5 million ballots were unstamped, and refused to recognize the official results. Large-scale pro-democracy protests erxploded following the results in order to protest the YSK's decision. In subsequent reports, the Organization for Security and Cooperation in Europe (OSCE) and Parliamentary Assembly of the Council of Europe (PACE) both criticised unfairness during the electoral campaign and declared the YSK's decision to be illegal.

An executive presidency has been a long-standing proposal of the ruling AKP and its founder Erdoğan. The MHP announced its co-operation for producing draft proposals with the government in October 2016. The total number of both AKP and MHP MPs being sufficient to put forward the amendments to a referendum following a parliamentary vote in January. Those in favour of a 'Yes' vote argued that the constitutional changes were necessary for a strong and stable Turkey. They claimed that an executive presidency would end to unstable coalition governments that had dominated Turkey since the 1960s up until 2002. The 'No' campaign have claimed that the proposals would concentrate too much power in the hands of the executive president, effectively disassembling the separation of powers and taking legislative authority away from the Grand National Assembly. 3 days before the referendum, one of Mr. Erdoğan's aides called for a federal system should the 'Yes' vote prevail, producing a backlash from the pro-Yes MHP.Both sides of the referendum campaign have been accused of using divisive and extreme rhetoric, with President Erdoğan accusing all 'No' voters of being terrorists siding with the plotters of the failed July 2016 coup.

The 'Yes' campaign were faced with campaigning restrictions by several EU countries, with the German, Dutch, Danish and Swiss governments all cancelling or requesting the suspension of 'Yes' campaign events directed at Turkish citizens living abroad. The cancellations caused a sharp deterioration in diplomatic relations and caused a diplomatic crisis between Turkish and the Dutch goverments. Some concerns were also raised about voting irregularities, with 'Yes' voters in Germany being caught trying to vote more than once and also being found to have been in possession of ballot papers before the overseas citizens' voting process had started. European election monitors told the vote did not meet international standards.

The AKP and MHP brought forward a total of 21 proposed amendments to the constitution on 10 December 2016. They began collecting signatures from MPs in order to begin the parliamentary procedures for initiating a referendum. After Turkish Grand National Assembly Commission talks, three proposals were withdrawn, leaving 18 amendments were remaining.

An English-language summary and interpretation of the 18 amendments are listed in the table below.

Definition of proposed amendments		
Proposal #	**Article**	**Definition of change**
1	Article 9	The judiciary is required to act on condition of neutrality.
2	Article 75	The number of seats in the Parliament is increased from 550 to 600.
3	Article 76	The age requirement to stand as a candidate in an election to be decreased from 25 to 18, while the condition of having to complete mandotory military service is to be removed. Citizens with relations to the military would be ineligible to run for election.
4	Article 77	Parliamentary terms are expanded from 4 to 5 years. Parliamentary and presidential elections will be held on the same day each 5 years, with presidential elections going to a run-off if no candidate wins a simple majority in the 1st round.
5	Article 87	The functions of Parliament are • Making, changing and removing laws. • Voting international contracts. • Argue, increase or decrease budget (on Budget Commission) and accept or reject the budget on parliament. • Appoint seven members of HSYK • And using other powers written in the Turkish Constitution
6	Article 89	To overcome a presidential veto, the Turkish Parliament needs to adopt the same law with an absolute majority (301).
7	Article 98	Grand National Assembly now detects cabinet and Vice President with *Parliamentary Research, Parliamentary Investigation, General Discussion* and *Written Question*. Interpellation is removed and replaced with *Parliamentary Investigation*. Vice President has to answer *Written Questions* within 15 days.
8	Article 101	In order to stand as a presidential candidate, a citizen requires the endorsement of 1 or more parties that won 5% or more in the preceding general elections and 100,000 voters. The elected president no longer needs to end their party membership if they have one.
9	Article 104	The Turkish President becomes both the head of state and head of government and could appoint and sack ministers and Vice President. The president could issue decrees about executive. If legislation makes a bill about the same topic that President issued an executive order, decree will become invalid and parliamentary bill become valid.
10	Article 105	Parliament could open parliamentary investigation with an absolute majority (301). Parliament discusses proposal in one month. After the

11		completion of Discussion, Parliamentary investigation could begin in Parliament with a hidden three-fifths (360) vote in favor. After the completion of investigations, the parliament could vote to indict the President with a hidden two-thirds (400) vote in favor.
11	Article 106	The President could appoint one or more Vice Presidents. If the Presidency falls vacant, then new presidential elections must be held within 45 days. If parliamentary elections are due within less than 1 year, then these two elections are held on the same day. If the parliament has over 1 year left before its term expires, then the freshly elected president serves until the end of the parliamentary term, after which both two elections are held. It does not count towards the President's 2-term limit. Parliamentary investigations into possible crimes committed by Vice Presidents and ministers could begin in Parliament with a three-fifths vote in favor. After the completion of investigations, the parliament could vote to indict Vice Presidents or ministers with a two-thirds vote in favor. If found delinquent, the Vice President or minister in question is only removed from office if their crime is one that inhibits them from running for election. If an incumbent MP is appointed as a minister or Vice President, their parliamentary membership will be end.
12	Article 116	The President and three-fifths of the assembly could decide to renew elections. In this case, the enactor also dissolves itself till elections.
13	Article 119	The President's ability to declare state of emergency is now subject to assembly approval to take effect. The Parliament could extend, remove or shorten it. States of emergency could be extended for up to 4 months at a time except during war, where no such limitation will be necessary. Each presidential decree issues during a state of emergency will need an approval of Parliament.
14	Article 125	The acts of the Turkish President are now subject to judicial review.
15	Article 142	Military courts are abolished except they are erected to investigate actions of military officers under conditions of warfare.
16	Article 146	The President used to appoint one Judge from High Military Court of Appeals, and one from the High Military Administrative Court. As military courts would be abolished, the number of Judges in the Constitutional Court would be reduced from 17 to 15. As a result, presidential appointees would be reduced from 14 to 12, while the Parliament would continue to appoint 3.
17	Article 159	Supreme Board of Judges and Prosecutors is renamed to "Board of Judges and Prosecutors" and the number of members are reduced to 13 from 22. Its departments are reduced to 2 from 3. 4 members are appointed by the Turkish President, 7 members will be appointed by the parliament. Supreme Board of Judges and Prosecutors (HSYK) candidates will have to get 2/3 (400) votes to pass 1st round and will need 3/5 (360) votes in 2nd round to be a member of HSYK.(Other two members are Justice Minister and Ministry of Justice Undersecretary, which is unchanged).
18	Article 161	President proposes fiscal budget to parliament 75 days prior to fiscal

			new year. Budget Commission members could make changes to budget but MPs could not make proposals to change public expenditures. If the budget is not approved by parliament, then a temporary budget will be proposed. If the temporary budget is also not approved, the previous year's budget would be used with the previous year's inflation ratio.
19	Several articles		Adaptation of many articles of the constitution with other changes, primarily transferring executive powers of cabinet to President
20	Temporary Article 21		Next presidential and General elections will take place on 3 November 2019. If parliament decides early elections, both will be held at the same day. Board of Judges and Prosecutors elections will be made within 30 days of approval of this bill. Military courts will be abolished once the bill comes into force.
21	Applicability of amendments 1-17		The amendments (2, 4, and 7) will come into force after next elections but other amendments (except temporary article) will come into force once newly elected president is sworn in. Annulled the article which elected Presidents forfeit their membership in a political party. This constitutional amendment will be voted in a referendum completely.

Table 25: Description of proposed amendments

The Parliamantery Commission completed the approval process on 30 December 2016 and rejected 3 of the 21 proposals in total.

Parliamentary Constitutional Commission scrutiny process results																					
Proposal	1	2	3	4	5	6	7	8	9	10	11	12	13	14	15	16	17	18	19	20	21
Result	✓	✓	✓	✓	✗	✓	✓	✓	✓	✓	✓	✓	✓	✗	✗	✓	✓	✓	✓	✓	✓

Table 26: Parliamentary Constitutional Commission scrutiny process results

Theoretical distribution of votes according to party lines							
Party		**Leader**	**Party position**	**Total MPs**	**Eligible to vote**	**Voting yes**	**Voting no**
AKP	Justice and Development Party	Binali Yıldırım	✓ Yes	317	315	315	0
CHP	Republican People's Party	Kemal Kılıçdaroğlu	✗ No	133	133	0	133
MHP	Nationalist Movement Party	Devlet Bahçeli	✓ Yes	39	39	33	6
HDP	Peoples' Democratic Party	Selahattin Demirtaş / Serpil Kemalbay	✗ No	59	48	*Boycotting*	
	Independents		✗ No (both)	2	2	0	2
Total				**550**	**537**	**348**	**141**

Table 27: Theoretical distribution of votes according to party lines

A final motion to present the approved amendments was approved by 339 votes, exceeding the 330-vote threshold to hold a referendum but falling short of the 367-vote threshold required to enact these amendments directly in parliament.

Choice	Nationwide votes	%	Overseas votes	%	Customs votes	%	Total votes	%
✓ Yes	24,325,633	51.18	778,833	59.46	52,997	54.17	25,157,463	51.41
✗ No	23,203,316	48.82	530,988	40.54	44,837	45.83	23,779,141	48.59
Valid votes	47,528,949	98.25	1,309,821	98.80	97,834	99.23	48,936,604	98.27
Invalid/blank votes	845,627	1.75	15,861	1.20	763	0.77	862,251	1.73
Turnout	48,374,576	87.45	1,325,682	44.60	98,597	3.32	49,798,855	85.43
Registered voters	55,319,222				2,972,676		58,291,898	

Table 28: The results of the constitutional referendum, 2017

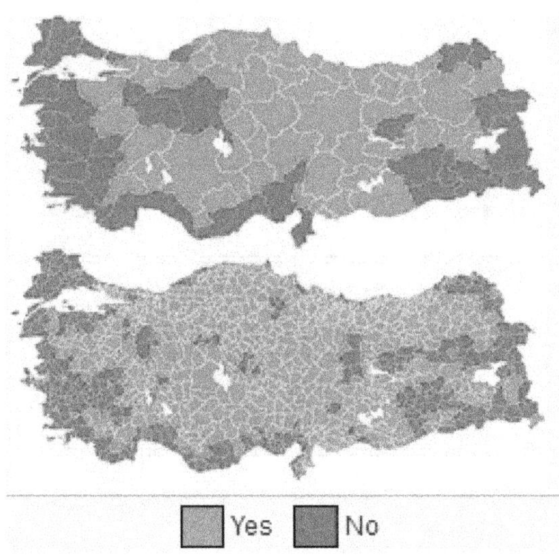

Figure 23: Constitutional referendum, 2017 results by province and districts

4.1.5. Presidential election, 2018

The presidential election were held on on 24 June 2018 as part of the 2018 general election, alongside parliamentary elections on the same date. After the approval of constitutional changes in a referendum held in April 2017, the elected Turkish President will be both the head of state and head of government, taking over the latter role from the to-be-abolished office of the PM.

The election was normally scheduled for November 2019. Altough insistence from the government that government would not be brought forward, speculation over a snap election continued since the 2017 referendum. After calls from MHP leader Mr. Bahçeli for an early election, President Mr. Erdoğan announced on 18 April 2018 that it would take place on 24 June 2018.

President Mr. Erdoğan declared his candidacy for the People's Alliance (In Turkish: Cumhur İttifakı) on 27 April 2018. Turkey's main opposition party, the CHP, declared Muharrem İnce, a member of the parliament known for his combative opposition and spirited speeches against Mr. Erdoğan. The HDP nominated the imprisoned ex-chairman Demirtaş. In addition to these candidates, Meral Akşener, leader of İyi Party (IP), Mr. Karamollaoğlu, the leader of the SP (Felicity Party) and Mr. Perinçek, the leader of the VP (Patriotic Party), have announced their candidacies and collected the 100,000 signatures from the citizens required for their nomination.

Campaigning for the election focused mainly on the faltering economy and the Turkish currency and debt crisis, with both government and opposition commentators warning of a more dangereous economic crisis following the election. The 2018 Gaza border protests, following the USA recognition of Jerusalem as capital of Israel, along with the Turkish military operation in Afrin, were also argued in the campaign.

Candidate	Party	Votes		
		#	%	±
Recep Tayyip Erdoğan	**Justice and Development Party (AKP)**	**26,330,823**	**52.59**	+0.80
Muharrem İnce	Republican People's Party (CHP)	15,340,321	30.64	New
Selahattin Demirtaş	Peoples' Democratic Party (HDP)	4,205,794	8.40	-1.36
Meral Akşener	İyi Party (İYİ)	3,649,030	7.29	New
Temel Karamollaoğlu	Felicity Party (SP)	443,704	0.89	New
Doğu Perinçek	Patriotic Party (VP)	98,955	0.20	New
Invalid/blank votes		1,129,275	–	–
Total		**51,188,524**	**100.00**	–
Registered voters/turnout		59,354,840	86.24	+12.11

Table 29: The results of the presidential election, 2018

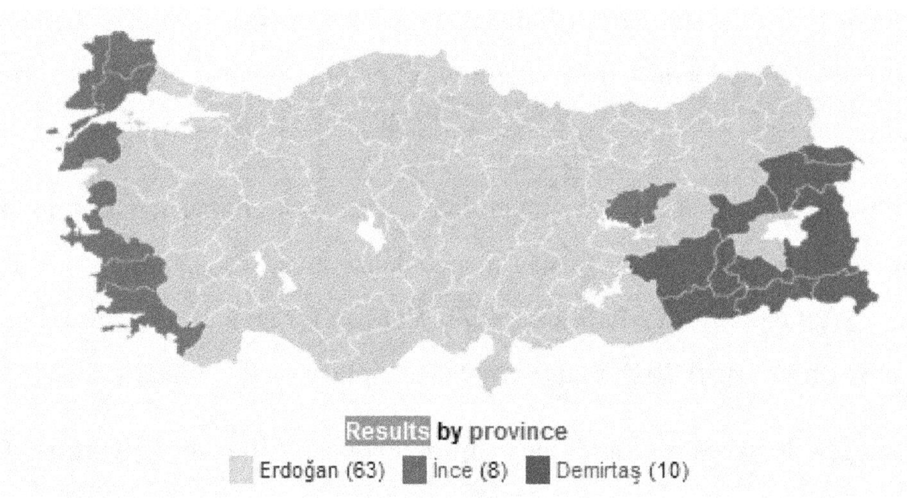

Figure 24: The presidential election, 2018 results by province

The 4th Erdoğan Cabinet is the 66th government of the Turkey, which was declared on 9 July 2018. It is the first cabinet after Turkey's transition into presidential system. Also, the first cabinet that doesn't need parliamentary approval.

In this presidential system, the number of ministries were reduced to 16 from 26. A statutory decree was issued to merge some ministries, and also to abolish specific organizational and functional laws of some ministries and institutions.

Previous name	Current name
Ministry of Labour and Social Security	Ministry of Labour, Social Services and Family
Ministry of Family and Social Policy	
Ministry of Science, Industry and Technology	Ministry of Industry and Technology
Ministry of Development	
Ministry of Customs and Trade	Ministry of Trade
Ministry of Economic Affairs	
Ministry of Food, Agriculture and Livestock	Ministry of Agriculture and Forest
Ministry of Forest and Water Management	
Ministry of Finance	Ministry of Finance and Treasury
Ministry of Transport, Maritime and Communication	Ministry of Transport and Infrastructure
Ministry of European Union Affairs	*Merged into the Ministry of Foreign Affairs*

Table 30: Changes of the number of ministries

Function	Portrait	Incumbent	Party	In office
President *Cumhurbaşkanı*		Recep Tayyip Erdoğan	AKP	9 July 2018 – present
Vice President *Cumhurbaşkanı Yardımcısı*		Fuat Oktay	Independent	10 July 2018 – present
Ministry of Foreign Affairs *Dışişleri Bakanı*		Mevlüt Çavuşoğlu	AKP	10 July 2018 – present
Ministry of the Interior *İçişleri Bakanı*		Süleyman Soylu	AKP	10 July 2018 – present
Ministry of Finance and Treasury *Maliye ve Hazine Bakanı*		Berat Albayrak	AKP	10 July 2018 – present
Ministry of Justice *Adalet Bakanı*		Abdulhamit Gül	AKP	10 July 2018 – present
Ministry of Energy and Natural Resources *Enerji ve Tabii Kaynaklar Bakanı*		Fatih Dönmez	Independent	10 July 2018 – present
Ministry of Agriculture and Forest *Tarım ve Orman Bakanı*		Bekir Pakdemirli	AKP	10 July 2018 – present
Ministry of Culture and Tourism *Kültür ve Turizm Bakanı*		Mehmet Ersoy	Independent	10 July 2018 – present
Ministry of Health *Sağlık Bakanı*		Fahrettin Koca	Independent	10 July 2018 – present
Ministry of National Education *Millî Eğitim Bakanı*		Ziya Selçuk	Independent	10 July 2018 – present
Ministry of National Defence *Millî Savunma Bakanı*		Hulusi Akar	Independent	10 July 2018 – present
Ministry of Industry and Technology *Sanayi ve Teknoloji Bakanı*		Mustafa Varank	Independent	10 July 2018 – present
Ministry of Labour, Social Services and Family *Çalışma, Sosyal Hizmetler ve Aile Bakanı*		Zehra Zümrüt Selçuk	Independent	10 July 2018 – present
Ministry of Transport and Infrastructure *Ulaştırma ve Altyapı Bakanı*		Cahit Turan	Independent	10 July 2018 – present
Ministry of Youth and Sports *Gençlik ve Spor Bakanı*		Mehmet Kasapoğlu	Independent	10 July 2018 – present
Ministry of Trade *Ticaret Bakanı*		Ruhsar Pekcan	Independent	10 July 2018 – present
Ministry of Environment and Urban Planning *Çevre ve Şehircilik Bakanı*		Murat Kurum	Independent	10 July 2018 – present

Table 31: Cabinet Erdoğan IV

4.1.6. General election, 2018

The Turkish parliamentary election were held on on 24 June 2018 as part of the 2018 Turkish general election, with a presidential election helding on on the same day. Normally scheduled for 3 November 2019, Mr. Erdoğan called an early election on 18 April after months of speculation. In the 2017 referendum, the number of MPs in parliament will be increased from the 550 to 600. These MPs will be elected by the constituents of the 87 electoral districts of Turkey by party-list proportional representation.

The referendum in 2017 caused Turkey's transition from a parliamentary to an executive presidential system. As such, the parliament will not be entitled to appoint the country's PM and cabinet after the 2018 elections. While the office of the PM of Turkey is set to be abolished altogether, ministers will primarily serve under the the pleasure of the President, who is to fill the mission both head of state and head of government.

In early 2018, the ruling AKP and the opposition party MHP brought forward joint proposals for an electoral alliance law. This attempt was widely speculated to be a result of the MHP's low poll ratings, which made it seemingly impossible to surpass the 10% threshold and win seats in parliament in future elections. The MHP had previously declared that it would support the re-election of AKP leader Mr. Erdoğan to the Presidency, and declared MHP was open to contesting future parliamentary elections in an alliance with the AKP.

The new electoral alliances law permitted parties to form alliances and submit them to the YSK, meaning that parties would be grouped together under their alliance name on the ballot paper. In addition, citizens would be given the option to vote for the alliance as a whole if citizens did not prefer a specific party. Votes cast for alliances rather than parties would then be shared to each party of the alliance at electoral district-level depending on their vote shares. For example, if Party A and Party B were in an electoral alliance and received 60 and 40 votes in an electoral district respectively, then 60% of votes cast for their alliance as a whole would be given to Party A while 40% of votes would be given to Party B. Thence, if 10 votes were cast for the electroal alliance, Party A would have a total number of 66 (60+6) votes and Party B would have a total of 44 (40+4) votes.

Parties contesting the election within an alliance would not be subject to the 10% electoral threshold. As long as the alliance in total won above 10% of the national threshold, any party within it would be eligible to win seats in parliament regardless of how low their vote share.

The election alliance law also contained several controversial changes to election law, containing the legalisation of unverified ballot papers to be incorporated in the count. The issue of counting unverified ballots triggered a huge controversy during the 2017 constitutional referendum, causing the opposition parties to allege large-scale electoral fraud and reject the results. On 31 May 2018, the Supreme Court rejected the opposition's bid to nullify the controversial changes.

After the approval of an election alliance law in early 2018, parties were given the ability to contest the election under official alliances as a means of jointly surpassing the election threshold. Totally, five parties decided to form 2 alliances by the 6 May deadline, with a more 2 parties contesting the election under the lists of these parties.

President Erdoğan formally declared the establishment of the People's Alliance (In Turkish: Cumhur İttifakı) between his party AKP and the MHP on 20 February 2018. The MHP had previously declared that it would support Mr. Erdoğan's re-election and was open to contest future elections under the AKP banner, which was widely seen as the main reason for the electoral alliances law to be passed in the first place. The Great Unity Party (BBP) joined the People's Alliance and declared that it would contest the elections under the AKP banner on 3 May 2018.

The People's Alliance is both a parliamentary and a presidential election alliance, although one of its supporters, the Free Cause Party (HÜDA-PAR) only supports this alliance in the presidential election while contesting in the parliamentary election as a stand-alone party.

The Nation Alliance was the opposition alliance launched on 1 May 2018 in rival to the People's Alliance. The alliance was formed of the main opposition CHP, the just formed nationalist İyi Party, the conservative Felicity Party and the centre-right Democratic Party. The structure of the alliance was criticised by the People's Alliance for being an alliance of 'non-conformists', referencing the secular ideology of the CHP in rival to the Islamist-conducted Felicity Party. However, this alliance crucially abolished the 10% threshold condition for the Felicity Party, which had at the last election won 0.68% of the vote. This meant that some Islamist leaning voters, which had previously voted for the AKP in order to not waste their vote, could now vote for the Felicity Party due to its presence in an electoral alliance that is polling above 10% altogether. The 4 parties were unable to agree on a joint presidential candidate despite speculation over the joint nomination of former president Mr. Gül. Thus, each party decided to nominate their own candidate for the presidential election.

The inclusion of the pro-kurdish Peoples' Democratic Party (HDP) was a largely discussed possibility, with the HDP openly calling for its containment. Hence the HDP is polling very close to the 10% threshold, its ultimate exclusion was criticised by some people. The key reason for the HDP's exclusion was seen to be their unclear association with the PKK terrorist organisation.

Alliance	Party	Votes			Seats		
		#	%	±	#	±	%
People's Alliance *Cumhur İttifakı*	Justice and Development Party* *Adalet ve Kalkınma Partisi*	21,335,579	42.56	-6.94	295	-22	49.17
	Nationalist Movement Party *Milliyetçi Hareket Partisi*	5,564,517	11.10	-0.80	49	+9	8.17
People's Alliance total		**26,900,096**	**53.66**	**-7.74**	**344**	**-13**	**57.33**
Nation Alliance *Millet İttifakı*	Republican People's Party* *Cumhuriyet Halk Partisi*	11,348,899	22.64	-2.68	146	+12	24.33
	İyi Party* *İyi Parti*	4,990,710	9.96	New	43	New	7.17
	Felicity Party* *Saadet Partisi*	673,731	1.34	+0.66	0	±0	0.00
Nation Alliance total		**17,013,340**	**33.94**	**+7.94**	**189**	**+55**	**31.50**
Peoples' Democratic Party *Halkların Demokratik Partisi*		5,866,309	11.70	+0.94	67	+8	11.17
Free Cause Party *Hür Dava Partisi*		157,612	0.31	+0.31	0	±0	0.00
Patriotic Party *Vatan Partisi*		117,779	0.23	-0.02	0	±0	0.00
Other *Diğer*		75,283	0.15	-1.44	0	±0	0.00
Invalid/blank votes		1,053,310	–	–	–	–	–
Total		**51,183,729**	**100.00**	–	**600**	**+50**	**100.00**
Registered voters/turnout		59.354.840	86.23	+1.05	–	–	–

Table 32: Summary of the 24 June 2018 parliamentary election

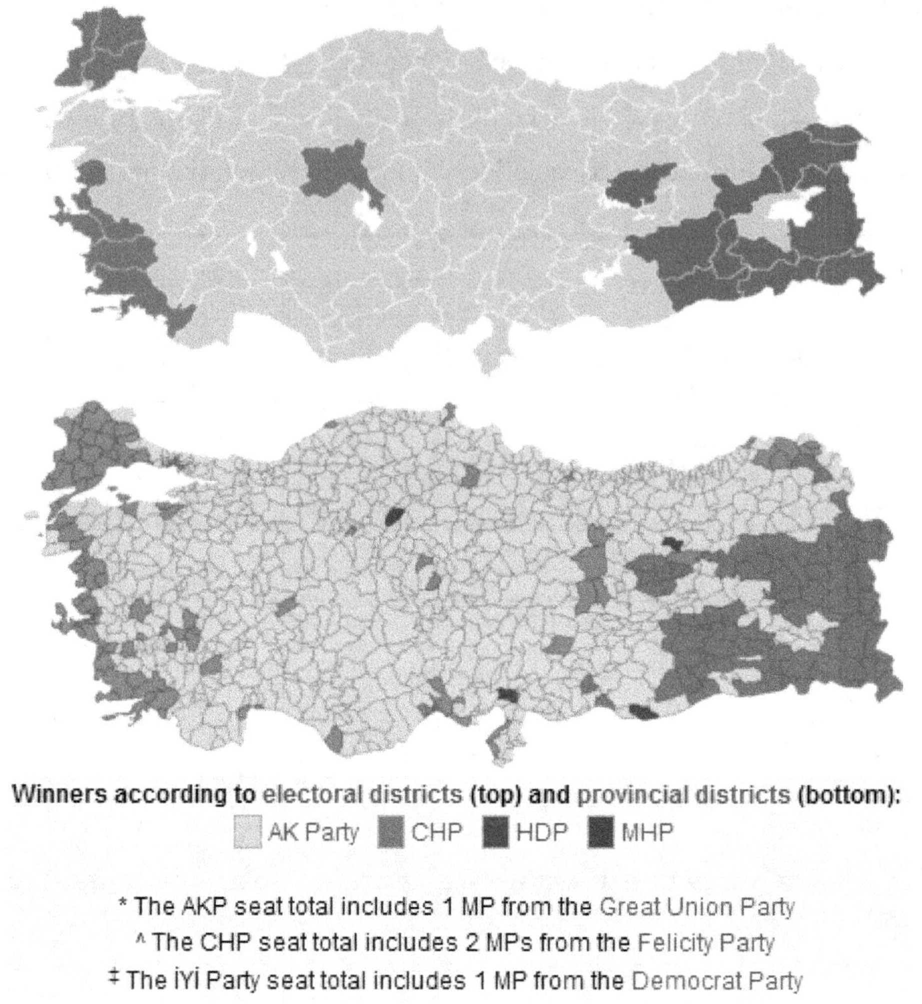

Figure 25: The general election, 2018 results by province

4.1.7. Local election, 2019

The Turkish local elections of 2019 were held on Sunday 31 March 2019 throughout the 81 provinces of Turkey. A total of 30 metropolitan and 1,351 district municipal mayors, alongside 1,251 provincial and 20,500 municipal councillors were elected, in addition to numerous local non-partisan positions such as neighbourhood wardens (muhtars) and elderly people's councils.

The governing Justice and Development Party (AKP) and the Nationalist Movement Party (MHP) contested the elections in many provinces under a joint People's Alliance. Likewise, the Republican People's Party (CHP) and the İYİ Party entered some of the races under the Nation Alliance banner. The Peoples' Democratic Party (HDP) did not openly announce support for either alliance, but did not field candidates in some areas to improve chances of opposition candidates.

Campaigning was described as distinctly negative and divisive, with the opposition criticising the government for Turkey's economic downturn, misuse of public funds and corruption. In response, the government alleged that the opposition parties were acting in the interests of 'foreign powers and terrorists'.[3] Particular controversy surrounded the AKP's allegations of financial fraud against the opposition's Ankara mayoral candidate Mansur Yavaş, which later turned out to have been made by an unverifiable source.[4] The use of video footage of the Christchurch terrorist attack by AKP leader and President Recep Tayyip Erdoğan during his election rallies additionally received international condemnation and caused diplomatic relations between Turkey and New Zealand to sour.[5] Five people were killed and two were injured during political violence on election day, in two separate incidents in Gaziantep and Malatya.[6][7] The election was criticised by observers due to excessive media bias in favour of the governing People's Alliance.

The members of the Nation Alliance were initially beset with issues concerning candidate selection and inner-party divisions, stemming from their general election loss in June 2018. However, both the CHP and the İYİ Party collectively managed to outperform expectations, securing 'shock' victories in Turkey's major metropolitan areas.[8] These included taking control of Ankara and Istanbul, Turkey's capital and largest city respectively. The CHP also held control of İzmir, Turkey's third largest city, and will now control 5 of Turkey's 6 largest population centres (the only exception being Bursa, where the governing coalition narrowly won). The Communist Party won control of a provincial capital, namely Tunceli, for the first time. In provinces where the AKP and MHP contested as separate parties, there was a substantial swing from AKP candidates to the MHP. Nevertheless, AKP leader and President Recep Tayyip Erdoğan claimed victory, announcing that the People's Alliance had secured 51.67% of the vote and thus maintained support from the majority of the electorate.[9].

The election was beset by a number of controversies, including an unexplained results blackout on election night just when the opposition were on the verge of victory in İstanbul. The Istanbul mayoral election, where CHP candidate Ekrem İmamoğlu defeated AKP candidate and former Prime Minister Binali Yıldırım by just under 14,000 votes (0.17%), remained disputed for two weeks after the vote. Numerous recounts, electoral complaints, legal disputes, alleged corruption, accusations of terrorist involvement and police operations took place after the election, initiated mainly by the AKP.[10][11] However, İmamoğlu was sworn in as Mayor on 17 April after most complaints were dismissed. The vote in three districts, where a clear winner could not be established, were annulled by the Supreme Electoral Council (YSK), with re-runs due to be held on 2 June.

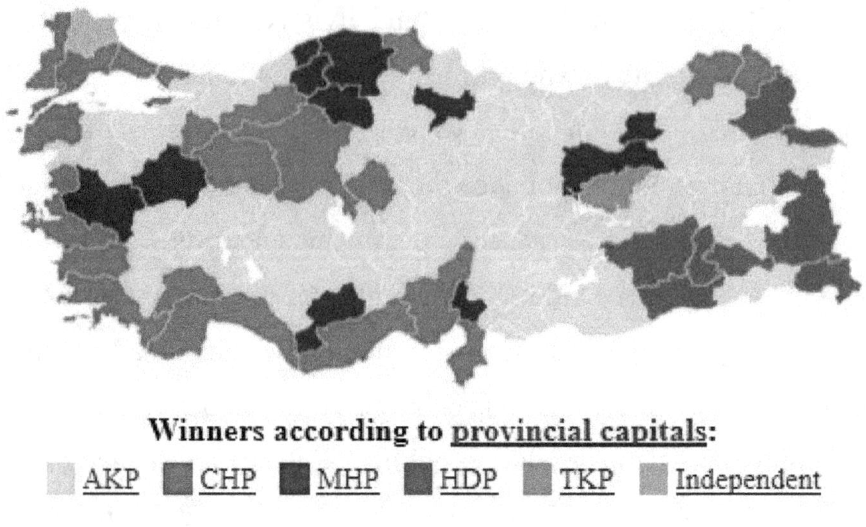

Figure 26: The local elections, 2019 results by province

5. Foreign Policy

The EU and NATO are the primary fixtures and the primary elements of continuity in Turkish foreign policy. "Turkey experienced the direct effect of the post-Cold War atmosphere of insecurity, which resulted in a diversity of security problems in Turkey's neighborhood. The most immediate issue for Turkish diplomacy, in this context, was to harmonize Turkey's effective power axes with the new international atmosphere."

"Throughout the Cold War, Turkey was a "wing country" under NATO's strategic framework, resting on the geographic environment of the Western alliance. On the other hand, NATO's strategic concept has evolved in the post-Cold War period and so has Turkey's account of its strategic environment. Turkish Military's presence in Afghanistan is a sample of this change."Turkey's involvement in NATO has increased during AKP government. Turkey also has advanced significantly in the European integration process compared with the last decade, when it was not even clear whether the EU was really considering Turkey's candidacy.

Turkey has been building relations with its neighbor countries (including Iran and Syria), under a doctrine called '0 problems with neighbors'. These developments worried many Western observers that Turkey, disappointed by its stalled EU accession drive among other things, is seeking to adjust its foreign relations, not just by moving closer to the Muslim countries but also by turning away from the Western world. On the other hand, AKP government rejected these claims.

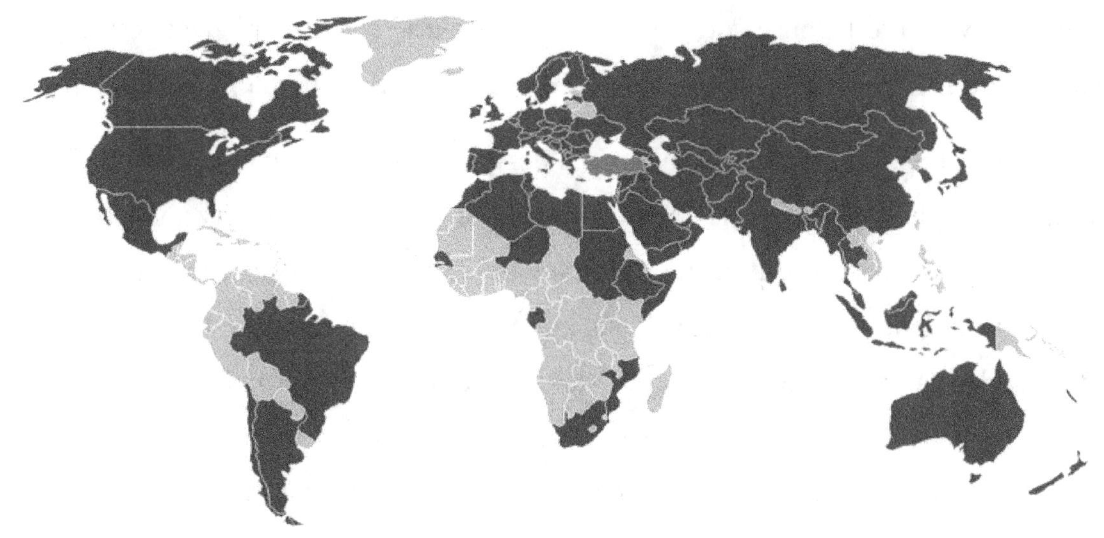

Figure 27: Map of international trips made by Recep Tayyip Erdoğan as prime minister

5.1. Turkey–United States relations

Turkey has remained a close ally of the United States, supporting it in the War on Terror in the post-September 11 climate. However, the Iraq War faced strong domestic opposition in Turkey and as such, the Turkish Parliament couldn't reach the absolute majority of 276 votes needed for allowing U.S. troops to attack Iraq from Turkey, the final tally being 264 votes for and 250 against. This led to a brief period of cooling in relations, particularly following the "hood event", which was perceived as an act of hostility in Turkey.

Ankara is particularly cautious about an independent Kurdish state arising from a destabilized Iraq. Turkey has fought an insurgent war against the Kurdistan Workers' Party (PKK), a Kurdish terrorist group (recognized as a terrorist organization by both the United States and the European Union) seeking Kurdish independence, in which more than 37,000 people have lost their lives. This has led Ankara to pressure the U.S. into clamping down on guerrilla training camps in northern Iraq, though the U.S. remains reluctant due to northern Iraq's relative stability compared to the rest of the country as well as its lack of spare forces to divert away from the more contentious areas of Iraq. On October 17, 2007, the Turkish Parliament voted in favour of allowing the Turkish Armed Forces to take military action against the PKK rebels based in northern Iraq. In response, U.S. President George W. Bush stated that he did not believe it's in Turkey's interests to send troops into Iraq.

In late 2007, Turkey recalled its ambassador to the United States after the House Committee on Foreign Affairs passed a United States resolution on the Armenian Genocide in the Ottoman Empire.

This resulted in a delay of a full House vote on Res. 106. Speaker Pelosi has pledged to bring the resolution to a full vote, but pressure from the White House and Turkey has kept her from doing so.

Nevertheless, the United States and Turkey share membership in NATO, the Organisation for Economic Co-operation and Development (OECD), the Organization for Security and Co-operation in Europe (OSCE) and the G-20, and continue to cooperate in important projects, such as the Joint Strike Fighter program. The United States also actively supports Turkey's membership bid to join the European Union, lobbying frequently on behalf of Ankara through its diplomatic missions in EU capital cities. In June 2008, The United States and Turkey began to cooperate on peaceful uses of nuclear energy with a pact that aims for the transfer of technology, material, reactors and components for nuclear research and nuclear power production in Turkey for an initial 15-year period followed by automatic renewals in five-year increments that provides a comprehensive framework for peaceful nuclear cooperation between the two nations under the agreed non-proliferation conditions and controls. A parallel U.S. bipartisan resolution has recently highlighted the importance for Turkish Republic's key role in providing her western (E.U. and U.S.) and regional allies Eurasian energy security.

The Center for Strategic and International Studies has recently started a one-year initiative project to evaluate and enhance the Turkish Republic - United States strategic partnership, aiming for a plan of implementation of the concluded framework at the end of this phase.

2009 U.S. presidential visit to Turkey

Relations between Turkey and the United States received a jumpstart during the Obama administration's first term, but the two countries were nevertheless unable to reach their ambitious goals. U.S. President Barack Obama made his first official visit to Turkey, stopping off in both Ankara and Istanbul, on April 6–7, 2009. There had been critics in the U.S. who claimed that Turkey should not be rewarded by an early presidential visit as its government had been systematically reorienting foreign policy onto an Islamist axis, but as former U.S. Ambassador to Turkey Mark Parris has stated, "Whatever the merits of this argument, the Obama administration, by scheduling the visit, have decisively rejected it."

During his visit, Obama urged Turkey to come to terms with its past and resolve its Armenian issues. Prior to this, during the 2008 U.S. Presidential election, he had criticised the then U.S. President George W. Bush for his failure to take a stance and stating that the "Armenian genocide is not an allegation, a personal opinion, or a point of view, but rather a widely documented fact supported by an overwhelming body of historical evidence".He responded positively to an announcement from sources in Ankara and Yerevan that a deal might soon be struck to reopen the border between the two states and exchange diplomatic personnel by indicating that although his own personal views on the subject remained unchanged, he may, in order to avoid derailing this diplomatic progress, refrain from using the word genocide in his upcoming April 24 speech on the question.

Turkish President Gül later referred to the visit as "evidence of a vital partnership between Turkey and the US," whilst Turkish Foreign Minister Ahmet Davutoğlu pointed out that, "You are changing the psychological atmosphere," of what was before "seen as a military relationship," but as Obama made clear, "We are not solely strategic partners, we are also model partners," and with this change in terminology, "The President wanted to stress the uniqueness of this relationship. This is not an ordinary relationship, it's a prototype and unique relationship." A U.S. House of Representatives Committee on Foreign Affairs hearing entitled The United States and Turkey: A Model Partnership under the chairmanship of the Head of the Subcommittee on Europe Robert Wexler was convened following, "the historic visit that Obama paid to Turkey," and concluded that, "This cooperation is vital for both of the two states in an environment in which we face serious security issues in Afghanistan, Iraq, Iran, the Balkans, Black Sea, Caucuses and the Middle East, besides a global financial crisis."

Following Obama's visit Turkish Prime Minister Recep Tayyip Erdoğan and Chief of the Turkish General Staff Gen. İlker Başbuğ played host to U.S. Chairman of the Joint Chiefs of Staff Adm. Mike Mullen in Ankara. In the course of the closed-door meeting they discussed the pledging of further Turkish support troops to Afghanistan and Pakistan where Turkish authorities have influence, the secure transport of troops and equipment from the port of İskenderun during the withdrawal of U.S. troops from Iraq, and the pro-Kurdish terrorists operating in south-eastern Turkey and northern Iraq.

On April 22, 2009, shortly after Obama's visit, Turkish and Armenian authorities formally announced a provisional roadmap for the normalisation of diplomatic ties between the two states.The U.S. responded positively with a statement from the office of U.S. Vice President Joe Biden, following a phone conversation with Armenian President Serzh Sargsyan, which stated that, "The Vice President applauded President Sargsyan's leadership, and underscored the administration's support for both Armenia and Turkey in this process."Turkish columnists however criticised the timing of the announcement believing it to have been made to placate the U.S. President in advance of his April 24 speech, with Fikret Bila writing in the Milliyet that, "the Turkish Foreign Ministry made this statement regarding the roadmap before midnight," as it would allow Obama to go back on his campaign promise, to refer to the incident as genocide, which the Turkish government denies profusely, by pointing out to the Armenian diaspora that, "Turkey reached a consensus with Armenia and set a roadmap," and, "there is no need now to damage this process."

Continued cooperation in the War on Terror

The 2009 U.S. Secretary of State's Country Report on Terrorism confirmed that cooperation in terrorism is a key element in America's strategic partnership with Turkey, before going on to praise Turkish contributions to stabilise Iraq and Afghanistan and highlighting the strategic importance of the İncirlik Air Base in Adana used by both U.S. and NATO forces for operations in the region.

Questions have been subsequently raised, however, over the continued presence of U.S. nuclear weapons, reportedly stationed at the air base during the Cold War as part of the NATO nuclear sharing programme, after recent parliamentary debates in Belgium and Germany called for the removal of weapons stationed there under the same programme. Bilkent University Professor Mustafa Kibaroğlu speculates that if the Obama administration presses for the withdrawal of these weapons, which Turkey wishes to maintain, then Turkey-U.S. relations may be strained.

The U.S. Secretary of State's report also contained information on the PKK and other terrorist groups operating in Turkey, whom the U.S. and Turkish authorities share intelligence on, highlighting the September 12, 2006 attack on Diyarbakır and the July 27, 2008 attack on Güngören before going on to mention the ongoing Turkish investigation into the Ergenekon network and concluding that, "the details of the case were murky, however, and Ergenekon's status as a terrorist organisation remained under debate at year's end."

A separate report presented to U.S. President Obama by the U.S. Commission on International Religious Freedom, which had previously urged him to raise the subject of religious freedom during his 2009 presidential visit to Turkey, concluded that Turkey's interpretation of secularism, "resulted in violations of religious freedoms for many of the country's citizens, including members of the majority and, especially, minority religious communities."

A U.S. Democratic Party delegation group including U.S. Senators Robert Casey, Edward E. Kaufman, Frank Lautenberg and U.S. Congressman Timothy Waltz met with Turkish officials in

Ankara on 30 May to confirm, "Turkey can always depend on the US, while the US can always rely on its close friendship with Turkey."

Turkey and the Iran Nuclear Deal

In April 2010, Washington stepped up its efforts to impose a new round of sanctions on Iran over its nuclear program. Key powers such as Turkey, India and China oppose the adoption of a new round of sanctions against Tehran. As a result, the U.S. Congress has delayed arms sales sought by the Turkish military.

2010 leaked diplomatic documents

According to leaked diplomatic cables, Erdoğan was described by U.S. diplomats as having "little understanding of politics beyond Ankara" and as surrounding himself with an "iron ring of sycophantic (but contemptuous) advisors". He is said to be "isolated", and that his MPs and Ministers feel "fearful of Erdogan's wrath". Diplomats state that "he relies on his charisma, instincts, and the filterings of advisors who pull conspiracy theories off the web or are lost in neo-Ottoman Islamist fantasies".

The alleged cables also highlight Turkish concerns that upgrades to General Dynamics F-16 Fighting Falcons had "precluded Turkish access to computer systems and software modification previously allowed".

Human rights and arms sales

In 2010, U.S. President Obama said that future arms sales would depend on Turkish policies.

The Arab Spring

The U.S. under President Obama was reluctant to get deeply involved in the Arab World and was generally supportive of Turkish efforts in the region.

For the Anatolian Falcon 2012 joint exercises, the United States sent the 480th Fighter Squadron to train with Turkish pilots in Suppression of Enemy Air Defenses.

Syrian Civil War, and the Kurdish question

Relations between the United States and Turkey have shown signs of deterioration during the Syrian Civil War and especially over the handling over the Kurdish question. The American forces in the Syrian Civil War are openly allied with the Kurdish YPG terrorists and support them militarily.

Turkey has considered the YPG fighters as "terrorists". Turkey overtly defied American orders of ceasing Turkey's military bombardment of the YPG terrorists in their bid to take the town of Azaz in northern Syria. Signs of strain were then displayed when Barack Obama refused to have a formal meeting with Erdogan when the latter visited the United States in March 2016.

Tensions following the 2016 coup

After the failed coup attempt in July 2016, Turkey demanded that the United States government extradite Fethullah Gülen, a cleric and Turkish national living in the U.S. state of Pennsylvania. However, the U.S. government demanded that Turkey first produce evidence that he was connected with the coup attempt. Due to perceptions that former U.S. Secretary of State and Democratic Party presidential nominee Hillary Clinton is friendly towards the Gülen movement, many Erdoğan supporters reportedly favored Republican Party presidential nominee Donald Trump in the United States' 2016 presidential election.

In a speech on July 29, 2016, President Erdoğan accused U.S. Central Command chief Joseph Votel of "siding with coup plotters", after Votel accused the Turkish government of arresting the Pentagon's contacts in Turkey. Yeni Şafak daily, a Turkish pro-government newspaper, claimed that the former commander of NATO forces in Afghanistan, now-retired U.S. Army General John F. Campbell, was the "mastermind" behind the coup attempt in Turkey.

The United States suspended all non-immigrant visas from Turkey "indefinitely", due to a US consulate employee's arrest, named in Turkish state media as locally hired Metin Topuz. He was charged under allegations that he had links to Pennsylvania-based opposition cleric Fethullah Gülen. He was arrested under "terror charges" by an Istanbul court, state media Anadolu said. Topuz is the second US government employee in Turkey to be arrested in 2017. Turkey retaliated against the US with suspensions of all US visas, including tourist visas, shortly after the US State Department made their announcement.

In December 2017, U.S. national security adviser General H.R. McMaster said that Turkey had joined Qatar as a prime source of funding that contributes to the spread of extremist ideology of Islamism: "We're seeing great involvement by Turkey from everywhere from western Africa to Southeast Asia," funding groups that help create the conditions that allow terrorism to flourish.

On August 1, 2018, the U.S. Department of Treasury imposed sanctions on top Turkish government officials who were involved in the detention of American pastor Andrew Brunson. Brunson was charged with terrorism and espionage. Daniel Glaser, the former Treasury official under President Obama, said: "It's certainly the first time I can think of" the U.S. sanctioning a NATO ally. On August 10, 2018, U.S. President Trump imposed punitive tariffs against Turkey after an impasse over Brunson's imprisonment, as well as other issues. The move prompted Turkish President Recep Tayyip Erdoğan said that the United States was "changing a strategic NATO partner with a pastor" and that the U.S. behavior would force Turkey to look for new friends and allies. The presidential spokesperson of Turkish President, İbrahim Kalın, tweeted that the U.S. is losing Turkey as a whole, the entire Turkish public is against U.S. policies. In addition, the Uşak Province decided to stop running digital advertisement on United States based social media platforms like Facebook, Google, Instagram, Twitter and YouTube canceling all of the budget as a response to the U.S. sanctions on Turkey. Furthermore, Turkey said that it would retaliate to the raising of steel and aluminium tariffs by the U.S. administration (The U.S. had already imposed 10 percent and 25 percent additional tariffs on aluminum and steel imports respectively from all countries on March 23, 2018, but in August 13, 2018 added additional tariffs on steel imports from Turkey). In addition, the Turkish President said that Turkey will boycott electronic products from the US giving iPhones as an example. The Keçiören Municipality in the Ankara has decided not to issue business licenses to American brands including McDonald's, Starbucks and Burger King. In addition, Turkey decided to increase tariffs on imports of a range of US products. Furthermore, in August 20, 2018 there were gunshots at the USA Embassy in the Ankara without casualties. Turkish authorities detained two men suspects.

Naturalized US citizen, Serkan Golge, has also been held since July 2018 on charges of participating in terrorism and conspiring against the government as a member of the Gülen movement.

5.2. Turkey-European Union Relations

Turkey signed a Customs Union agreement with the EU in 1995 and was officially recognised as a candidate for full membership on 12 December 1999, at the Helsinki summit of the European Council.

Negotiations for full membership were started on 3 October 2005. Progress was slow, and out of the 35 Chapters necessary to complete the accession process only 16 had been opened and one had been closed by May 2016. The early 2016 refugee deal between Turkey and the European Union was intended to accelerate negotiations after previous stagnation and allow visa-free travel through Europe for Turks.

Turkish accession talks came to a halt as a result of the 2016–17 purges in Turkey. On 24 November 2016 the European Parliament voted to suspend accession negotiations with Turkey over human rights and rule of law concerns, though this decision was not binding. On 13 December, the Council of the European Union (comprising the ministers of the member states) resolved that it would open no new areas in Turkey's membership talks in the "prevailing circumstances", as Turkey's path toward autocratic rule made progress on EU accession impossible. By 2017, and especially following the passage of the constitutional referendum, Turkish accession talks had effectively stopped.

The European Commission's long-term budget proposal for the 2021-2027 period released on 2 May 2018 includes a Western Balkan Strategy for further enlargement, but omits Turkey, thus treating Turkey as a neighbouring country rather than a candidate country.

2000s

The next significant step in Turkey–EU relations came with the December 2002 Copenhagen European Council. According to it, "the EU would open negotiations with Turkey 'without delay' if the European Council in December 2004, on the basis of a report and a recommendation from the Commission, decides that Turkey fulfills the Copenhagen political criteria."

The European Commission recommended that the negotiations should begin in 2005, but also added various precautionary measures. The EU leaders agreed on 16 December 2004 to start accession negotiations with Turkey from 3 October 2005. While Austria and Germany initially wanted to leave open the possibility that negotiations with Turkey would lead to a privileged partnership, less than full membership, accession negotiations were ultimately launched with the "shared objective" of membership.

Turkey's accession talks have since been stalled by a number of domestic and external problems. Both Austria and France have said they would hold a referendum on Turkey's accession. In the case of France, a change in its Constitution was made to impose such a referendum, but later another constitutional change has enabled the parliament (if a large majority of its members agrees) to prevent such a referendum. The issue of Cyprus continues to be a major obstacle to negotiations. European officials have commented on the slowdown in Turkish reforms which, combined with the Cyprus problem, led the EU's Enlargement Commissioner Olli Rehn in March 2007 to warn of an impending 'train crash' in the negotiations. Due to these setbacks, negotiations again came to a halt in December 2006, with the EU freezing talks in 8 of the 35 key areas under negotiation.

In December 2009, the Republic of Cyprus blocked 6 chapters of Turkish accession negotiations, including those on Judiciary and Fundamental Rights, Energy and Education and Culture, arguing that Turkey needs to first normalise relations with Cyprus. As a result, no chapter has been opened since June 2010. Hence, there is no chapter Turkey can open other than the difficult and economically detrimental chapters Competition Policy, Social Policy and Employment, and Public Procurement that most candidate countries open at the end of accession as all other chapters are blocked. In February 2013, Turkish Deputy Undersecretary of the Ministry for EU Affairs, Burak Erdenir, claimed that the EU had yet to communicate to Turkey the benchmark criteria for opening chapters 23 and 24, Judiciary & Fundamental Rights and Justice, Freedom & Security, which was to be done after screening of the chapters was completed in 2006, thus making it impossible to comply with them. He also suggested this was a deliberate attempt to slow their accession process.

Positive Agenda

After over 2 years of no chapter openings, the European Commission set up a "Positive agenda" designed to focus on common EU-Turkey interests. EU Commissioner for expansion Stefan Füle describes that the goal was "to keep the accession process alive and put it properly back on track after a period of stagnation which has been a source of frustration for both sides." The EU Commission mentioned a broad range of areas as the main elements of the Agenda such as "intensified dialogue and cooperation on political reforms", "visa", "mobility and migration", "energy", "fight against terrorism", "further participation of Turkey in Community programmes", "town twinning", "trade and the Customs Union" and "supporting efforts to align with the acquis, including on chapters where accession negotiations cannot be opened for the time being". The proposal was considered favorably on the condition that it serves as an instrument in support of and complementary to the negotiation process with the EU.

In the framework of "Positive Agenda", Working Groups were established on 8 chapters ("3-Right of Establishment and Freedom to Provide Services", "6-Company Law", "10-Information Society and Media", "18-Statistics", "23-Judiciary and Fundamental Rights", "24-Justice, Freedom and Security", "28-Consumer and Health Protection" and "32-Financial Control"). The "Positive Agenda" kick-off meeting was held on 17 May 2012 in Ankara with the participation of Stefan Füle, EU Commissioner for Enlargement and European Neighbourhood Policy. As a result of the Working Groups meetings held so far, a total of four closing benchmarks were confirmed to have been met by Turkey in three chapters (Company Law, Consumer and Health Protection and Financial Control chapters).

Recent developments

In 2007, Turkey stated that they were aiming to comply with EU law by 2013, but Brussels refused to back that as a deadline for membership. In 2006 European Commission President José Manuel Barroso said that the accession process will take at least until 2021. In a visit to Germany on 31 October 2012, Turkish Prime Minister R.T. Erdoğan made clear that Turkey was expecting membership in the Union to be realised by 2023, the 100th Anniversary of the Turkish Republic, implying that they could end membership negotiations if the talks had not yielded a positive result by then. Turkish President Abdullah Gül said that upon completing the accession process Turkey will hold a referendum for Turkish membership in the European Union.

On 20 June 2013, in the wake of Ankara's crackdown on mass demonstrations in Taksim Square, Germany blocked the start to new EU accession talks with Turkey. According to the Financial Times, one Turkish official said that such a move could potentially break off political relations with the bloc.

A Eurobarometer poll in September 2013, which included EU countries and candidate countries as well, showed that 43% of Turks viewed the EU positively, as compared with 60% six months previously. In the same poll, 29% of Turks polled expressed support for an EU Constitution, the lowest level of support among EU countries and candidates polled. Germany says that its reservation stems from a technical issue, but Angela Merkel, an opponent of Turkish entry into the EU, has described herself as "shocked" after Ankara's use of overwhelming police force against mostly peaceful demonstrators. France stated that they would not waive their veto over unfreezing four accession chapters with Turkey until after elections for the European Parliament in June 2014.

The crackdown following the 2016 Turkish coup d'état attempt by President Erdogan damaged relations with the EU. Erdogan has indicated his approval of reinstating the death penalty to punish those involved in the coup, with the EU suggesting that this would end its EU ambitions. Erdogan stated in November 2016 that he was considering putting Turkey's continued negotiations with the EU on membership to a referendum in 2017. In November 2016, the European Parliament voted in favour of a non-binding resolution to request that the European Commission temporarily suspend membership negotiations due to the "disproportionate repressive measures" of the government to the coup. On 13 December, the European Council (comprising the heads of state or government of the member states) resolved that it would open no new areas in Turkey's membership talks in the "prevailing circumstances"; Turkey's path toward autocratic rule makes progress on EU accession impossible.

In April 2017, the Parliamentary Assembly of the Council of Europe (PACE) voted to reopen its monitoring procedure against Turkey. This vote is widely understood to deal a major blow to Turkey's perspective of eventual EU membership, as exiting that process was made a precondition of EU accession negotiations back in 2004.

The European Commission's long-term budget proposal for the 2021-2027 period released on 2 May 2018 includes a Western Balkan Strategy for further enlargement, but omits Turkey, thus treating Turkey as a neighbouring country rather than a candidate country.

5.3. Turkey-Russia Relations

For centuries, Turkey and Russia have been rivals for regional supremacy. With the rise of the Erdoğan government, the two countries have realised that friendly relations are in the interest of them both. Accordingly, co-operation rather than rivalry appears to dominate the ties.

In 2002, trade between Turkey and Russia was worth some $5 billion. By the end of 2010, this figure reached almost $30 billion.

In December 2004, Russian President Vladimir Putin visited Turkey. This was the first Presidential visit in the history of Turkish-Russian relations besides that of the Chairman of the Presidium, Nikolai Podgorny in 1972. In November 2005, Putin attended together with the inauguration of a jointly constructed Blue Stream natural gas pipeline in Turkey. This sequence of top-level visits has brought several important bilateral issues to the forefront. The two countries consider it their strategic goal to achieve "multidimensional co-operation", especially in the fields of energy, transport and the military. Specifically, Russia aims to invest in Turkey's fuel and energy industries, and it also expects to participate in tenders for the modernisation of Turkey's military.

President Medvedev described Turkey as "one of our most important partners with respect to regional and international issues." He continued "We can confidently say that Russian-Turkish relations have advanced to the level of a multidimensional strategic partnership."

On May 12, 2010, Ankara and Moscow signed 17 agreements to enhance cooperation in energy and other fields, including pacts to build Turkey's first nuclear power plant and furthering plans for an oil pipeline from the Black Sea to the Mediterranean Sea. The leaders of both countries have also signed an agreement on visa-free travel. Tourists will be able to get into the country for free and stay there for up to 30 days.

In May 2009, Turkish Prime Minister Recep Tayyip Erdoğan flew to Sochi, Russia for a working visit with Russian Prime Minister Vladimir Putin at which he stated, "Turkey and Russia have responsibilities in the region. We have to take steps for the peace and well being of the region. This includes the Nagorno-Karabakh problem, the Middle East dispute, the Cyprus problem." Putin responded that, "Russia and Turkey seek for such problems to be resolved and will facilitate this in every way," but, "As for difficult problems from the past – and the Karabakh problem is among such issues – a compromise should be found by the participants in the conflict. Other states which help reach a compromise in this aspect can play a role of mediators and guarantors to implement the signed agreements." Whilst on the subject of energy security Erdoğan stated that, "The agreement on gas supplies through the so-called Western route signed in 1986 is expiring in 2012. We have agreed today to immediately start work to prolong this agreement."

In May 2010, the visit by the Russian President Medvedev to Turkey saw the signing of numerous deals such as the lifting of visa requirements. A multibillion-dollar deal was signed for the construction of a nuclear power plant in Akkuyu, Mersin.

According to a 2013 BBC World Service poll, 30% of Turks viewed Russia's influence positively, with 46% expressing a negative view.

On 24 November 2015, within weeks of the start of the Russian military intervention in support of Syria's President Bashar al-Assad, Turkish F-16 combat aircraft shot down a Russian Su-24 during an airspace dispute close to the Turkish-Syrian border. Russian President Vladimir Putin described the incident as "a stab in the back by the accomplices of terrorists" and further stated that "today's tragic events will have significant consequences including for relations between Russia and Turkey". In response, Russia imposed a number of economic sanctions on Turkey. These included the suspension of visa-free travel to Russia for Turkish citizens, limits on Turkish residents and companies doing business in Russia and restrictions on imports of Turkish products. Russian tour operators were discouraged from selling Turkish package holidays and asked to stop charter flights to Turkey while Russian football clubs were banned from signing Turkish players and discouraged from organizing winter training camps in Turkey. The day after the jet was shot down, a Russian law-maker, Sergei Mironov, introduced a bill to the Russian parliament that would criminalize the denial of the Armenian Genocide, a political move that Turkey has strongly opposed when countries like France and Greece adopted similar laws.

The Pan-Orthodox Council, which had been originally scheduled to be held in Istanbul's Hagia Irene in 2016 had to be shifted to Crete, Greece, after the Russian Orthodox Church indicated that it did not want to go to Turkey due to the crisis between the two countries following the downing of the Russian jet.

The process of normalisation of ties between the two countries was started in June 2016 with Recep Erdoğan expressing regret to Putin for the downing of the Russian warplane. Putin and Erdogan held a telephonic conversation on 29 June which was described as being productive by Russian and Turkish government officials. The Russian government later lifted the travel restrictions on Russian citizens visiting Turkey and ordered normalisation of trade ties.

On 9 August 2016, the countries' leaders held a meeting in St Petersburg, Russia, which was described by a commentator as a "clear-the-air summit" — the first time the pair met since they fallout over the Russian fighter jet downing by the Turkish air force as well as Erdoğan's first trip abroad since the failed coup attempt in Turkey. The BBC commented that the summit, at which Erdoğan thanked Putin for his swift support during the coup attempt, "unnerved the West".

Following the assassination of Russian ambassador to Turkey Andrei Karlov on 19 December 2016, the countries' leaders sought to contain any possible damage to relations between the two countries. In December 2016, the two countries initiated the Astana peace talks on Syria peace settlement, subsequently, along with Iran, agreeing to create de-escalation zones in Syria.

During Putin's visit to Ankara at the end of September 2017, the Turkish and Russian presidents said they agreed to closely cooperate on ending Syria's civil war. Vladimir Putin's visit to Ankara in December that year was the third face-to-face meeting between the countries' leaders in less than a month and their seventh in a year.

On 12 September 2017, Turkey announced that it had signed a deal to purchase the Russian S-400 surface-to-air missile system; the deal was characterised by American press as "the clearest sign of Recep Tayyip Erdoğan's pivot toward Russia and away from NATO and the West" that "cements a recent rapprochement with Russia". Despite pressure to cancel the deal on the part of the Trump administration, in April 2018 the scheduled delivery of the S-400 batteries had been brought forward from the first quarter of 2020 to July 2019.

In June 2018, the Russian government-controlled news agency Sputnik, shut down its website in Kurdish language without mentioning any particular reason for the decision. Former employees of Sputnik said that the news agency decided to shut it down at Turkey's request.

In mid-August 2018, Russia and Turkey backed one another in their respective disputes with the United States. Russia condemned U.S. sanctions against Turkey over the detention of Andrew Brunson, while Turkey stated its opposition to U.S. sanctions on Russia over the annexation of Crimea and alleged interference in the 2016 U.S. elections.

5.4. Turkey-China Relations

Chinese–Turkish relations are foreign relations between China and Turkey. Diplomatic relations were established in 1934 and Turkey recognized the People's Republic of China (PRC) on 5 August 1971. Turkey conforms to the One-China policy and recognizes the PRC as the sole legal representative of China. The PRC has an embassy in Ankara, and a consulate–general in Istanbul whereas Turkey has an embassy in Beijing and 2 consulates–general in Hong Kong and Shanghai. China and Turkey have maintained a good relationship throughout, despite the China's conflicts with Turkic Uyghur separatists. Recently, regional and global cooperation between the two countries have also been growing, with both sides seeking for closer ties.

In the 16th century, there emerged travelogues of both Ottoman travelers to China and Chinese travelers to the Ottoman world.

According to the official history of the Ming Dynasty, some self-proclaimed Ottoman envoys visited Beijing to pay tribute to the Ming emperor in 1524. However, no Ottoman sources substantiate any official diplomatic mission to China at that time.

Kaiser Wilhelm II was so alarmed by the Chinese Muslim troops in the Boxer Rebellion that he requested the Caliph Abdul Hamid II of the Ottoman Empire to find a way to stop the Muslim troops from fighting. The Caliph agreed to the Kaiser's request and sent Enver Pasha (not the future Young Turk leader) to China in 1901, but the rebellion had ended by that time.

Turkish government officials received a Chinese Muslim delegation under Wang Zengshan who denounced the Japanese invasion of China.

In 1950, United Nations Resolution 83 requested military aid for South Korea following its invasion by North Korean forces, which were assisted by China and the Soviet Union. The 5,000-strong

Turkish Brigade was attached to the U.S. 25th Infantry Division, served within United Nations Command.

The Turkish Brigade fought in several major actions, including the Battle of Wawon (27–29 November 1950), against elements of the 38th Group Army of the Chinese People's Liberation Army and Battle of Kumyangjang-Ni (25–26 January 1951), against elements of the Chinese 50th Army. The brigade was awarded Unit Citations by both South Korea and the United States.

On 28 November 2008, Jia Qinglin, China's top political advisor and the chairman of the People's Political Consultative Conference, gave an official goodwill visit to Turkey as guest of Turkish Parliament Speaker Köksal Toptan. In Ankara, Jia met Turkish President Abdullah Gül and Prime Minister Recep Tayyip Erdogan. After visiting Ankara, Jia attended a business forum entitled "Turkish-Chinese Economic and Commercial Opportunities Forum" in İstanbul.

Turkish President Abdullah Gül has become the first Turkish president to visit China in 14 years with his official visit between on 24–29 June 2009. Gül said one of the major goals of his visit was to boost economic relations. In Beijing, Gül hold talks with his Chinese counterpart Hu Jintao and attended a Turkey-China business forum. Following the meetings, seven cooperation agreements were signed between the two countries in the fields of energy, banking, finance and culture. After Beijing, Gül visited Xian, and he was awarded with an honorary doctorate by the Xian Northwest University.In the third leg of his China trip, Gül visited Shenzhen. Upon an invitation of the Beijing administration, Gül also visited Ürümqi, and has become the first Turkish president visiting Xinjiang Uyghur Autonomous Region.

Initially in response to the July 2009 Ürümqi riots, the Foreign Ministry of Turkey urged the Chinese authorities to find the perpetrators and bring them to justice but some officials disagreed: a deputy from ruling Justice & Development (AK) Party resigned from the Turkey-China Interparliamentary Friendship Group, and in his personal capacity, Turkey's industry and trade minister called on Turks to boycott Chinese goods to protest the continuing ethnic violence, to which the Chinese chargé d'affaires in Ankara expressed "surprise".After daily demonstrations in Ankara and Istanbul, Prime Minister Recep Tayyip Erdoğan strengthened his rhetoric and said "These incidents in China are as if they are genocide. We ask the Chinese government not to remain a spectator to these incidents."China demanded that Recep Tayyip Erdogan retract his accusation; editorials in the state-run China Daily pointed out that 137 of the 184 victims of the unrest were Han Chinese. A phone conversation between China and Turkey's respective foreign ministers reaffirmed the importance of Turkish-

Chinese relations, and Turkish Foreign Minister Ahmet Davutoglu said that Turkey did not intend "to interfere with the domestic affairs of China".

On 7 October 2010, China and Turkey signed eight cooperation agreements relating to trade, cultural and technical exchange, marine cooperation, and other things. At the signing ceremony attended by both of the countries' prime ministers, both pledged to increase bilateral trade to $50 billion by 2015, and to cooperate in building high-speed rail to link Ankara to Istanbul. Later in November, Turkish Foreign Minister Ahmet Davutoğlu toured China for six days and met with his counterpart Yang Jiechi, after Chinese premier Wen Jiabao visited Turkey and upgraded the China–Turkey relationship to a "strategic partnership". Among the joint pledges the foreign ministers made in China were to start a Turkish industrial zone in Xinjiang and to jointly crack down on separatism and terrorism, including on anti-China separatist activities in Turkey. Commentators have cited these stronger ties as further proof of a realignment of Turkish foreign policy to the "East".

Rebiya Kadeer claimed that Turkey is hampered from interfering with Uyghurs because Turkey recognizes its own Kurdish issue problems, which China may interfere with in retaliation.

In February 2019, Turkish government denounced China for "violating the fundamental human rights of Uyghur Turks and other Muslim communities in the Xinjiang Uyghur Autonomous Region."

On 4 July 2015, 2,000 Turkish nationalists protesting against China fasting ban mistakenly attack Korean tourists in Istanbul which led to China issuing travel warning to its citizens traveling to Turkey. The ruling AKP party in power in Turkey has different factions; some of which are nationalists who want to inflame tensions with China over Uyghurs, and other members who want to maintain good relations with China and believe the Uyghur issue is being abused to spoil relations between China and Turkey by the United States. Some Islamist AKP members have accused Rebiya Kadeer of being an "American agent" and "infidel". Turkey has had to follow its own country's interests first with a pragmatic approach to the situation of Turkic peoples in other countries like Uyghurs, Gagauz, and Crimean Tatars.

Devlet Bahçeli, a leader from Turkey's MHP (Nationalist Movement Party), said that the attacks by MHP affiliated Turkish youth on South Korean tourists were "understandable", telling the Turkish news paper Hurriyet that: "What feature differentiates a Korean from a Chinese? They see that they both have slanted eyes. How can they tell the difference?". Another translation of his remarks was : "What is the difference between a Korean and a Chinese anyway? They both have slitty eyes. Does it make any difference? "A Uighur staffed, Turkish owned Chinese restaurant was assaulted by Turkish nationalists, who have also attacked the Dutch consulate which they thought was the Russian consulate. Anti-Chinese violence in Turkey motivated by Chinese treatment of Uyghurs targets believed Chinese nationals, but often these nationals are Uyghurs holding Chinese citizenship.

5.5. Turkey-Israel Relations

In Turkey 2002 election the Justice and Development Party, also known as AKP, won a landslide victory. Prime minister Recep Tayyip Erdoğan visited Israel in 2005 offering to serve as a Middle East peace mediator and looking to build up trade and military ties. Erdoğan brought a large group of businessmen on his two-day trip, which included talks with Prime Minister Ariel Sharon and President Moshe Katsav. Erdoğan also laid a wreath at the Holocaust memorial, Yad Vashem. Erdoğan told Sharon that his Justice and Development Party regarded anti-Semitism as "a crime against humanity." He added that Iran's nuclear ambitions were a threat not just to Israel but to "the entire world."

In early 2006, the Israeli Foreign Ministry described its country's relations with Turkey as "perfect. A joint Israeli-Palestinian industrial park was being developed under Turkey's aegis. Israeli President Shimon Peres and Palestinian Authority President Mahmoud Abbas addressed the Grand National Assembly of Turkey a day apart. Peres described Turkey as an "important player in the Middle East in relation to the United States, Syria and the Palestinians, as well as us."According to a report in the Jerusalem Post, a spokeswoman for the Syrian Foreign Ministry said that Turkey was serving as a "channel of communication" between Syria and Israel.

On a three-day visit to Ankara in November 2007, Israeli President Shimon Peres met with Turkish President Abdullah Gül, and addressed the Grand National Assembly of Turkey. Gül promised to help free three abducted Israeli soldiers: Gilad Shalit, Ehud Goldwasser and Eldad Regev.

Deterioration of relations

The Turkish government's condemnation of the 2008–2009 Israel–Gaza conflict strained relations between the two countries. In December 1987, Turkey had already declared support for the Palestinians' right to self-determination. In 2004, Turkey had denounced Israeli assassination of Sheikh Ahmed Yassin. It described Israeli policy in the Gaza Strip as "state-sponsored terrorism". There were demonstrations across Turkey against Israeli actions in Gaza.

On 5 March 2009, the Israeli daily newspaper Haaretz reported that "secret reconciliation talks at the highest level" had been held to get the Israeli-Turkish relations back on track. This report was cited in the Turkish press.

On 11 October 2009, a military aerial exercise was to consist of Turkey, Israel, the United States, and Italy. However, Turkey barred Israel from the Anatolian Eagle military exercise.

In October 2009, following Turkey's banning Israel's participation in the Anatolian Eagle military exercise, Israeli Prime Minister Benjamin Netanyahu objected to Turkey as a mediator, stating "Turkey can't be an honest broker", between Syria and Israel.

Turkey's Prime Minister Recep Tayyip Erdoğan criticizes Israeli policy and leaves the World Economic Forum in Davos, Switzerland.

Erdoğan harshly criticized Israel's conduct in Gaza at the World Economic Forum conference in Davos, Switzerland in January 2009. After the assembled audience applauded Peres, Erdoğan said: "I find it very sad that people applaud what you said. You killed people. And I think that it is very wrong." The moderator, Washington Post columnist David Ignatius asked Erdoğan to finish, saying that people needed to go to dinner. Erdoğan complained about the fact, that he was given 12 minutes to talk, whereas Peres talked for a duration of 25 minutes. Erdoğan then proceeded to leave the stage.

In October 2009, Ayrılık, a prime-time serial on Turkish state television channel TRT 1 featured fictionalized scenes of Israeli soldiers shooting Palestinian children and mistreating elderly Arabs. Israeli Foreign Minister Avigdor Lieberman criticized the program, and rebuked the Turkish Ambassador in front of assembled media. Lieberman subsequently apologized after Turkey threatened to withdraw its ambassador.

After Hamas leader Khaled Mashal paid an official visit to Turkey, relations began to cool off. In January 2010, Israel protested when an episode ("Ambush") of the Turkish soap opera Valley of the Wolves depicted Israeli intelligence spying inside Turkey and kidnapping Turkish babies. The series depicted a fictional Mossad attack on the Turkish embassy in Tel Aviv in which the ambassador and his family are taken hostage. On 11 January 2010, Israeli Deputy Foreign Minister Danny Ayalon met with Turkish ambassador Ahmet Oğuz Çelikkol, who was seated on a stool that was lower than Ayalon's. Ayalon allegedly turned to his aide and quipped, "The main thing is that you see that he is seated low and that we are high ... that there is one flag on the table (the Israeli flag) and that we are not smiling."

Moshe Ya'alon, Israel's Minister of Strategic Affairs, accused Turkey of cooperating with Hamas and Iran. According to the Shin Bet, Hamas established a command post in Turkey and has used it to recruit operatives and oversee operations in the Middle East. David Ignatius has reported that in 2012, Turkey revealed the names of Mossad agents to Iran.

Gaza Flotilla incident

On 31 May 2010, nine activists (eight Turkish citizens and one Turkish-American with dual citizenship) were killed and many more wounded by Israeli troops and seven Israeli soldiers were injured on the Mavi Marmara, part of the "Gaza Freedom Flotilla", a convoy of six ships carrying 663 people from 37 nations, including pro-Palestinian activists. Following the raid, which took place in the Mediterranean Sea in international waters, tension between the two countries mounted. One of the ships taking part was flying a Turkish flag. Turkish Prime Minister Erdoğan described the raid as "state terrorism". Turkey recalled its ambassador from Israel, and summoned the Israeli ambassador to demand an explanation. The Turkish Foreign Ministry stated that the incident could lead to irreparable consequences in bilateral relations.

On 2 September 2011, Turkey downgraded diplomatic ties with Israel and suspended military co-operation after the UN released its report of the Mavi Marmara raid. A statement from the Israeli prime minister's office said, "Israel hopes to find a way to overcome the dispute and will continue to work towards this goal". Turkey demanded an Israeli apology and compensation over the 31 May 2010 incident aboard the Mavi Marmara in which eight Turkish nationals and an American man of Turkish descent died when the vessel was stormed by Israeli commandos. The Israeli government refused to give one.

In September 2011, Turkey expelled Israel's ambassador after a UN report found that the blockade of Gaza was legal according to international law although excessive force was used when boarding the ship. Israeli officials stated that they hoped to restore ties but reiterated that they would not apologize. Hamas praised Turkey's decision.

Kemal Kılıçdaroğlu, Turkey's opposition leader, condemned the downgrade in relations with Israel, stating "No good can come of it and there is no need for us to risk our interest with petty action."Faruk Logoglu, a deputy chairman of the opposition Republican People's Party, criticized Erdoğan, stating that "The probability that (Turkey's ruling) party has carried Turkey to the brink of a hot conflict is saddening and unacceptable." Alon Liel, a former Israeli ambassador to Turkey, stated that it was unlikely that Turkish forces would penetrate Israeli waters, but speculated that Turkey might to disrupt future Israeli gas exports to Cyprus and warned of a new Turkish-Egyptian alliance that could isolate Israel in the Mediterranean.

Israeli Defense Minister Ehud Barak predicted that the rift would pass in time. At the U.N. General Assembly in September 2011, U.S. President Barack Obama asked Erdoğan to resolve the crisis with Israel.

Further Turkish actions (2012–13)

The Turkish Foreign Ministry called on the international community and the United Nations to take the necessary initiatives to stop Israel's military operation in Gaza on late 2012, which it described as another example of Israel's hostile policies. Turkish Foreign Minister Ahmet Davutoğlu see in this attack another of Israel's "crimes of humanity." Turkish Prime Minister Recep Tayyip Erdogan accused the United Nations on 19 November of failing to act over the deadly Israeli air bombardments of Gaza, calling Israel a "terrorist state" that "massacres innocent children".

During his speech in Vienna on 1 March 2013 at a United Nations event, Turkish Prime minister Recep Tayyip Erdoğan devoted to dialogue between the West and Islam, decrying the rising racism in Europe and the fact that many Muslims "who live in countries other than their own" often face harsh discrimination. Erdoğan described Zionism as "a crime against humanity" saying, "It is necessary that we must consider—just like Zionism, or anti-Semitism, or fascism—Islamophobia." In an interview to the Euronews, Shimon Peres argued that Erdoğan's statements are based on ignorance and they raise the flames of hatred. On March 20, Erdoğan began an official visit to Denmark with an effort to clarify his remarks he made on February 27 at a UN conference in Vienna referring to Zionism as a crime against humanity. "Let no one misunderstand what I said. Everyone knows that my criticism of Israel focuses on some critical issues. It's directed especially toward Israeli policies on Gaza," Erdoğan said in an interview with Politiken, a Danish newspaper. Erdoğan claimed February comments were not anti-Semitic but rather a criticism of Israel's policies.

Failure of reconciliation attempts

Following US pressure on both sides, reconciliation took off in early 2013. On 22 March 2013, during a phone call with Turkey's Prime Minister Recep Tayyip Erdoğan, Israel's Prime Minister Benjamin Netanyahu apologized for the Gaza Flotilla incident. An official statement by the Israeli government said that Netanyahu expressed regret over deterioration in bilateral relations and described the incident as unintentional, regretful and—according to an investigation—involving "operational errors". Mr. Erdogan later issued a statement, where he accepted the apology on behalf of the Turkish people. Israel also vowed to compensate the victims' families. An Israeli statement first said that the countries had agreed to restore normal diplomatic relations, including the return of ambassadors and cancellation of Turkish legal proceedings in absentia against Israeli troops involved in the raid, but this statement was later omitted.

U.S. President Barack Obama, whose visit to Israel coincided with the development and who was credited with brokering the reconciliation, said that the U.S. "attached great importance to the restoration of positive relations between Israel and Turkey in order to advance regional peace and security."

In August 2013, the Hürriyet reported that Erdoğan had stated to a meeting of the AKP's provincial chairs that Israel was responsible for the recent military coup in Egypt which overthrew Mohammad Morsi. Erdoğan reportedly stated "Who is behind this? Israel. We have evidence" - specifically, Erdoğan cited a video posted online of Tzipi Livni speaking with French intellectual Bernard-Henri Levy. Erdoğan claimed that Levy had stated:

"   "The Muslim Brotherhood will not be in power even if they win the elections, because democracy is not the ballot box."   "

However, according to the Hürriyet, what Levy actually stated was:

"   "If the Muslim Brotherhood arrives in Egypt, I will not say democracy wants it, so let democracy progress. Democracy is not only elections, it is also values...I will urge the prevention of [the Muslim Brotherhood] coming to power, but by all sorts of means."   "

The Israeli Foreign Ministry spokesman later stated that Erdoğan's accusation was "a statement well worth not commenting on." Egypt's interim government rejected Erdoğan' claim, describing it as "baseless," "very bewildering," and charged that "Its purpose is to strike at the unity of Egyptians."

With the scandal over alleged Turkish involvement in exposure of Israeli special agents in Iran in October 2013, the relations between Israel and Turkey have hit a new low.

Negotiations for the normalisation of diplomatic ties (2015-present)

In December 2015, Turkey and Israel began talks to restore diplomatic ties; however disagreements on normalising relations between both sides still continue.

March 2016 Istanbul bombing

On 19 March 2016, a suicide bombing by ISIL took place in Istanbul's Beyoğlu district. Among those killed were two dual Israel-US nationals and one Israeli national. Following the attack Erdogan wrote a letter of condolences to Israeli President Reuven Rivlin, saying he was "very sorry" to hear that three Israelis were killed and 10 wounded in the attack. The letter stated: "I want to send my deepest condolences to the Israeli people and the families that lost their loved ones in this traitorous attack."

On 20 March, Dore Gold, the director-general of the Israeli Foreign Ministry, came to Istanbul to hold talks with the undersecretary of the Turkish Foreign Ministry Feridun Sinirlioğlu and the governor of Istanbul Vasip Şahin about the ISIL attack. On 21 March, Gold thanked the Turkish government for what it did in the aftermath of the attack and underlined the need for an alliance in the fight against terror. Furthermore, he said: "I want to thank first and foremost the government of Turkey, which did everything to its capacity and helped the families of Israelis that came to take care of beloved ones. It helped us to get through any bureaucracy in the Turkish hospitals and bring the wounded as well as deceased back home to Israel."

Reconciliation agreement

Turkish ambassador to Israel Kemal Ökem presents his Letter of credence to the president of Israel Reuven Rivlin on December 12, 2016

A reconciliation agreement was announced on 27 June 2016 to end the six-year rift in the relation between both countries.

The Turkish Parliament will pass a law canceling all appeals against Israeli soldiers involved in the killing of nine Turkish citizens during the Gaza flotilla raid and will also block any future claims.

Commitment to stop terrorist or military activity against Israel on Turkish soil including funding and aid to such activities from Turkey. Palestinian movement Hamas will be allowed to operate on Turkish soil but only as a political movement.

Turkey will accept to send all aid to the Gaza Strip through Israel and then from Israel to Gaza on land.

Israel will allow Turkey to advance humanitarian projects in the Gaza Strip, such as building an hospital, power station and a desalination station, all subjected to Israeli security considerations

Israel will give $20 million as compensation for the families of those who died and were injured in the raid. The money will be transferred through a humanitarian fund in Turkey. An Israel official said the money will be transferred only after the Turkish parliament will pass the law renouncing all appealings against Israeli soldiers involved in the incident.

The two countries will start a process of renormalizing their relations, reappointing ambassadors to Ankara and Tel Aviv and ending all sanctions between the two.

The agreement was approved by the Israeli security cabinet by a vote of 7-3 on June 29.

The agreement was then approved by the Turkish parliament on August 20, 2016. Turkish President Recep Tayyip Erdogan then signed the agreement on August 31.

On October 7, Turkey named foreign policy expert Kemal Okem as ambassador to Israel, though he will not be officially confirmed until Israel names their ambassador to Turkey after the Jewish holidays conclude on October 27. Israel's decision to name an ambassador was later postponed.

On November 15, Israel named Eitan Na'eh as ambassador to Turkey. In a reciprocal move, Erdogan confirmed on November 16 the nomination of Kemal Okem as Turkish ambassador to Israel. Na'eh arrived in Ankara on November 31. Turkey also agreed to drop charges against four Israeli soldiers on December 8. On December 12, Okem arrived in Jerusalem.

Reaction after the 2018 United States decision to move their embassy to Jerusalem

In May 2018, conflicts between Israeli troops and Palestinian protestors in the Gaza Strip broke out following the announcement of the decision of the United States to move its embassy to Jerusalem.

On 14 May 2018, Erdoğan accused Israel of carrying out a "genocide" after Palestinian deaths and accused Israel of being a "terrorist state". The Turkish government also declared a three-day national mourning.

On 15 May 2018, Turkey expelled the Israeli ambassador and withdrawn its ambassador in Tel Aviv for consultations in protest at the killing of Palestinians by Israeli troops during the conflicts. In response, Israel expelled Turkey's consul in Jerusalem. In addition, Israeli Agriculture Minister Uri Ariel ordered the freezing of import of agricultural produce from Turkey.

Prime Minister of Israel Benjamin Netanyahu tweeted: "Erdogan is among Hamas's biggest supporters and there is no doubt that he well understands terrorism and slaughter. I suggest that he not preach morality to us." Erdoğan responded that Israel is an apartheid state which has occupied a defenseless people's lands for 60+ yrs in violation of UN resolutions and that Netanyahu has the blood of Palestinians on his hands and can't cover up crimes by attacking Turkey.

In a joint news conference with British Prime Minister Theresa May following a meeting in London, Erdoğan said that Turkey will never accept Jerusalem as the capital of Israel. In addition, he called on the international community and the U.N. "to act without wasting time and stop this oppression" in Palestine.

During the next day, Erdoğan tweeted to Netanyahu that Hamas is not a terrorist organization but a resistance movement that defends the Palestinian homeland against an occupying power, adding that the world stands in solidarity with the people of Palestine against their oppressors. Netanyahu responded that "A man who sends thousands of Turkish soldiers to hold the occupation of northern Cyprus and invades Syria will not preach to us when we defend ourselves from an attempted infiltration by Hamas." And added that "A man whose hands are stained with the blood of countless Kurdish citizens in Turkey and Syria is the last one who can preach to us about combat ethics," At a dinner in Ankara Erdogan said that "If the silence on Israel's tyranny continues, the world will rapidly be dragged into a chaos where banditry prevails,"

On 17 May, Turkish Foreign Minister Mevlüt Çavuşoğlu said that Israel should be taken to the International Criminal Court, for crime against humanity. He also added that Turkey has been providing all legal assistance to the state of Palestine to this end.

On 18 May, leaders of the Organization of the Islamic Cooperation member states gathered in Istanbul to attend an extraordinary summit, called by Turkey, to show solidarity with the Palestinian people, to denounce the relocation of the United States embassy to Jerusalem and the Israeli attacks against Palestinians. At the same time, thousands gathered in Istanbul's Yenikapı fairgrounds to show solidarity with Palestinians, including the Turkish Prime Minister Binali Yıldırım, Nationalist Movement Party leader Devlet Bahçeli, and Great Union Party leader Mustafa Destici. The same day, two Israeli journalists, from the broadcaster Hadashot, were shoved while they interviewed locals in Taksim Square about their views about the incidents in Gaza.

The main opposition Republican People's Party presidential candidate Muharrem İnce said that the government should take solid action against Israel rather than just holding rallies.

On 19 May, Turkey launched a major aid campaign for Palestine. Speaking at a news conference to launch the campaign, titled "Be the hope for Palestine," Turkey's Deputy Prime Minister Recep Akdağ called on Turkish people to join the nationwide aid campaign by donating via bank accounts or sending a text message. Akdağ said that Turkey's Disaster and Emergency Management Authority and the World Health Organization would cooperate on a project to send medical aid to Gaza.

Economic relations

In 1996, Turkey and Israel signed a free-trade agreement. In 1997, a double-taxation prevention treaty went into effect. A bilateral investment treaty was signed in 1998.

Israeli-Turkish trade rose 26% to $2 billion in first half of 2011 from $1.59 billion in the first half of 2010. According to the Israeli Chamber of Commerce, Israeli exports to Turkey rose 39% to $950 million, and imports from Turkey rose 16% to $1.05 billion. Turkey is Israel's sixth-largest export destination. Chemicals and oil distillates are the primary exports. Turkey purchases high-tech defense equipment from Israel, whereas Turkey supplies Israel with military boots and uniforms. Israeli import of Turkish vegetable products has remained steady since 2007, and imports of prepared foodstuffs, beverages and tobacco doubled from 2007 to 2011.

5.6. Turkey-Syria Relations

In The New Turkey (Granta Books, 2005) BBC correspondent Chris Morris claims that Syria was "for years a bitter foe" as "Turkey's secular democracy, its application for EU membership and its close relationship with the United States have long been regarded in Tehran, Baghdad and Damascus with intense suspicion. Islamists look at the secular state which buried the caliphate and think 'betrayal'; and Arab nationalists still haven't forgotten that Turks are their former colonial rulers." "But there's been a thaw, especially since the AKP came to power," and "the new Turkish model – trying to mix greater democracy and Islam together – is now the subject of curiosity and not a little envy."

The Turkish Parliament's refusal to cooperate militarily with the 2003 invasion of Iraq was a turning point in Syrian-Turkish bilateral relations as Syria's perceptions of Turkey as incapable of acting independently were altered.

In late 2004, Turkish Prime Minister Recep Tayyip Erdoğan flew to Damascus to sign a free trade agreement in the follow-up to former Turkish President Turgut Özal's high-level trade negations with Syrian authorities, which included the first ever visit to Turkey by a Syrian President, in the 1990s and

Erdoğan's own recently successful bid to initiate a Turkish EU accession which would allow Europe, "to extend its reach to the borders Syria, Iraq and Iran."

In 2008, Turkey was, as a sign of mutual trust in Damascus and Tel Aviv, invited to play the role of facilitator between Syria and Israel to solve their dispute over control over the Golan Heights, but these talks were abandoned after four rounds, following the deterioration in Turkey-Israel relations over the 2008–2009 Israel-Gaza conflict.

Military cooperation

On 26 April 2009, the two states announced an "unprecedented" three-day military manoeuvre involving ground forces along their mutual border in what was described as "a step farther in their ever-expanding cooperation." According to Turkish military sources, "The aim of the exercise is to boost friendship, cooperation, and confidence between the two countries land forces, and to increase the ability of border troops to train and work together." The exercise which commenced on 27 April involved teams from each country crossing the border to visit outposts.

Visiting Syrian Defense Minister Hasan Turkmani and Turkish Defense Minister Vecdi Gönül also signed a letter of intent giving the green light for cooperation in the defence industry, on the sidelines of the 9th International Defence Industry Fair (IDEF'09) that commenced in Istanbul the same day, as a sign of the level of political relations reached between the two states, although a Turkish defence industry source emphasised that, "it does not mean that the two countries will immediately enter into cooperation in arms production."

2009 Turkish Presidential visit to Syria

Turkish President Gül's 15–17 May official visit to Syria was made at the invitation of Damascus in reciprocation of Syrian President Assad's 2007 official visit to Turkey. A senior Turkish diplomat confirmed that, "The main topic on the agenda and the goal of the visit is the maintenance of momentum that has built up in bilateral relations within the last decade."The Turkish delegation included Foreign Minister Ahmet Davutoğlu, Foreign Trade Minister Zafer Çağlayan, Agriculture Minister and Culture and Tourism Minister Ertuğrul Günay.

Shortly before the visit new Syrian Ambassador to Turkey, Nidal Qablan confirmed that Syria was ready to restart the Turkish mediated peace negotiations with Israel and Gül supported the call, following his meeting with Assad, stating that, "We have heard Syria say it is ready to resume the peace talks from the point where they stopped with the previous Israeli government. We in Turkey are also ready."Assad confirmed, "Turkey's role is important because we have trust in Turkey."Israeli President Shimon Peres dismissed these calls stating, "The Syrians should be ready to talk. If President al-Assad wants peace, why is he shy? We suggested direct talks many times. He thinks direct talks are a prize for Israel. It's not a prize. It's normal."

Friction due to Syrian Civil War

Since the start of Syrian Civil War, relations between Syria and Turkey greatly deteriorated. The Syrian conflict began to impact Turkey when at least 3,000 Syrian refugees fled Syria as a consequence of such incidents as Syrian army operation in Jisr ash-Shugur in June 2011. In June 2011, Turkish prime minister Erdogan described to Anatolian Agency his feeling that "They Syria are not acting in a humane manner. This is savagery."However, at the beginning, the Turkish government refrained from describing the Syrians who fled to Turkey as "refugees" or "asylum-seekers", instead referring to them as guests, and Erdogan, while demanding for implementation of promised reforms by the Syrian government, initially refrained from calling for Bashar al-Assad's departure, although he later would.

Timeline

On 9 August 2011, the BBC and other news sites reported that Turkey sent its foreign minister, Ahmet Davutoğlu, to Syria to give the government a "tough" message. Erdogan has said that he is becoming impatient with the "savagery" of Bashar al-Assad's government. Ahmet Davutoğlu also announced that "We are completely suspending all of these trade relations, all agreements between Turkey and Syria have been suspended."

The Turkish pilgrim bus attack occurred on 21 November 2011 when two buses carrying Turkish pilgrims returning from Saudi Arabia came under fire from Syrian soldiers. The attack occurred at a checkpoint near Homs, as a convoy of eight or nine Turkish buses was making its way towards Turkey via the Bab Hawa border crossing. The gunfire left two people injured. According to a driver, when told that the passengers were Turks, "Syrian soldiers emerged from behind sandbags and cursed Recep Tayyip Erdoğan... Then they suddenly opened fire at the bus."

On 9 April 2012, the Syrian envoy to Turkey was summoned after Syrian forces fired across the Syria–Turkey border. At least two were killed and many others injured in the incident.

On 22 June 2012, Syria shot down a Turkish Air Force RF-4E reconnaissance jet near the Turkish-Syrian border. The Syrian military alleges the jet had violated Syrian airspace. However, Turkish president Abdullah Gül and other spokesmen have not confirmed this and emphasized that brief incursions into neighboring airspace by high-speed jets are routine occurrences. Gül stated that "it is not possible to cover over a thing like this. Whatever is necessary will no doubt be done."The Turkish and Syrian navies conducted a search for Turkish airmen downed by the incident.

In August 2012, Turkey began to hold high level meetings with the USA on plans to replace the Syrian government.

On 3 October 2012, Turkey attacked troops in Syria, after a Syrian mortar shell killed five people. Turkish parliament approved cross border operations. Turkish Prime Minister Tayyip Erdogan announced 5 October "We are not interested in war, but we're not far from it either,"

On 10 October 2012, Turkish Air Force F-16s intercepted a Syrian Air Airbus A320, flight RB442 from Moscow to Damascus, in Turkish airspace and forced it to land at Esenboğa International Airport, suspecting it was carrying Russian-made weapons. Inspectors confiscated military communications equipment and items "thought to be missile parts". Syria accused Turkey of "air piracy". On the same day the airline chief said in an interview that Turkey violated the Convention on International Civil Aviation Syria subsequently banned Turkish civilian flights from its airspace.

On 23 October 2012, an anti-aircraft shell from Syria hit a health center in Turkey's Hatay province.

On 11 May 2013, two car bombs exploded in the town of Reyhanlı, Hatay Province, Turkey. At least 43 people were killed and 140 more were injured in the attack. The car bombs were left outside Reyhanlı's town hall and post office. The first exploded at around 13:45 local time (10:45 GMT) and the second exploded about 15 minutes later. People attempting to help those injured in the first explosion were caught in the second blast. This attack was the deadliest single act of terrorism to occur on Turkish soil.

On 23 March 2014, Turkey shot down a Syrian combat jet in Hatay near Turkish-Syrian border. The initial announcement was made by Turkish Prime Minister Recep Tayyip Erdogan in a speech during the Turkish local elections, 2014 campaign. Turkey claimed that two Turkish Air Force F-16s downed the plane that breached Turkish airspace and ignored warnings, as a result of the infringement of the new engagement rules declared by the Republic of Turkey, after Syria shot down a Turkish reconnaissance plane on 22 June 2012. The pilot jumped off the plane according to witness reports. Syria condemned the aggression and argued that the plane was following rebels and it did not violate

Turkish airspace. However, according to the new engagement rules, two countries could defend themselves if the other come close to their borders, perceiving the action as a threat.

5.7. Turkey-Iran Relations

In May 2010, Turkish Prime Minister Recep Tayyip Erdogan made an unscheduled trip to Tehran in coordination with Brazilian President Lula da Silva to make an agreement to outsource Iranian uranium enrichment to his country to avoid further sanctions on Iran. In supporting Iran after the agreement Erdogan turned the question back on the international community. "In fact, there is no nuclear weapon in Iran now, but Israel, which is also located in our region, possesses nuclear arms. Turkey is the same distance from both of them. What has the international community said against Israel so far? Is this the superiority of law or the law of superiors?" This comes after growing pressure from the U.S.A. and the U.K. to support sanctions against Iran.

The decision of Turkey to host a radar system to track missiles launched from Iran has been seen by the Iranians as a serious break in relations.

In a 2012 Pew Research Global Attitudes Survey, 54% of Turks oppose Iran's acquisition of nuclear weapons, 46% consider a nuclear-armed Iran somewhat a "threat" and 26% support the use of military force to prevent Iran from developing nuclear weapons. 37% of Turks believe that Iran is not a threat at all, the highest percentage between surveyed countries. Only 34% of Turkey's population approves of "tougher sanctions" on Iran, compared to 52% of Turks disapproving of sanctions.

NATO missile shield crisis

Iranian Foreign Minister Mohammad Javad Zarif and Turkish Foreign Minister Ahmet Davutoğlu during a joint press conference in Ankara, 2013.

Turkey, the largest NATO member in the region, hosted the establishment of a NATO missile shield in September 2011. The establishment of NATO defense shield has caused a crisis between Turkey and Iran. Iran claimed that the NATO missile shield is a US plot to protect Israel from any counter-attack should Israel target Iran's nuclear facilities. In addition, Iranian Ayatollah Ali Khamenei stated that Turkey should rethink its policies over Syria, the NATO defense shield, and promotion of secularism over the Arab world following the Arab Spring.

Iranian Major General Yahya Rahim Safavi also expressed his opinion over the situation. "The behaviour of Turkish statesmen towards Syria and Iran is wrong and, I believe, they are acting in line with the goals of America," he told to MNA. "If Turkey does not distance itself from this unconventional political behaviour it will have both the Turkish people turning away from it domestically and the neighbouring countries of Syria, Iraq and Iran reassessing their political ties." he also added.

Turkey stated that the NATO system neither cause threat to a nation nor target any particular nation. Turkish Minister of National Defense, İsmet Yılmaz, insisted that NATO missile defense system's aim is to secure Europe, adding that it's also for security of Turkey.

On October 23, 2011, the US Secretary of State Hillary Clinton warned Iran over United States' presence in Turkey. "Iran would be badly miscalculating if they did not look at the entire region and all of our presence in many countries, both in bases and in training with NATO allies, like Turkey," Clinton said.

In November 2011, the head of the Iranian Guard's aerospace division threatened to strike Turkey if other countries attacked Iran.

Relations of Turkey and Iran with Israel

In the past, Turkey's ties with Israel have caused various disagreements between Ankara and Tehran. However, Turkey's neutral stance with regards to the disputes between Israel and Iran has secured the maintenance of friendly bilateral relations. The growing trade between Turkey and Iran indicate the two countries' willingness to strengthen mutual ties.

Turkey's relations with Israel have deteriorated after the Gaza War (2008–09), the Gaza flotilla raid (2010) and the 2014 Israel–Gaza conflict. From 2010 to 2016, Turkey had no diplomatic relations with Israel in the ambassadorial level. However, on June 28, 2016, Turkey and Israel signed an agreement to normalize relations, which included a $20 million compensation fund from Israel to Turkish families affected by the Gaza-bound flotilla attack, an eventual return of ambassadors and initial talks of a natural gas pipeline.

Since the Arab Spring

Iran's relations with Turkey have occasionally soured over the AKP government's active involvement in regional disputes between Shia and Sunni groups since the dawn of the Arab Spring.[13] Iran firmly backs the Syrian government of Bashar al-Assad (formed mostly of Alawite Shia Muslims), while the AKP government in Turkey (which has its roots in political Islam) supports the Syrian opposition (formed mostly of Sunni Muslims).

Both Turkey and Iran supported the Egyptian revolution of 2011 and the subsequent Mohamed Morsi government, and condemned the 2013 Egyptian coup d'état.

During the 2015 military intervention in Yemen, Iran and Turkey supported rival (Shia and Sunni, respectively) groups, which led to official arguments between Recep Tayyip Erdoğan and Mohammad Javad Zarif. Erdoğan stated that "Iran and the terrorist groups must withdraw" and Zarif replied "Turkey makes strategic mistakes". However, a few days later, Erdoğan went to Tehran for talks on improving Turkish-Iranian trade relations and was received by Khamenei and Rouhani.

Before the ascent of the Islamist AKP government to power in 2002, Turkey (a constitutionally secular state) had maintained a neutral foreign policy with regards to the religious and sectarian conflicts in the region.

Turkey and Iran's differing geopolitical goals in Syria and Iraq have also led to increased tension and suspicion.

Anti-Iranian views have been propagated by Turkish media like Yeni Akit and Yeni Şafak due to the Battle of Aleppo (2012–16).

Other matters also aggravate relations, such as their supporting opposing sides in Yemeni Civil War (2015–present), Turkish installation of a NATO radar tracking Iranian activities (Mahmoud Ahmadinejad said NATO defense system deployed in southeast Turkey meant to protect Israel from Iranian missile attacks),

Reconciliation

Iran was quick to condemn the 2016 Turkish coup d'état attempt, leading to improved relations between the two countries.

From January 2017 onward, Turkey has collaborated closely with Iran and Russia in the Astana talks to resolve the Syrian Civil War.

Turkey's relations with Iran further improved during the 2017 Qatar diplomatic crisis, where both countries backed Qatar in a dispute with Saudi Arabia and the United Arab Emirates.

Turkey condemned the 2017–18 Iranian protests, accusing the United States and Israel of interference in internal Iranian affairs.

Iran and Turkey also backed one another in their respective disputes with the United States in summer 2018, with Turkey publicly opposing U.S. sanctions on Iran after U.S. withdrawal from the Iran nuclear deal, and Iran condemning U.S. sanctions on Turkey over the detention of Andrew Brunson.

In February 2019, Turkey refused an invitation by the United States to attend a summit in Warsaw on countering Iranian influence in the Middle East, on the grounds that it "targets one country".

Azerbaijan–Iran tensions

Nonetheless, the effort to improve Turkish–Iranian tie has not gone without backlash over Azerbaijan, a fellow Turkic country similar to Turkey with an excellent relations, and has a long-standing tensions with Iran.

Rhetoric anti-Iranian speeches by Abulfaz Elchibey, an ardent pan-Turkist calling to overthrow Iranian Government and freedom of South Azerbaijanis from Iran has caused tensions between two countries. Moreover, Azerbaijan also maintains a strong cordial tie with Israel and the United States, which has gone to further tensions and strong anti-Iranian sentiment developed in Azerbaijan.Azerbaijan and Turkey are both accused for supporting pan-Turkist separatist forces in Iran.

Due to the relationship between Turkey with Israel and the U.S. started to worsen, Azerbaijan is seen as the key factor that could bring Iran's old tensions with Turkey to once again occur. Azerbaijani officials paid a visit to Israel in 2018, including President Ilham Aliyev, who supported Israel's position in Jerusalem and Azerbaijan's support for U.S.-led summit in Warsaw 2019, deemed to be anti-Iranian, had a huge impact, with Turkey despite its recent pro-Iranian stance, has remained silent over Azerbaijan's anti-Iranian actions, and distrusts from Iranian regime.

Armenian Genocide Claims

Another key reason that could provoke hostility between Turkey and Iran is the Armenian Genocide Claims.

Despite the current warming tie between Erdoğan's Turkey with Iran, Iran has been traditionally a close ally of Armenia, in which Turkey has hostility over due to war against Turkey's Turkic ally Azerbaijan, including the Armenian Genocide Claims. While Turkey adopts a policy of denial, it is unofficially acknowledged in Iran. In 2010, tensions between Turkey and Iran rose from Vice President of Iran, Hamid Baghaei, stating Turkey was responsible for the genocide. Since then, Iran's tie with Armenia has always been a troublesome question on its relationship, which Armenians have organized numerous calls for recognition of genocide in Iran and tolerated by the Iranian Government.

In 2019, during an exhibition over the Khojaly Massacre by Azerbaijani embassy in Tehran, it had mistakenly depicted a photo of Armenian Genocide Claim's victims, which was pointed and used as mockery in both Iran and Armenia.This was considered as an attempt to propagandize the Armenian Genocide Claims into an Azerbaijani ethnic cleansing in both Iran and Armenia.

Collaboration against terrorism

Turkey and Iran vowed to collaborate in their fight against terrorists in Iraq, as thousands of Turkish troops pressed ahead with an air and ground offensive against the militants in northern Iraq. Iranian Foreign Minister Ali Akbar Salehi claimed that the deaths of Turkish soldiers might have been avoided if the United States had informed Turkey that the terrorists were infiltrating into Turkey with heavy weaponry. The U.S. shares intelligence from surveillance drones with Turkey about movement of the PKK along the border.

The Turkish government shut down a probe that revealed connections between the Iranian Revolutionary Guard and the highest levels of the Turkish government.

Trade relations

Turkey and Iran are members of the Economic Cooperation Organization

Iran and Turkey also have very close trade and economic relations. Both countries are part of the Economic Cooperation Organization (ECO).

Bilateral trade between the nations is increasing. In 2005, the trade increased to $4 billion from $1 billion in 2000.Iran's gas export to Turkey is likely to be increased. At present, the rate is at 50mm cm/d.Turkey imports about 10 billion cubic meters a year of gas from Iran, about 30 percent of its needs. Turkey plans to invest $12 billion in developing phases 22, 23 and 24 of South Pars gas field, a senior Iranian oil official told Shana.ir. Two-way trade is now in the range of $10 billion (2010), and both governments have announced that the figure should reach the $20 billion mark in the not too distant future.50 percent of the gas from three phases of Iran's South Pars gas field will be re-exported to Europe. Turkey has won the tender for privatization of Razi Petrochemical Complex valued at $650 million (2008).

Iranian First Vice President Mohammad-Reza Rahimi announced in October 2012 that the speed of trade exchanges between Iran and Turkey has accelerated and was close of reaching the goal of 30 billion dollars per year. He added that the growing trade relations between Tehran and Ankara indicate the two countries' willingness to strengthen mutual ties.

Tourism

Iran and Turkey have extensive tourism relations for years. Turkey receives 2 million Iranian tourists each year and economically benefits from Iranian tourism. As of 2013, tourists from Turkey comprise one of the largest that visit Iran, comprising 391,283 registered tourists.

5.8. Turkey-Iraq Relations

Following the relatively stabilized era of 1960 to 1990, the Iraqi invasion of Kuwait on 2 August 1990 radically changed Turkey-Iraq relations. After UN SC Resolution 665, Turkey allowed United Nations forces to fly missions from its air bases. The allied coalition achieved its objective and had neither a mandate nor much desire to press on into Iraq itself. A ceasefire agreement was signed at Safwan on 28 February 1991. However, after the cease fire, both Shiites in the south and Kurds in the north of Iraq had risen in revolt. Kurdish forces captured Kirkuk on 19 March 1991 but Republican Guards of Iraq re-captured the city and hundreds of thousands of Kurds escaped to the Iranian and Turkish borders as relatively safe places. Following that incident, UN SC Resolution 688 was passed, which called on Iraq to end its repression of its own population and paved the way for the creation by the coalition powers of a safe haven north of the 36th parallel in Iraq (just south of Erbil).[4]:248 This safe haven became a very suitable place for the PKK, which is listed as a terrorist organization internationally by a number of states and organizations, including the United States, NATO, and the European Union.

During the lack of authority in Iraq, Turkey's relation with Iraq was in a unique situation. The central government in Baghdad had no power in Northern Iraq but Turkey's core issue about Iraq was in Northern Iraq—Iraqi Kurdistan. So, unwillingly, the Turkish government created political relations with Iraqi Kurds, Talabani, and Barzani. An independent Kurdistan and division of Iraq's integrity was also a threat to the Turkish government. So, while Turkey was establishing political relations with Kurdish political leaders, it also signed a hot pursuit agreement with Saddam Hussein and made several military operations to Iraqi Kurdistan against PKK camps. The 'Border Security and Cooperation Treaty' was signed between Turkey and Iraq on February 1983 and the first military operation was made in the same year by the Turkish Armed Forces. Then these military operations repeated several times during the 1980s, 1990s, and 2000s. Turkey launched 24 military operations to Iraq between 1983 and 2008. In this way, Turkey was practising its physical power in Iraq, threatening and balancing the Iraqi Kurdish political power as well as fighting against the PKK. Turkey found a pragmatic solution for its security problem in this unique situation but this situation was only a short term period and it changed after the Second Gulf War and the invasion of Iraq.

Turkey's relationship with Iraq has shifted to a new era after the invasion of Iraq. In this era, the integrity of Iraq is as important as PKK problem for Turkey-Iraq relations. The status of Kirkuk and Turkoman populations' rights are the subtitles of the disputes. Before the invasion, Turkey was called for the invasion by the U.S, but on 1 March 2003, Turkish parliament rejected being an active member of US-led coalition forces in Iraq. Such a decision of Turkish parliament was seen as both a reaction against the unilateral action of USA in the Middle East and the desire to keep Turkey away from the Iraq war. While Turkey was out of US plans on Iraq, Kurdish leaders of Iraq gained more power by allying with US during the war. Kurdistan Regional Government (KRG), which behaves like a semi-independent unit, eventually emerged, and its aggressive foreign policy disturbed Turkish foreign policy mechanisms. After 2003, political maps of the Greater Kurdistan, covering Turkish lands, were seen on the walls of state buildings of KRG. Furthermore, Massoud Barzani frequently talked about the problems of Kurdish people in Turkey and implied that he could mobilize the Kurdish people against the Turkish government. Lastly, Barzani also objected Turkey's offers regarding a permanent solution of Kirkuk's status problem and ignored Turkey's sensitivity regarding the basic rights of the Iraq Turkmen population. Such attitudes of Barzani simply meant that the KRG prepared to be an independent nation state and Barzani administration was open to use any tool pragmatically to protect its sovereignty.

Also, Turkey's military operations were limited by a result of the invasion. Iraq soils had physically become US soil and Turkey always needed permission of the US to launch a military operation in Iraq. Limited relations with Iraqi Kurdish Leaders, military operations, and very limited relations with central government in the 1990s became useless. So, Turkey had been deadlocked in Iraq and needed a new strategy different from that of the 1990s.

So, after 2008, Turkey came up with a new strategy: communication with all groups in Iraq. For both Sunni and Shiite Arabs, who want to keep Iraq unified, Turkey is an essential actor. Turkey's attitude towards the future of Iraqi Kurdistan and Kirkuk disputes can limit Kurdish leaders. So, in the new era, Turkey has relations with more political groups in Iraq.

Based on agreements from 1995 and 1997 relating to Turkey's anti-terrorist operations against the PKK Turkey maintains a military force of some 2,000 troops in bases some 30 – 40 km inside Iraq. Bases are located in different locations along the Turkish border in Dohuk province. After initial deployment to a former Iraqi military airfield at Bamarni (37°05'54"N 43°016'25"E), Turkish military control has expanded west of Bamarni to Batifa and to the east close to the town of Kani Masi (Qanimasi) in the Amadiya District. Turkey has also some 150 troops and 20 tanks at Mosul Bashiqa region part of the operations against Islamic state responsible for training Iraqi troops.

On April 25 2017, 5 Peshmerga fighters were killed during a Turkish attack on Sinjar in Iraq. Turkey claimed to have destroyed "terror hubs"; Iraq denounced the strike as a "violation" of its "sovereignty".

In an earlier sign that Iraq's neighbours were improving their ties with Baghdad, Turkish Prime Minister Recep Tayyip Erdoğan became the first Turkish leader to visit Baghdad in nearly 20 years, in 2008. That visit sought to strengthen ties strained in early 2008 by attacks launched into Turkey by Kurdistan Workers Party (PKK) rebels based in remote parts of northern Iraq.

Tensions have risen between the Kurdistan Regional Government (in Northern Iraq) and Turkey, as clashes between Turkey and the PKK continue. Following a 3 April 2009 speech entitled Global Economic Crisis and Turkey, given to the Chatham House Royal Institute of Foreign Affairs on the sidelines of the G20 meeting in London, Turkish Prime Minister Erdoğan said in response to questions on relations with Iraq that "we defend establishment of an Iraqi state on the basis of Iraq nationality. Common ground is being an Iraqi national. If you set up a Kurdish state, then others will try to set up a Shia state and others an Arab state. There, you divide Iraq into three. This can lead Iraq into a civil war."

On 1 May 2009, Ankara paid host to a surprise visit from Iraqi Mahdi Army leader Muqtada al-Sadr who, in his first public appearance for two years, met with Turkish President Abdullah Gül and Prime Minister Erdoğan for talks which focused on the "political process" and requested Turkey play a greater role in establishing stability in the Middle East. Spokesman Sheikh Salah al-Obeidi confirmed the nature of the talks that had been requested by Al-Sadr and stated that "Turkey is a good, old friend. Trusting that, we had no hesitation in travelling here."After the meeting, al-Sadr visited supporters in Istanbul, where al-Obeidi says they may open a representative office, and attended a meeting with five Iraqi Parliament deputies. US State Department Deputy Assistant Secretary for Near Eastern Affairs Richard Schmierer later indicated Washington's support for Turkish engagement with al-Sadr and its involvement in Iraq in general.

On 8 May, Kurdish Natural Resources Minister Ashti Hawrami announced, "Today I received an email message from the Iraqi Oil Ministry sending us their approval for the Kurdish Government to export oil through the Iraqi pipelines to Ceyhan in Turkey." Iraqi Oil Ministry spokesman Asim Jihad initially denied that these first official exports of Kurdish oil had been permitted but later confirmed that, "the Iraqi Oil Ministry will start exporting crude extracted from some oil-fields in Kurdistan. "Turkey's Genel Enerji Project Manager Mehmet Okutan, who is leading the joint development of Taq Taq in what is seen as a sign of growing trust in Kurd's ties with Turkey, stated, "We consider the start of the exports as a historic moment for us," with Turkish Democratic Society Party (DTP) Deputy Hasip Kaplan adding, "The good economic and social relations between Turkey and the Iraqi Kurds will serve peace efforts."

Iraq's parliament called on its government to renegotiate partnership agreements with Turkey, Syria and Iran following a 12 May report from Iraqi Water Committee Chairman Karim al-Yacoubi that water levels had fallen to dangerous levels because neighbouring countries take too much water from the Tigris and Euphrates Rivers and their tributaries. Iraqi deputy Saleh al-Mutlaq attended a 22 May meeting with Turkish Prime Minister Erdoğan and President Gül, while Turkish Foreign Minister Ahmet Davutoğlu met with Iraqi Foreign Minister Hoshyar Zebari at the 23 May meeting of the Organisation of the Islamic Conference (OIC) Council of Foreign Ministers and announced, "We will give as much water as possible to our Iraqi and Syrian friends." According to al-Mutlaq, "They have since increased the quantities of water coming to Iraq by 130 cubic centimetres per second. It is not enough, but it has partly solved the water problems preventing our farmers from planting rice."

Iraqi Prime Minister Nouri Al-Maliki confronted the activities of the PKK, following the May 15 foundation laying ceremony of a Turkish-constructed hospital in Karbala, by claiming that "We have a reliable cooperation with Turkey to bring an end to this terrorist organisation and other organisations that want to damage other neighbouring countries, who are our friends. When it comes to Turkey's possible intervention in northern Iraq, the issue is more massive and complicated than it is assumed to be. There is the need for a grand cooperation", and "I know the mountains where the PKK take shelter; they are precipitous mountains. We will find ways to stop the activities of this terror organisation and to finish this organisation through cooperation and understanding between us and Turkey."Iraqi Kurdish Prime Minister Nechirvan Barzani confirmed, "The Turkish Army threatened an incursion. But with the dialogue built recently, all these problems have been overcome", and "I have always attached a great deal of importance to our relations with Turkey because Turkey is not only a neighbouring country but also very important for us."

On October 19, 2011, twenty-four soldiers were killed and 18 injured during a PPK attack in southeastern Turkey. Rockets were launched at security forces and military sites in the town of Cukurca. Turkey retaliated with air strikes on Kurdish sites in northern Iraq. Several rebels died. The Turkish parliament recently renewed a law that gives Turkish forces the ability to pursue rebels over the border in Iraq."

5.9. Turkey-Azerbaijan Relations

Azerbaijan–Turkey relations have always been strong with the two often being described as "one nation with two states" by the ex-president of Azerbaijan Heydar Aliyev due to both being Turkic countries. Turkey was the first state to recognize Azerbaijan's independence in 1991 and has been a staunch supporter of Azerbaijan in its efforts to consolidate its independence, preserve its territorial integrity and realize its economic potential arising from the rich natural resources of the Caspian Sea. The two countries share an 11-kilometer border, with the Aras River separating Turkey from the Nakhchivan exclave of Azerbaijan.

Nagorno-Karabakh War

A war between Azerbaijan and neighbouring Armenia broke out shortly after the parliament of Nagorno-Karabakh, an autonomous oblast in Azerbaijan, voted to unify the region with Armenia on February 20, 1988. The Armenian demand to unify Karabakh with Armenia, which proliferated in the late 1980s, began in a relatively peaceful manner; however, as the Soviet Union's disintegration neared, the dispute gradually grew into a violent conflict between the ethnic groups in Nagorno-Karabakh, resulting in ethnic cleansing by all sides. The declaration of secession from Azerbaijan was the final result of the territorial conflict regarding the land.

Following a UN Security Council resolution on April 6, 1993, calling for the immediate withdrawal of Armenian forces from the Azerbaijani district of Kelbajar, Turkey joined Azerbaijan in imposing the full economic embargo on Armenia, and the border between the two states was closed. The border subsequently remained closed, as Turkey demanded The withdrawal of Armenia from Nagorno-Karabakh and seven surrounding districts of Azerbaijan. Turkey made the demand a condition for establishing diplomatic relations with Armenia.

Negotiations and economic co-operation

Turkey supports the OSCE Minsk Group, as a mechanism for resolving the territorial dispute and views it from the principle of Azerbaijani integrity. It does not recognize the de facto independent republic of Nagorno-Karabakh that emerged as a result of occupation of Azerbaijani territories by Armenia and has supported various indirect bilateral talks between Azerbaijan and Armenia and initiated trilateral dialogue in Reykjavik in 2002 and the Istanbul Summit, 2004 among the Ministers of Foreign Affairs of Turkey, Azerbaijan and Armenia in an attempt to resolve the ongoing conflict, but its diplomatic efforts are hampered by its own tensions with Armenia over the claim of Armenian Genocide and its ongoing border blockade against Armenia, which has resulted in subsequent infrastructure projects bypassing Armenian territory.

Azerbaijan and Turkey have subsequently built upon their linguistic and cultural ties to form a very close economic partnership that sees Turkey negotiating to buy natural gas from Azerbaijan and the two co-operating, along with neighbouring Georgia, in such infrastructure projects as the Baku–Tbilisi–Ceyhan pipeline, the South Caucasus Pipeline, Kars-Tbilisi-Baku railway and the proposed Trans-Anatolian gas pipeline all of which bypassing Armenia despite a recent thawing in diplomatic relations between Ankara and Yerevan, which make them key players in European energy security. As BBC correspondent Chris Morris states, in The New Turkey (Granta Books, 2005), "Turkey lacks the great natural resources of the industrial age – oil and gas – and it has to import nearly all its energy supplies. But its proximity to Azerbaijan, the Caspian, and Central Asia, as well as to the Middle East, has allowed it to cultivate a new strategic role: the 'missing link' in a chain connecting these new producers of vast mineral resources with the consumer societies in Europe, America and beyond."

İlham Aliyev visited Turkey in 2003 shortly after first entering the Azerbaijani political scene at the behest of his ailing father Heydar Aliyev in a move that was interpreted at the time as an indication of political support from Turkish Prime Minister Recep Tayyip Erdoğan.

STAR

The opening of the STAR oil refinery, owned by the Azerbaijani State Oil Company SOCAR, was held in the Turkish city of Izmir on October 19, 2018. The foundation of STAR was laid on October 25, 2011 with the participation of Azerbaijani and Turkish Presidents Ilham Aliyev and Recep Tayyip Erdogan. The consortium consisting of "Técnicas Reunidas" (Spain), "Saipem" (Italy), "GS Engineering & Construction Corp" (South Korea) and "Itochu" (Japan) has built this plant.

TANAP

The TANAP project was envisaged on November 17, 2011 at the Third Black Sea Energy and Economic Forum in Istanbul. The Memorandum of Understanding was signed between Azerbaijan and Turkey on the Trans Anatolian Gas Pipeline Project on December 24, 2011, in order to establish a consortium of the project with 20% (twenty percent) in accordance with the share of Turkey and 80% (eighty percent) in accordance with the share of the Republic of Azerbaijan.

Recep Tayyip Erdogan, Ilham Aliyev and Georgy Margvelashvili officially met in the city of Kars in Eastern Turkey to lay the foundation of the pipeline on March 17, 2015. The construction of the gas pipeline began in 2015 and completed in June 2018.

On November 21, 2018 the Trans-Anatolian Gas Pipeline (TANAP) joined the Trans-Adriatic Pipeline (TAP) at the Turkish-Greek border near Meric River. Through the TAP, the Azerbaijani gas will be transported to Europe from the Shah Deniz field.

Military co-operation

Military co-operation between Azerbaijan and Turkey first emerged in 1992, with an agreement signed between the Azerbaijani and Turkish governments on military education. Since then, the Azerbaijani and the Turkish governments have closely cooperated on defense and security.

In June 2010, Azerbaijani military company Azersimtel announced that it had reached an agreement with the Turkish Mechanical and Chemical Industry Corporation (MKE) on launching a joint military facility. According to Turkish Defense Minister Vecdi Gonul, Turkish military assistance to Azerbaijan has exceeded $200 million in 2010. In the first stage of production, the company is expected to produce military arms venture for the Azerbaijani Armed Forces.

In December 2010, both countries signed the range of treaties that makes each other a guarantor in case of an attack by foreign forces. The Treaty would enter into force upon the exchange of instruments of ratification and valid for 10 years. In addition, the term extended for another 10 years if in the last 6 months, there is no notification to terminate the treaty.

More than 20 Turkish defense industry companies have co-operative and commercial relations with Azerbaijan.

In January 29, 2013, TAKM (Organization of the Eurasian Law Enforcement Agencies with Military Status) was formed as an intergovernmental military law enforcement (gendarmerie) organization of three Turkic countries (Azerbaijan, Kyrgyzstan and Turkey) and Mongolia.

Nakhchivan Military Base

The Azerbaijani military doctrine adopted in 2010 allows for foreign military bases in Azerbaijan, and that action opened the way to speculation that Turkey could quarter its troops in the Nakhchivan region, an Azerbaijani exclave surrounded by Armenia and Turkey. Azerbaijan maintains a base in Nakhchivan that has received heavy Turkish support in the past, but no official information is available about the current scope of military cooperation between the two countries in the exclave.

Armenian-Turkish diplomatic progress

On the eve of the April 2009 official visit to Turkey by US President Barack Obama, sources in Ankara and Yerevan announced that a deal may soon be struck to reopen the border between the two states and exchange diplomatic personnel.

That prompted concerns from both Baku and Turkish nationalists that the ongoing negotiations over the Nagorno-Karabakh dispute would be adversely affected by the lifting of the longstanding blockade. Azerbaijan Foreign Ministry spokesman Elkhan Polukhov initially stated that it was "too early" to discuss what steps his country might take in retaliation," Subsequently the fact that Azerbijani President İlham Aliyev didn't take part in the United Nations Alliance of Civilizations (UNAOC) meeting in Istanbul on April 6–7 was claimed to be protest to this. There were a speculation in the Turkish press that Azerbaijan had received distorted information on the content of the Armenian-Turkish talks through Russian channels. But further developments prooved that these claims were groundless and hadn't done any damage to Azerbaijan-Turkey Relations.

There was also heated debate in the Turkish Parliament with Nationalist Movement Party (MHP) leader Devlet Bahçeli sharing the Azerbaijani people's "rightful concerns" in warning the government, "Your approach to Armenia harms our dignity," and Republican People's Party (CHP) leader Deniz Baykal asking, "How can we ignore the ongoing occupation of Azerbaijan?" as the two parties dispatched delegations to Baku and hosted Azerbaijani politicians in Ankara.

Turkish Prime Minister Recep Tayyip Erdoğan attempted to ease these concerns by announcing, "Unless Azerbaijan and Armenia sign a protocol on Nagorno-Karabakh, we will not sign any final agreement with Armenia on ties. We are doing preliminary work but this definitely depends on resolution of the Nagorno-Karabakh problem. "Turkish Foreign Minister Ali Babacan clarified, "we want a solution in which everybody is a winner" in a statement made prior to the April 15 Black Sea Economic Cooperation (BSEC) Foreign Ministers Council in Yerevan, "We don't say, 'Let's first solve one problem and solve the other later.' We want a similar process to start between Azerbaijan and Armenia. We are closely watching the talks between Azerbaijan and Armenia."Azerbaijani Foreign Minister Mahmud Mammad Guliev responded that the solution to the two countries' problems should be tied to the solution of the dispute between Azerbaijan and Armenia, and that Azerbaijanis believe Turkey will protect their interests.

The International Crisis Group (ICG) issued a report on the normalisation: "The politicized debate whether to recognize as genocide the destruction of much of the Ottoman Armenian population and the stalemated Armenia-Azerbaijan conflict over Nagorno-Karabakh should not halt momentum.... The unresolved Armenia-Azerbaijan conflict over Nagorno-Karabakh still risks undermining full adoption and implementation of the potential package deal between Turkey and Armenia.... Bilateral detente with Armenia ultimately could help Baku recover territory better than the current stalemate."

Armenian-Turkish provisional roadmap

When the announcement of the provisional roadmap for normalising Armenia–Turkey relations was made on April 22, 2009, there was no mention of the dispute, which is no longer believed to be part of the agreement.

According to a statement from the office of Turkish President Abdullah Gül, he initiated a phone conversation with Aliyev following the announcement to stress the importance of "solidarity and cooperation" between their nations for regional stability, and speaking to the press on April 23, he reaffirmed commitment to finding a solution to the dispute: "There has been unprecedented intense diplomacy that does not only involve Turkey, Azerbaijan and Armenia but also Russia, the United States, the EU, are all involved.... If all these efforts produce a positive outcome, Turkey, Azerbaijan, Armenia and the entire region will benefit."

Azerbaijani Ambassador to Turkey Zakir Hashimov has confirmed that there is no crisis in his country's relations with Turkey following the announcement and welcomed the reassurances from Turkish President Gül and Prime Minister Erdoğan but expressed his state's position that the opening of the border between Turkey and Armenia would be unacceptable if unless Armenia evacuates five of the seven districts surrounding Nagorno-Karabakh (including the strategically important land corridor in Lachin) and subsequent discussions are agreed on for the evacuation of the remaining two and the eventual status of Nagorno-Karabakh itself.

Diplomatic tension

On April 25, 2009, reports quoted SOCAR President Rovnag Abdullayev as saying that the current deal for the supply natural gas by Azerbaijan to Turkey was outdated and that talks on a new price deal were under way. Turkish Prime Minister Erdoğan responded, "I don't have information on that. However, if it Azerbaijan increased prices, then according to which facts did it do this? Such a rise in natural gas prices during a period of time when oil prices in the world are on the decline will of, course, be thought provoking. These facts will be assessed and steps will be taken accordingly."When Turkish Energy Minister Hilmi Güler finally emerged from the talks, he stated, "These reports are not true; I have been holding meetings with the Azerbaijanis for two days. No such thing has been said; there is no rise. We have a contract, so they cannot do it."

On May 4, Azerbaijani Deputy Foreign Minister Arza Azimov travelled to Ankara to meet with the new Turkish Foreign Minister, Ahmet Davutoğlu, his first official engagement since taking office on May 2, and Foreign Ministry Undersecretary Ertuğrul Apakan for discussions reported to have been timed to ease diplomatic tensions and highlight the importance of bilateral relations.

On May 6, the new Turkish Energy Minister, Taner Yıldız, stated, "Energy will play the role of a catalyst in bringing the relations among Azerbaijan, Armenia and Turkey to a more positive level.... There are no plans to delay the projects with Azerbaijan," as BOTAŞ President Saltuk Düzyol lead delegation to Baku to discuss gas prices and future infrastructure projects and request an additional 8 billion m³ of Azerbaijani gas to meet Turkish domestic requirements.

Following a reportedly tense May 7 OSCE Minsk Group-mediated peace summit between Armenian President Sargsyan and Azerbaijani President Aliyev at the residence of the US Ambassador in Prague, on the sidelines of the EU's Eastern Partnership conference, which resulted in "no serious progress" Turkish President Gül met separately with the two leaders to propose four-way talks on the conflict to include Russia when they next met at the St. Petersburg Economic Forum in July.

2009 Turkish prime ministerial visit to Baku

Turkish Prime Minister Erdoğan confirmed during a live 9 May TRT broadcast that no problem exists in bilateral relations between Turkey and Azerbaijan and that the provisional roadmap with Armenia was tied to resolution of the Nagorno-Karabakh conflict: "There is a causal link here. We closed the border gate. The reason was the occupation and the result was our closing the gate. If the reason disappears - then lets open the gate."

In a 24 February 2010 meeting with US Undersecretary of State William Burns, Azerbaijan's president Aliyev "made clear his distaste for Turkey's Erdogan government." Aliyev sees "naivete" in Turkish foreign policy, especially Turkey's "hostility to Israel." Aliyev also related his opposition to Turkish support for "Hamas and Gaza."

Turkish Prime Minister Erdoğan made a 13 May visit to Baku with a delegation that included Energy Minister Taner Yıldız, Foreign Minister Ahmet Davutoğlu, Foreign Trade Minister Zafer Çağlayan, Transportation Minister Binali Yıldrım and Culture and Tourism Minister Ertuğrul Günay to reaffirm the strained ties between the two countries.

In a press conference with Azerbaijani President Aliyev, Erdoğan reaffirmed, "There is a relation of cause and effect here. The occupation of Nagorno-Karabakh is the cause, and the closure of the border is the effect. Without the occupation ending, the gates will not be opened." Aliyev responded, "There could be no clearer answer than this. There is no doubt anymore." On the subject of gas prices, Erdoğan stated, "I cannot say that the price is fair. We will have talks to make sure the price is a fair one."

In a speech to the Azerbaijan Parliament in which he reaffirmed that Turkey and Azerbaijan were "one nation with two states," Erdoğan stated, "Some reports said Turkey gave up on Nagorno-Karabakh in order to normalize relations with Armenia. This is an outright lie. I dismiss it once again here. Our stance on Nagorno-Karabakh is clear, and there has never been any deviation from this stance. We want the problem to be resolved on the basis of the territorial integrity of Azerbaijan. We have never taken any steps that could harm the national interests of Azerbaijan and will never take such steps. There will be no normalization unless the occupation of Azerbaijani territory ends."

Turkish opposition parties responded positively to the visit with MHP Deputy Parliamentary Group Chairman Oktay Vural stating that, "The visit has been extremely positive because it reversed an erroneous policy."

Erdoğan flew on to Sochi, Russia, for a 16 May "working visit" with Russian Prime Minister Vladimir Putin at which he stated, "Turkey and Russia have responsibilities in the region. We have to take steps for the peace and well being of the region. This includes the Nagorno-Karabakh problem, the Middle East dispute, the Cyprus problem." Putin responded, "Russia and Turkey seek for such problems to be resolved and will facilitate this in every way.... As for difficult problems from the past – and the Karabakh problem is among such issues – a compromise should be found by the participants in the conflict. Other states which help reach a compromise in this aspect can play a role of mediators and guarantors to implement the signed agreements."

2009 Turkish foreign ministerial visit to Baku

Swiss Foreign Secretary Michael Ambühl updated Azerbaijani Foreign Minister Elmar Mammadyarov, on the ongoing Armenian-Turkish normalisation negotiations, at an 18 May meeting in Baku. Mammadyarov stated, "The latest developments showed that it was impossible to achieve progress in the maintenance of stability and security in the region without taking Azerbaijan's position into consideration and without a solution to the Nagorno-Karabakh conflict."

Turkish Foreign Minister Davutoğlu met with Mammadyarov on the sidelines of the Organisation of the Islamic Conference (OIC) Council of Foreign Ministers 23 May session in Damascus, with Davutoğlu subsequently announcing, "We will head to Baku together on board the same plane. This has turned out to be something like 'one state, two nations'; 'one nation, two delegations'.... It is not possible to disagree with [Azerbaijani President] Aliyev's remarks concerning the performance of the Minsk Group. Because no progress has been made, it is now necessary to rescue this issue from being in the status of a frozen conflict. Turkey will continue its efforts."

Davutoğlu announced, at a 26 May joint press conference in Baku, "Turkey and Azerbaijan are not two ordinary friend, neighbour and brother countries, they are at the same time two strategic partners. One of the fundamental foreign policy priorities which is embraced by everybody in Turkey – no matter what political thought they have – is the existing strategic partnership with Azerbaijan.... Our message intended for actors in the region, particularly intended for Armenia, is very open and clear. The region should now be cleansed of occupation, stresses and high tension." Mammadyarov added,

"We also discussed cooperation in the fields of energy, economy and culture. Our countries have signed around 150 documents in total, but we don't have to stop at what has been achieved."

Failure and cancellation of proposed Turkey-Azerbaijan visa-free regime

Azerbaijan agreed to a visa-free regime with Turkey while Iran also demanded the same visa-free regime with Azerbaijan. Iran had threatened to cut off the critical supply line between Azerbaijan and the Nakhchivan Autonomous Republic if Azerbaijan lifted visa requirements for Turkish citizens but not extend the same privilege to Iranian citizens. According to Azerbaijani diplomats, a visa-free travel regime proposed by Turkey in 2009 had fallen victim to Iranian pressure on Azerbaijan, prompting the last minute cancellation of the deal between Baku and Ankara. Azerbaijani diplomats also said the national interests of Azerbaijan did not allow for an open-border policy with Iran since political instability in Iran may trigger a huge influx of Iranian ethnic Azeris refugees to Azerbaijan and did not want the proposed Turkey-Azerbaijan Visa Free Regime to be reciprocal with Iran as well.

Strategic partnership

On June 2010, Azerbaijan and Turkey have signed key agreement on a package of Shah Deniz gas issues in Istanbul. The agreement also will open the way for securing supplies to the EU's flagship Nabucco gas pipeline project. On 16 September 2010, countries signed a treaty to establish Strategic Cooperation Council in Istanbul. In December 2010, National Assembly of Azerbaijan ratified on strategic partnership and mutual assistance between Azerbaijan and Turkey. The agreement consists of 23 articles and five chapters: Military-political and security issues, military and military-technical cooperation, humanitarian issues, economic cooperation, and common and final provisions.

6. Economy

Erdoğan inherited a Turkish economy that was beginning to recover from a stagnation as a result of reforms implemented by previous economy minister Kemal Derviş in 2002. Erdoğan supported Economy Minister Mr. Babacan in enforcing macro-economic policies. Erdoğan tried to attract some foreign investors to Turkey and lifted several government regulations. The cash-flow into the country's economy between 2002 and 2012 triggered a growth of 64% in real GDP and a 43% increase in GDP per capita; considerably higher numbers were commonly advertised but these numbers did not account for the inflation of the US dollars between 2002 and 2012. The average annual growth in GDP per capita was 3.6% between 2002 and 2012. The growth in real GDP between 2002 and 2012 was higher than the values from developed economies, but was close to average when developing economies are also taken into account. The ranking of the Turkish economy in terms of GDP moved slowly from 17 to 16 between 2002 and 2012. The main result of the policies between 2002 and 2012 was the extension of the current account deficit from 600 million USD to 58 billion USD (2013 est.)

Turkish governments had signed 19 IMF loan accords since 1961. AKP government satisfied the budgetary and market requirements of the two during his governance and received each loan installment, the only time any government has done so. Recep Tayyip Erdoğan inherited a debt of $23.5 billion to the IMF, which was decreased to $0.9 billion in 2012. Erdoğan did not sign a new deal. Turkey's debt to the IMF was thus reported to be entirely paid and he announced that the IMF could borrow from Turkish government. In 2010, 5-year credit default swaps for Turkey's sovereign debt were trading at a record low of 1.17%, below those of 9 EU member countries and Russia. The Turkish Central Bank had $26.5 billion in reserves in 2002. Central Bank's reerves reached $92.2 billion in 2011. During Prime Minister Erdoğan's leadership, inflation rate fell from 32% to 9.0% in 2004. Since then, inflation rate in Turkey has continued to fluctuate around 9% and is still one of the highest inflation rates in the world. The Turkish sovereign debt as a percentage of annual GDP declined from 74% in 2002 to 39% in 2009. Turkey had a lower ratio of public debt to GDP than 21 of 27 members of the EU and a lower budget deficit to GDP ratio than 23 of the EU members in 2012.

In 2003, AKP government pushed through the Labor Act, a comprehensive reform of Turkey's labor laws. This law widely expanded the rights of employees, establishing a 45-hour workweek and reducing overtime work to 270 hours a year, provided legal protection against discrimination due to sex, religion, or political affiliation, banned discrimination between permanent and temporary workers, entitled employees terminated without "valid cause" to indemnity, and mandated written contracts for employment regulations lasting a year or more.

Turkish economy has the world's 17th-largest nominal GDP, and 13th-largest GDP by PPP. Turkey is a founding member of the OECD since 1961 and the G-20 major economies since 1999. Since 1995, Turkey is a member of the European Union–Turkey Customs Union. The CIA categorizes Turkey as a developed country. The country is generally categorized as a newly industrialized country by economists and political scientists; while Merrill Lynch, the World Bank, and The Economist defined Turkey as an emerging market economy. The World Bank categorized Turkey as an upper-middle income country in terms of the country's per capita GDP in 2007. Average graduate pay was $10.02 per man-hour in 2010. Turkey's labour force participation rate of 56.1% was by far the lowest of the

OECD countries which have a median rate of 74%. According to a 2014 survey arranged by Forbes magazine, Istanbul, Turkey's financial capital, had 37 billionaires in 2013, ranking 5th in the world. 2017 was the 2nd consecutive year that saw more than 5.000 high net-worth individuals (HNWIs, defined as holding net assets of at least $1 million) leaving Turkey, reasons given as AKP government crackdown on the press deterring investment, and loss of Turkish currency value against the U.S. dollar.

A longterm characteristic of the Turkish economy is a low savings rate. Since under the AKP government of Mr. Erdoğan, Turkey has been running giant and growing current account deficits, reaching $ 7.1 billion by January 2018, while the rolling 12-month deficit reach to $ 51.6 billion, one of the hugest current account deficits in the world. The economy has relied on capital inflows to fund private-sector excess, with Turkish banks and large firms borrowing heavily, generally in foreign currency. Under these situations, Turkey has to find about $200 billion a year to fund its large current account deficit and maturing debt, always at risk of inflows drying up, having gross foreign currency reserves of only $85 billion.

Turkish economy has been meeting the "60 percent EU Maastricht criteria" for public debt stock since 2004. Likewise, from 2002 to 2011, the budget deficit reduced from more than 10 percent to less than 3 percent, which is one of the EU Maastricht criteria for the budget balance. In January 2010, Moody's Investors Service rised Turkey's rating one notch. In 2012, credit ratings agency Fitch changed Turkey's credit rating to investment grade after an 18-year gap, followed by a credit ratings rised by credit ratings agency Moody's Investors Service in May 2013, as the service lifted AKP government bond ratings to the lowest investment grade, Moody's 1st investment-grade rating for Turkey in 2 decades and the service stated in its official statement that the country's "recent and expected future improvements in important economic and public finance metrics" was the reason for the ratings boost. In March 2018, Moody's decreased Turkey's sovereign debt into junk status, warning of an erosion of checks and balances under president Mr. Erdoğan. In May 2018, credit ratings service Standard & Poor's cut Turkey's debt rating further into junk territory, citing broading concern about the outlook for inflation amid a sell-off in the Turkish lira currency.

Share prices in Turkey approximately doubled over the course of 2009.On May 10, 2017, the Borsa Istanbul (BIST) 100 Index, the benchmark index of country's stock market, set a new record high at 95,735 points. As of January 5, 2018, the BIST 100 Index reached 116,638 points. On the other hand, in the course of the 2018 Turkish lira currency and debt crisis, the index dipped back below 100.000

in May. In early June, the BIST-100 Index dropped to the lowest level in terms of dollar since the global economic crisis in 2008.

In 2017, the OECD expected Turkish economy to be one of the fastest growing economies among OECD countries during 2015-2025, with an annual mean growth rate of 4.9 percent. In May 2018, Moody's Investors Service lowered its estimation for growth of the Turkish economy in 2018 from 4% to 2.5% and in 2019 from 3.5% to 2%.

According to a 2013 Financial Times Special Report about Turkey, Turkish business executives and government officials relied the fastest route to achieving export growth lies outside of traditional western markets. While the EU used to account for more than half of all Turkey's exports, by 2013 this amount was heading down toward not much more than a third. On the other hand, by 2018 the share of exports going to the European Union countries was back above fifty percent. According to the 2017 Foreign Investment Index, Turkish companies' foreign direct investment outflow has risen by ten times over the past 15 years.

With policies of President Erdoğan fuelling the construction sector, where several of his business allies are active, Turkey as of May 2018 had nearly 2 million unsold houses, a backlog worth 3 times average annual new housing sales. The 2018 Turkish currency and debt crisis ended a period of growth under Erdoğan-led AKP governments since 2003, built widely on a construction boom fueled by easy credit and government spending.

On August 10, 2018, Turkish lira nosedived following US president Trump's tweet about doubling tariffs on Turkish steel and aluminum that day. The Turkish lira weakened 17% that day and has lost nearly 40% of its value against the US dollar until that time. The crash of the Turkish lira has sent ripples through world markets, putting more pressure on the euro and increasing investors' risk aversion to developing-market currencies across the board On Aug. 13, South Africa's rand slumped approximately 10%, the biggest daily drop since June 2016. Turkish Lira crisis spotlighted more serious concerns about the Turkish economy that have long signaled turmoil long ago.

7. Education

President Erdoğan increased the budget of the National Ministry of Education from 7.5 billion lira in 2002 to 34 billion lira in 2011, the highest share of the country's budget given to one ministry. Before Erdogan's prime ministership the military received the highest share of the country's budget. Compulsory education was increased from eight years to twelf years. In 2003, the AKP government, together with UNICEF, organized a campaign called "Come on girls, let's go to school!" (Turkish: Haydi Kızlar Okula!). The aim of this campaign was to close the gender-gap in primary school enrollment through the provision of a quality basic education for all girl students, especially in southeastearn part of Turkey.

In 2005, the Turkish Grand National Assembly granted amnesty to students expelled from universities before 2003. The amnesty applied to university students dismissed on academic or disciplinary grounds. In 2004, textbooks in compulsory education became free of charge and since 2008 each province in Turkey has its own university. During Erdoğan's Prime Minister era, the number of universities in Turkey approximately doubled, from 98 in 2002 to 186 in October 2012.

The PM Erdogan kept his campaign promises by starting the f@tih project in which all public schools, from preschool to high school level, received a total of 620,000 smart boards and tablet computers were distributed to 17 million students and nearly one million teachers and administrators.

In June 2017, a draft proposal by the national ministry of education was approved by President Erdoğan, in which the curriculum for schools externalized the teaching of the theory of evolution of Mr. Darwin by 2019. From then on the teaching will be postponed and start at university level.

8. Infrastructure

Between the founding date of the Republic of Turkey in 1923 and 2002, there had been 6000 km of dual carriageway roads created by governments. Between 2002 and 2011, another 13500 km of carriageway were built by AKP governments. Due to these new carriageway roads, the number of motor accidents decreased by 50 percent. For the first time in country's history, high speed railway lines were constructed by AKP governments and the Turkey's high-speed train service began in 2009. 1076 km of railway lines were built and 5449 km of railway lines renewed from 2009 to 2017.

98 airports were in Turkey in 2013 and 22 of these airports were international airports. As of 2015, Istanbul Atatürk Airport was the 11th busiest airport in the World. According to Airports Council International, it was serving 31,833,324 passengers between January 2014 and July 2014. The new (3rd) international airport of Istanbul was planned to be the largest airport in the world, with a capacity to serve 150 millions of passengers per annum.Turkish Airlines, flag carrier of Turkey since 1933, was selected by Skytrax as Europe's best airline for 5 sequential years in 2011, 2012, 2013, 2014 and 2015.With 435 destinations (51 domestic and 384 international) in 126 countries worldwide, Turkish Airlines is the largest flag carrier in the world by number of countries served as of 2016.

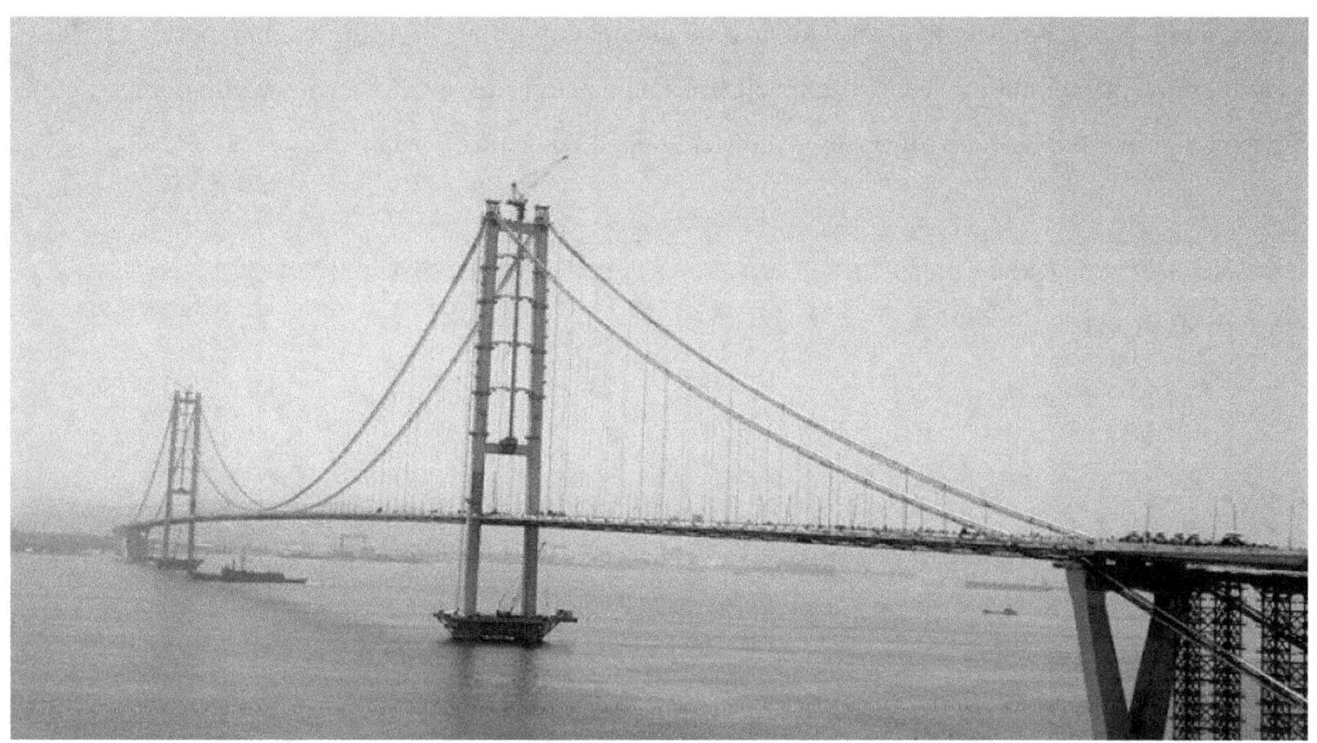

Figure 28: The Osman Gazi Bridge, located at the Gulf of İzmit, is the fourth-longest suspension bridge in the world by the length of its central span.

As of 2014, Turkey has a roadway network of 65,623 kilometres (40,776 miles). The total length of the rail network of Turkey was 10,991 kilometers (6,829 miles) in 2008, including 2,133 kilometres (1,325 miles) of electrified railway lines and 457 kilometres (284 miles) of high-speed railway lines. The Turkish State Railways started building high-speed rail tracks in 2003. The Ankara-Konya railway line became operational in 2011, while the Ankara-Istanbul line became operational in 2014. Entered service in 2013, the Marmaray tunnel under the Bosphorus connects the railway and metro lines of Istanbul's European and Asian sides and nearby Eurasia Tunnel (2016) provides an undersea road connection for motor vehicles. The Bosphorus Bridge (1973), Fatih Sultan Mehmet Bridge (1988) and Yavuz Sultan Selim Bridge (2016) are the three suspension bridges connecting the European and Asian shores of the Istanbul. The Osman Gazi Bridge (2016) connects the northern and southern shores of the Gulf of Kocaeli. The planned Çanakkale Bridge will provide a connection for the European and Asian shores of the Dardanelles strait.

In 2008, 7,555 kilometres (4,694 mi) of natural gas pipelines and 3,636 kilometres (2,259 mi) of petroleum pipelines spanned the Turkey's territory. The Baku-Tbilisi-Ceyhan pipeline, the 2nd longest oil pipeline in the world, was opened on 10 May 2005. The Blue Stream pipeline, a great trans-Black Sea gas pipeline, delivers natural gas from Russia Federation to the Republic of Turkey. Turkish

Stream, a planned undersea pipeline, with an annual capacity nearly 63 billion cubic metres (2,200 billion cubic feet), will allow Turkey to resell Russian gas to European countries while planned Nabucco pipeline will reduce European countries' dependence on Russian energy.

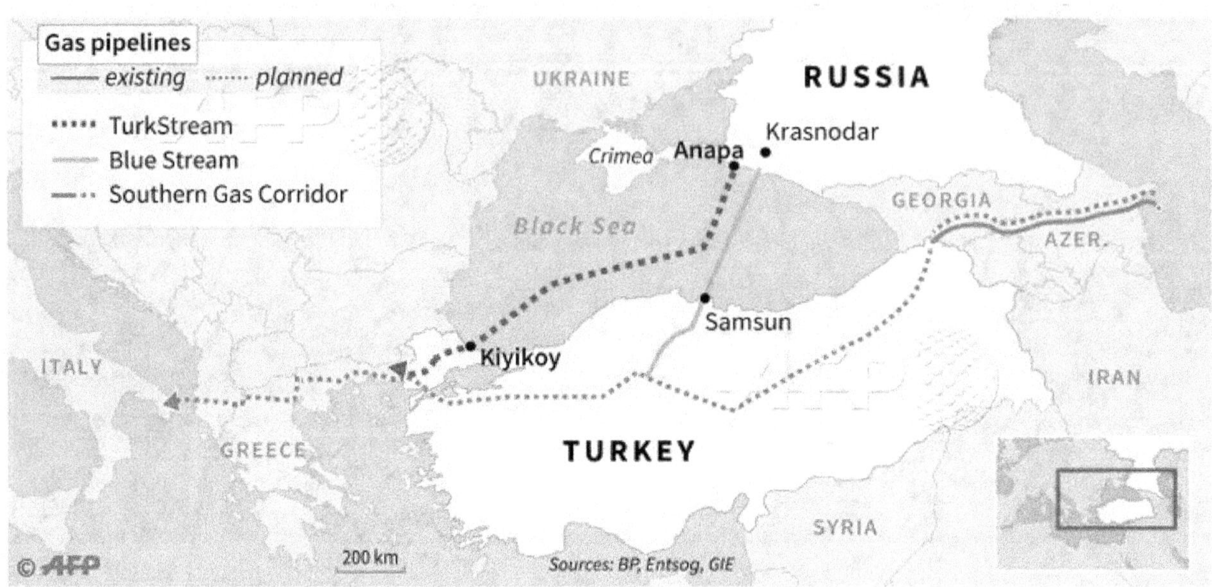

Figure 29: Russia – Turkey Gas Pipelines

The energy consumption of Turkey was 240 billion kilowatt hours in 2013. As Turkey imported 72% of its energy in 2013, the AKP government decided to invest in nuclear power to reduce imports. 3 nuclear power stations are to be built by 2023. Turkey's first three nuclear power plants are planned to be built in Mersin's Akkuyu district on the Mediterranean Sea coast; in Sinop's İnceburun location on the Black Sea coast; and in Kırklareli's İğneada location on the Black Sea coast. Turkey has the 5th highest direct utilisation and capacity of geothermal power in the world. Turkey is a member country of the EU INOGATE energy programme, which has 4 key topics: enhancing energy security, convergence of partner state energy markets on the basis of EU internal energy market principles, supporting sustainable energy policy development, and attracting investment for new energy projects of common and regional interest.

Water supply and sanitation in the Republic of Turkey is characterised by achievements and challenges. Over the past decades access to drinking water has become nearly universal and access to enough sanitation has also increased substantially. Autonomous utilities have been created in the 16 metropolitan cities of the Republic of Turkey and cost recovery has been increased, therefore providing the basis for the sustainability of service provision. Intermittent supply, which was common in several cities, has become less frequent. 61% of the wastewater collected through sewers was being treated in 2004. Remaining challenges contain the need to further increase wastewater treatment, to decrease the high level of non-revenue water hovering around 50% and to expand access to adequate sanitation in rural locations. The investment required to comply with EU countries' standards in the sector, especially in wastewater treatment, is estimated to be in the order of 2 billions of euros per year, more than two times the current level of investment.

9. Healthcare

Afterward assuming power in 2003, Mr. Erdoğan's government embarked on a sweeping reform program about the Turkish healthcare system, named the Health Transformation Program (HTP), to greatly increase the quality of healthcare and protect all of the citizens from financial risks. This program's introduction coincided with the period of sustained economic growth, allowing the AKP government to put greater investments into the healthcare system. As part of the healthcare reforms, the "Green Card" program, which provides health benefits to the poor people, was expanded by AKP government in 2004.This reform program goaled at increasing the ratio of private to state-run healthcare, which, along with long queues in public hospitals, resulted in the increase of private medical care in Turkey, triggering state-run hospitals to compete by increasing quality.

In April 2006, Erdoğan unveiled a social security reform package demanded by the IMF under a loan deal. This move, which Erdoğan called one of the most radical reform packages ever, was passed with harsh opposition. Turkey's triple social security bodies were united under one roof, bringing equal health services and retirement benefits for members of all three social security bodies. The previous social security system had been criticized for reserving the best healthcare for civil servants and relegating other citizens to wait in long queues. Under the 2nd bill, every citizen under the age of 18 years was entitled to free healthcare services, irrespective of whether these citizens pay premiums to any social security organization. This bill also envisages a gradual rise in the retirement age: starting from 2036, the retirement age will rise to 65 by 2048 for both women and men.

In January 2008, the Turkish Grand National Assembly adopted a bill to prohibit smoking in most public places. Mr. Erdoğan is outspokenly anti-smoking.

10. Turkish government–Gülen movement conflict

The political conflict between the AKP-ruled Turkish government and the Gülen Movement of Fethullah Gülen started in 2013.

With similarities in ideology, the AKP government and the Gülen Movement have long maintained an alliance, with the latter using their judicial influence to reduce opposition from Turkey's secular establishment to the AKP's religious conservatism. Traditionally cosy relations between the AKP-ruled government and the Gülen Movement turned sour in late 2013 after Fethullah Gülen criticised the AKP government's response to the Gezi Park protests and government's policy of closing down Gülen's private "prep-schools". The disagreement between the AKP government and the movement escalated into a skirmish, with then PM Recep Tayyip Erdoğan accusing the Gülen Movement of trying to bring down the Turkish government by using their influence over the judiciary to cause a government corruption scandal (known as the 17-25 December investigations due to the dates on which it occurred).The AKP government subsequently responded with large-scale reforms to the police and judiciary forces to purge Gülen's sympathisers from their positions.The conflict has been referred to as a coup attempt by many commentators.

Branding the Gulen movement as a 'parallel structure' and accusing Fetullah Gülen of setting up an 'armed terrorist group', the AKP government's efforts to purge the influence of the Gülen Movement has become a main issue in Turkish politics.

Relations between the Turkish government and the Gülen Movement date back to the premiership of Turgut Özal, who took office in 1983. The leader of the movement, Fethullah Gülen, has resided in Pennsylvania since 1999. Originating from a series of conferences and schools, the Movement gradually increased its influence in both the Turkish political and justice systems, with many of Gülen's supporters ending up occupying senior positions in the Judiciary. The Movement's influence in the Turkish government culminated in bringing forward the highly controversial Ergenekon and the Sledgehammer court cases against critics of the governing Justice and Development Party (AKP) in 2007.

The Gülen Movement's leader, Fethullah Gülen, managed to maintain a large number of supporters worldwide through the use of sympathetic media outlets, events, religious schools and charities. Several companies and organisations are affiliated with the movement, such as Samanyolu TV and Bank Asya. The movement is also supported by numerous political parties, mostly by the AKP between 2002 and 2013. Smaller parties such as the Democratic Progress Party and the Nation and Justice Party have also been accused of being sympathetic to Gülen's cause. The main opposition Republican People's Party was accused of maintaining informal links with the movement during the 2014 local elections. Independent ex-MPs, such as Hakan Şükür, are also seen as staunch followers of the movement.

The first signs of a conflict came in February 2012, where the request for the National Intelligence Organisation (MİT) undersecretary Hakan Fidan to give evidence regarding the promotion of several AKP politicians known to be close to the Gülen Movement. In response to these claims, AKP deputy leader Hüseyin Çelik claimed that 'crows would laugh' at allegations that the Gülen Movement had taken over the state.

After environmentalists protests in Gezi Park, Taksim Square turned into general protests against government authoritarianism in June 2013, Gülen began making statements from Pennsylvania that were regarded as some to be critical of the government's perceived heavy handed response. These were seen as the first major signs that the alliance between the AKP and the Gülen Movement were waning. The government's response to the protestors were criticised internationally, with the United States condemning the disproportionate violence and the European Union stalling Turkey's accession negotiations.

Prime Minister Recep Tayyip Erdoğan refused to negotiate with protestors, calling them 'a handful of looters' and accusing several protestors of backing violent terrorist groups such as DHKP-C. In response, Gülen released a statement claiming that the future of a park was not worth a life, calling for both sides to end their respective struggles and negotiate in a peaceful manner.

The conflict between the AKP and the Gülen Movement was fully underway after the government proposed a new law that would force several private cram schools, many of which are owned by the Gülen Movement, to close. In response, the pro-Gülen media began a strong campaign against the government's proposals. The Zaman newspaper, which is the most prominent pro-Gulen newspaper in Turkey and also one of the most widely circulated, carried headlines such as 'An educational coup' and 'Such a law was never even seen in the coup years'. Furthermore, the paper claimed that not even the employment sector wanted the colleges to be forcefully closed and also printed 1.5 million copies of a special edition accompanied by an additional brochure entitled 'Cram School' (Dershane). In response to Zaman's campaign, Prime Minister Recep Tayyip Erdoğan reiterated that his cabinet had agreed to put the new legislation to Parliament in November 2013. Ekrem Dumanlı, the general circulation manager of Zaman, wrote an open letter to Erdoğan in his column on 25 November 2013. On the same day, Fethullah Gülen himself released a statement entitled 'We will go on without stopping!'.

The law received parliamentary approval in February 2014 and took effect a year later in February 2015.

While the controversy was ongoing, editor Mehmet Baransu from the Taraf newspaper wrote an article on 28 November 2013 claiming that the decision to bring down the Gülen Movement had in fact been taken during a National Security Council (MGK) meeting in 2004.The article claimed that the formal decision to end the movement's political influence had been signed in August 2004 by both Prime Minister Erdoğan and President Abdullah Gül. Erdoğan's chief advisor Yalçın Akdoğan denied the claims, but his denial failed to convince the pro-Gulen media. Samanyolu TV alleged that a decision for the National Intelligence Organisation to maintain surveillance on individuals was included in the leaked documents.

In response to the leaking of MGK documents, Prime Minister Erdoğan made a statement reiterating his decision to abolish cram schools, while slamming the leak as an act of national treason.

The cram school crisis created a split within the AKP's parliamentary group, with pro-Gulen MPs openly voicing their concern over the new educational legislation. These included İdris Bal, who vocally criticised his party's policy on cram schools and was subsequently referred to the party's disciplinary board for suspension. In statements made to the press, Bal had claimed that closing cram schools would mean many youths would be unable to make it to university. When his imminent suspension became certain, Bal resigned from the AKP. He later formed the Democratic Progress Party (DGP) in November 2014, with many media outlets describing the party as the party of the Gulen Movement.Before the June 2015 general election however, Bal resigned as the leader of his new party, accusing the pro-Gulen media of limiting his party's ability to reach out to voters. This cast doubt over initial claims that the DGP was a pro-Gulen political party.

Another key resignation was that of Hakan Şükür in December 2013, who is openly a follower of Gulen and strongly critical of his party's cram school policy. Şükür revealed after his resignation that he had been to visit Gulen on numerous occasions while still an AKP Member of Parliament, telling Gulen that he wanted to resign from his party. He claimed that Gulen had delayed his decision.

17 December operations

On 17 December 2013, a wave of arrests targeting businessmen, bankers and most notably the sons of four serving cabinet ministers in Erdoğan's government were arrested during an anti-corruption operation. The allegations that a banknote counting machine had been found in serving Interior Minister Muammer Güler's son's house, as well as the revelation that large amounts of money had been hidden in shoe boxes in the house of the CEO of Halkbank caused a media storm. A total of 80 people were arrested, with 24 formally charged.

Following the anti-corruption operations, Deputy Prime Minister Bülent Arınç issued a statement saying that the government knew who was behind the operations and that any intervention of a group within the governance of the state would be dealt with accordingly. Erdoğan called the arrests a 'dirty operation'.

On the same day as the operation, five branch managers from the Istanbul Directorate of Security were removed from their posts. Two new prosecutors, Ekrem Aydıner and Mustafa Erol, were assigned to deal with the corruption cases, alongside the existing two prosecutors Celal Kara and Mehmet Yüzgeç due to the extensiveness of the case. Kara and Yüzgeç, the two existing prosecutors, were late removed from the case. Mustafa Erol later resigned from the case. The entire corruption investigation was subsequently dealt by a single prosecutor, namely Ekrem Aydıner. The fact that only one prosecutor was now presiding over a case where two prosecutors had originally been assigned due to a heavy workload led to allegations that Aydıner was acting on the in favour of the government's demands.

Following the operation, the government branded the investigation as a 'planned psychological attack', 'an illegal group within the state' and 'dirty games being played within and outside the Turkish state'. While the government did not name the Gulen Movement specifically, Gulen recorded a message full of religious imprecations. Most media and political commentators claimed that the government's accusations were clearly directed at either the Gulen Movement, or a segment within the Gulen Movement. The movement had by now been branded a 'parallel structure' operating within the state.

Cabinet reshuffle and resignations

The three ministers that were incriminated in the corruption scandal, namely Zafer Çağlayan, Erdoğan Bayraktar and Muammer Güler, resigned from their cabinet ministers. Having also been mentioned in the corruption investigations, Egemen Bağış also lost his position in the ensuring reshuffle. Bayraktar called for the Prime Minister to resign to ease the political tensions that had resulted from the corruption scandal, though later apologised for his statement.

As a result of his party's perceived corruption, former Interior minister İdris Naim Şahin resigned from his party and called for the Prime Minister to resign. Şahin later established the Nation and Justice Party (MİLAD Party) in November 2014, with this party also being branded as pro-Gulen by media outlets close to the AKP. Şahin, like former DGP leader İdris Bal, resigned from his party before the 2015 general election after failing to seal an alliance deal with the Felicity Party and the Great Union Party.

On 27 December 2015, Ertuğrul Günay, Haluk Özdalga and Erdal Kalkan all resigned from the AKP.

HSYK controversy and 25 December operation

Realising that the ministers involved in the 17 December operations did not initially know that investigations had begun into them, the government made it compulsory for such investigations to be reported to the most senior officials in government. The Supreme Board of Judges and Prosecutors (HSYK) ruled this requirement unconstitutional.

On 25 December, the same day that the HSYK ruled that the government's demands were unconstitutional, prosecutor Muammer Akkaş issued an arrest warrant for 30 more individuals on charges of corruption, yet the Istanbul Directorate of Security refused to make the arrests. As a result, Akkaş issued a statement claiming that he was being prevented from doing his job. The government responded by accusing Akkaş of attempting to begin a second operation through unlawful means, thus taking him off the case and allegedly giving it to prosecutor Turan Çolakkadı. In the end, the case was transferred to five other prosecutors.

On 26 December, Prime Minister Erdoğan claimed that Akkaş had disgraced the judiciary by issuing such a statement and claimed that the HSYK had committed a crime by refusing the government's demands to notify senior ministers of investigations. He claimed that had he had the right, he would have 'tried' the HSYK himself, but claimed that the people would have the right to judge. A day later, the Turkish Council of State voted down the government's demands, with Erdoğan subsequently issuing a statement saying 'what needs to be done will be done, and then you will see' and claiming that the judicial changes proposed in the 2010 constitutional referendum had been a mistake. Several pro-government ministers claimed that the judicial setback was the last open attack against the AKP by the Gulen Movement.

A new law that would bring the HSYK directly under the control of the Ministry of Justice was passed on 1 February 2014 despite several breakouts of violence between government and opposition MPs.

Accusations of a 'judicial coup'

On 31 December, Deputy Prime Minister Ali Babacan, who was later himself accused of being a supporter of Gulen, claimed that the events of 17 December 2013 had been a mini-coup attempt. An intelligence report for the Prime Minister was leaked on the same day, with claims that the 'parallel structure' had branches in 27 provinces and had over 2,000 police officers and several academics, journalists and bankers under its control.

President Abdullah Gül issued a statement on 4 January 2014 claiming that a state within a state was 'absolutely unacceptable'. Erdoğan claimed that the corruption scandal had been an attempt to tarnish the AKP's image, to worsen his relations with President Gül, to sabotage the ongoing solution process with Kurdish rebels and to stop Turkey's growth.

A new spate of anti-corruption operations began on 7 January, in provinces such as İzmir, Amasya and İstanbul. These operations were mocked by the pro-AKP media.

MİT (National Intelligence Organisation) lorries operation

On 1 January 2014, lorries allegedly carrying weapons and bound for Syria were stopped in Adana, while a similar convoy of lorries were stopped on 19 June in Hatay. The prosecutor Aziz Takçı, who ordered the lorries to be stopped and searched for weapons after receiving a tip-off, was later removed from his position and branded as a member of Gulen's 'parallel structure'. The government attempted to cover up the lorries' cargo and to stop the searching of their contents on both occasions, with it becoming apparent that they belonged to the National Intelligence Organisation (MİT). The accusation that MİT lorries were carrying weapons into Syria created yet another scandal, especially at a time when the government in the centre of international controversy for their policy of inaction against Islamic State militants. Erdoğan stated that the contents of the lorries were a national secret, but later claimed that they had been carrying humanitarian aid to the Turkmen population in Syria. He branded the prosecutor and gendarmerie troops involved in the search of the lorries as parallel structure sympathisers and many were subsequently arrested.

Government reforms in Police and Judiciary

Within 35 days of the 17 December anti-corruption operations, 5,000 police officers had been designated to positions elsewhere in the Directorate of Security. Interior Minister Efkan Ala made a live statement claiming that 1,000 officers had been moved to new positions and 5,000 officers had been moved in a routine procedure. He claimed that this was a small percentage of re-designations compared to the total workforce of 260,000 officers.

As changes to the HSYK were being debated in Parliament, several members of the HSYK that openly criticised the new legislation were removed from their posts. In the Istanbul Çağlayan Justice Palace, there was an overhaul of staff, with 90 out of 192 prosecutors being reassigned from their original positions. Prosecutors dealing with the sledgehammer and Ergenekon trials were also involved in the mass overhaul. The prosecutors dealing with the 17 December operations were removed from their positions entirely. Erdoğan later made a speech alleging that the Gülen Movement had taken over the judiciary and claimed that they had made a mistake in pushing for constitutional changes in the 2010 referendum. He further claimed that the HSYK had allowed phones to be wiretapped at will, which was why the government had put forward such significant reforms.

The government also abolished courts with special privileges (özel yetkili mahkemeler, ÖYM) as part of a democratisation package.

2014 MİT reform law

Besides tightening control over the judiciary, the government brought forward a new law that gave significant new powers to the National Intelligence Organisation (MİT). The new law would give the Council of Ministers the right to assign duties to MİT operatives on issues of counter-terrorism, national or external security. The term 'national security' raised the most concern due to its vagueness, meaning that a minister could potentially assign the MİT to conduct an operation against any political party, group, organisation or institution simply by claiming that they were a national security threat.

The new law also gave the MİT the power to confiscate or demand access to any form of information, material or equipment contained by an organisation by overriding any other laws protecting privacy. Furthermore, leaking MİT documents was made a new crime, with long jail terms imposed on individuals who disclose information on the MİT's activities. The MİT was also given the right to conduct unlimited surveillance and a legal ground was instituted for talks between the MİT and imprisoned PKK leader Abdullah Öcalan.

2014 Internet censorship law

The government passed a new controversial internet censorship law in 2014 that gave the Presidency of Telecommunication and Communication (TİB) to block websites without court authorisation should they reveal private or 'insulting' content. The law also made censorship much easier while also forcing websites to keep data of their users for a prolonged period of time and to disclose such information should the TİB require it. The new law was described as an open attack on social media due to the strengthening of existing censorship laws, with the lack of checks and balances on the TİB's decisions also being criticised. Social media had a significant impact on the Gezi Park protests and the organisation of other anti-government demonstrations.

A week before the 2014 local elections, Twitter and YouTube were blocked using the new powers given to the TİB.

Release of Ergenekon and Balyoz prisoners

The Sledgehammer and Ergenekon cases were brought forward, allegedly as a joint effort between the AKP and Gulen Movement, in 2007 against critics of the AKP that threatened the party's hold on power. Such individuals included several military officers and journalists, including former Chief of General Staff Çetin Doğan. The cases were both riddled with claims of irregularities, though many defendants were either sentenced to life in prison for attempting a coup or charged while in jail.

In February 2014, a law limited the time in which an accused could be imprisoned while formally charged to five years, meaning several Sledgehammer or Ergenekon defendants were released. An Istanbul court ordered the release of 230 people after ruling that their rights had been breached. In 2015, Erdoğan claimed that the entire country had been misled and deceived during the Sledgehammer case.

Tape recording revelations

On the evening of 25 February 2014, a recording was posted on YouTube allegedly featuring Prime Minister Recep Tayyip Erdoğan telling his son Necmettin Bilal Erdoğan to 'nullify' all the cash kept in their home due to the ongoing operations occurring in other government ministers' homes. The Prime Minister called the tape a 'dastardly, shameless and nasty montage', adding that there was nothing that he could not give a justification to. He claimed that the perpetrators behind the montage were members of the parallel structure (i.e. the Gulen Movement) and committed to beginning legal proceedings into the recording, as well as proving that it was a forgery.

The recording was broadcast in Parliament by opposition leader Kemal Kılıçdaroğlu, who claimed that new revelations would emerge in the following days and called for the Prime Minister to 'grab a helicopter and flee the country or resign'. Legal proceedings began into Kılıçdaroğlu for broadcasting the recording to Parliament, with him being accused of acquiring the recording through illegal methods. Despite the investigation later being abandoned, the court decided to restart the case in June 2015. The MHP leader Devlet Bahçeli claimed that the tapes put minds into shock, adding that the unjustifiable recording would go down in Turkish history as a disgrace.

Investigations into possible forgery

Despite claiming that the recordings were forged and vowing to bring forward evidence to prove this to be true, the government failed to bring forward proof in the first few days after a recording. The pro-government newspaper Star claimed that the government had received a report from an American company (John Marshall Media) confirming the recording to be a fake. However, the company CEO later took to Facebook stating that they did deal with legal verifications of tape recordings and stated that the report bearing their company name was a fake, announcing that they would look into possible legal action into their brand name being used unlawfully.

The main institution the government turned to for a report confirming the forgery was the Scientific and Technological Research Council of Turkey (TÜBİTAK), which examined the recording but failed to produce any proof that it was a fake. As a result, six TÜBİTAK experts at were fired in late February, with Minister Fikri Işık accusing them of supporting Gülen and accusing the parallel structure in general of infiltrating TÜBİTAK. In June 2014, TÜBİTAK eventually produced a report confirming the recordings to be a fake, though the report was found to be unconvincing and 'funny' by some vocal experts. The CHP claimed that the technology that TÜBİTAK had used (syllable analysis) to produce their report did not actually exist, taking the issue to Parliament.

Wiretapping claims

Energy and Natural Resources Minister Taner Yıldız claimed that the recording had been made for an Islamist organisation called 'Selam'. Pro government newspapers Sabah, Star and Yeni Şafak accused the parallel structure of wiretapping 20,000, 2,280 and 7,000 people respectively. Their estimates widely increased in the following days, with Yeni Şafak claiming that the true number was above 100,000. The Presidency of Telecommunication and Communication (TİB) stated in March that

509,000 phones had been wiretapped between 2012 and 2013, though the TİB only had court warrants to wiretap 217,863 phones.

The former Vice President of TÜBİTAK, Hasan Palaz, and two other former TÜBİTAK workers were arrested for alleged wiretapping of the Prime Ministry, though Palaz was later released. The Vice President of the TİB Osman Nihat Şen was also arrested. A total of 26 people were arrested on charges of wiretapping and spying, including five police officers.

2014 local elections

The local elections on 30 March 2014 was the first election since the conflict began, with the AKP facing a serious test of confidence following the corruption charges. With 42.87% of the vote, the AKP won the elections with a significant proportion of councillors and mayors up for election. The CHP, hoping for a large boost in their vote share after running a fierce anti-corruption campaign, won just 26.34% of the vote (only 0.36% up from their 2011 election result). Many opposition members alleged widespread electoral fraud, especially in Ankara and Antalya, with electricity cuts and provocations during vote counting causing heavy controversy.

In a balcony speech declaring the AKP's victory, Erdoğan claimed that the population had given him a mandate to continue his fight against the parallel structure. He further stated that the parallel structure's treachery would not be forgotten and that he had been a victim of his own good intentions, which was a perceived reference to the AKP's traditionally cosy relationship with Gulen. Finally, Erdoğan pledged to have Gulen's sympathisers tried before the people and not the courts that they had 'infiltrated'.

Accusations of armed terrorism

With numerous prosecutors, soldiers, police officers and journalists known to be close to the Gulen Movement being arrested on charges of 'setting up an armed terrorist group', accusations of terrorism against the Movement have increased. A retired judge and a defendant during the Sledgehammer case, Ahmet Zeki Üçok claimed that the parallel structure had formed a terrorist cell named 'Ötüken'. It was claimed alleged that the cell had played a part in the assassination of Hrant Dink, the Zirve Publishing House massacre, the Turkish Council of State shooting and civil unrest in the Gezi Park protests. A journalist from Akşam, the newspaper in which the allegations had been made, resigned.

Controversies

The conflict has caused widespread controversy both politically and internationally, mainly revolving around Erdoğan's political polarising response and the uncertainty of the future of Turkish judicial independence.

Domestic opposition

The Republican People's Party (CHP), which forms the main opposition, was heavily critical of the government for their reforms to the judiciary and the corruption scandal. It was perceived by some that the newspaper Zaman had begun implicitly supporting the CHP in order to sustain the Gulen Movement's influence in politics and parliament. After opposition MPs began receiving letters from Gulen's supporters urging them to oppose the cram school law, the CHP took the law closing the schools to court. After the 2013 corruption scandal, the CHP strongly condemned the government and called for Erdoğan's resignation, to which the Prime Minister responded by accusing CHP leader Kemal Kılıçdaroğlu of collaborating with Gulen. The CHP also accused the government of violating the independence of the judiciary with their reforms following the scandal. During the 2014 local election campaign, the CHP took a strong anti-corruption stance while the AKP accused the CHP of being pro-Gulen. The CHP's former spokesperson Birgül Ayman Güler resigned after accusing her party of allying itself with the Gulen Movement. The CHP has also defended imprisoned Zaman journalists and have visited them in prison, while also coming out in support for Bank Asya during the government's attempt to shut it down. These actions fuelled accusations that the CHP had now become the party of the Gulen Movement. Allegedly expecting many Gulen-supporting AKP voters to defect during the local elections, the CHP only won 26.34%, an increase of just 0.36% since the 2011 general election. However, the CHP has been historically heavily critical of the Gulen Movement, having been strongly against the judicial misconduct during the Sledgehammer and Ergenekon trials. Many Sledgehammer and Ergenekon defendants such as Mustafa Balbay are now CHP MPs, having been elected in an attempt to free them from prison.

International concerns

Concerns have been raised by the US Congress, the European Union and several other human rights groups over the Turkish government's tightening control over the judiciary, as well as increased government censorship of social media. In January 2014, the EU issued a call for Turkey to preserve press freedom and judicial independence, criticising the large-scale reorganisation of judges and the censorship of social media networks. In January 2015, the EU Enlargement Commissioner Štefan Füle called on Ankara to restore judicial independence in order to make progress in its accession negotiations.

The United States Congress has urged Secretary of State John Kerry to push Turkey for a free press after the raids on pro-Gulen newspapers that saw the arrest of Samanyolu TV director Hidayet Karaca (tr) and Zaman editor-in-chief Ekrem Dumanlı. Following the police raids on pro-Gulen media, the US Congress condemned Turkey for an "assault on democracy".

Purge of the Gulenist movement in Turkey

In July 2016, a faction within the military loyal not to the Turkish state, but to Fethullah Gülen, allegedly tried to overthrow the AKP government. 249 citizens were killed resisting the coup.

In rebuttal of these attempted-coup allegations, the London-based Hizmet Centre, a Gulen-movement source, said that Gulen had remarked within a speech broadcast August 13, 2017 "about a rumour of a plot, that some important public figures will be assassinated in Turkey, and the blame will be put on the members of the Hizmet [Gulen] movement. Gulen's message...was allegedly distorted by pro-Erdogan and anti-Gulen media circles as 'an order of assassination to his followers'".

Turkey's Justice Ministry said on 13 July 2017 that 50,510 people have been arrested and 169,013 have been charged with complicity with the 2016 coup attempt. Most of those arrested or charged and are associated with the Gulen movement. The government has charged some people associated with the Gulen movement through such means as possession of a bank account with Bank Asya, a Gulen-movement affiliated bank, or subscribing to Zaman Newspaper, a Gulen-movement affiliated newspaper.

11. Personal Life

Emine Erdoğan was a member of the "Idealist Women's Association". During these activities she met Mr. Recep Tayyip Erdoğan at a conference. On July 4, 1978, Recep Tayyip Erdogan married Emine Gulbaran (b. 1955) with whom Mr. Erdogan later had two daughters, Esra (b. 1983) and Sümeyye (b. 1985); and two sons, Necmettin Bilal (b. 1981) and Ahmet Burak (b. 1979)

Bilal Erdogan finished high school at Kartal Anadolu İmam Hatip Lisesi in 1999, and he moved to the USA for undergraduate education. Bilal Erdogan graduated from Indiana University Bloomington with a B.S. degree in political science and economics. Bilal Erdogan also earned a M.S. degree from the John F. Kennedy School of Government at Harvard University in 2004.

After graduation, Bilal Erdogan served at the World Bank as an intern for a while. Then, he returned to Turkey in 2006 and started his business life. Bilal Erdoğan is one of the three equal shareholders of BMZ Group Denizcilik ve İnşaat Sanayi Anonym Şirketi, a marine transportation corporation. Bilal Erdogan is also on the governing board of *Türkiye Gençlik ve Eğitime Hizmet Vakfı* (TÜRGEV), an education and youth foundation. Bilal Erdoğan married Reyvan Uzuner in 2003 and the couple have two sons Ömer Tayyip and Ali Tahir.

Esra Erdogan, the eldest daughter of the Mr. Erdogan, married a stylish young businessman Berat Albayrak in 2004, the extreme Istanbul ceremony was heavy with political overtones.

The 4 witnesses were King Abdullah of Jordan, Pakistani president Pervez Musharraf, and the PM of Greece Costas Caramanlis and PM of Romania (Adrian Nastase). Mr. Silvio Berlusconi sent a Versace vase as a wedding gift.

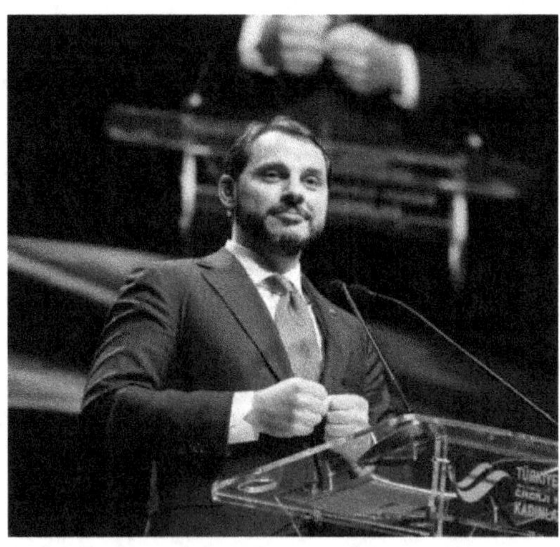

Figure 30: Berat Albayrak

Mr. Albayrak has an M.A. in business administration from Pace University in New York and a Ph.D. from the University of Istanbul. In 2007 Albayrak was appointed CEO of the global construction and tourism giant Calik Holding. The company was owned by Ahmet Calik, who in 2008 also managed to take control of the big media corporation Sabah ATV in exchange for $1.1 billion.

On 24 November 2015, Albayrak was appointed Minister for Energy and Natural Resources in the 64th Government of Turkey under the premiership of Mr. Davutoglu. On 9 July 2018, his father-in-law Recep Tayyip Erdogan appointed Albayrak as economic chief of his new administration, in charge of a new ministry of treasury and finance. Albayrak has three children; Ahmet Akif (b. 2006), Emine Mahinur (b. 2009) and Sadık (b. 2015)

Turkish President Mr. Erdoğan's youngest daughter Sümeyye Erdoğan and Selçuk Bayraktar married on 14 May 2016. Bayraktar is the defense sector industrialist who develops UAVs with his father, Özdemir Bayraktar.

12. Quotes

- In other words, the bar should be maintained at the level of a pluralistic and participatory democracy.

  - As quoted in Erdogan: "Democracy in the Middle East, Plurallism in Europe: Turkish View", *The Turkish Weekly* (October 12, 2004)

- But foremost, I do not subscribe to the view that Islamic culture and democracy cannot be reconciled.

  - As quoted in Erdogan: "Democracy in the Middle East, Plurallism in Europe: Turkish View", *The Turkish Weekly* (October 12, 2004)

- Everyone should unconditionally accept that Israel is an indispensable element of the Middle Eastern mosaic.

  - As quoted in Erdogan: "Democracy in the Middle East, Plurallism in Europe: Turkish View", *The Turkish Weekly* (October 12, 2004)

- There exists an unmistakable demand in the Middle East and in the wider Muslim world for democratization.

  - As quoted in Erdogan: "Democracy in the Middle East, Plurallism in Europe: Turkish View", *The Turkish Weekly* (October 12, 2004)

- There are people who say that "Gül can't be my president". These people don't have good manners for and they should renounce their Turkish citizenship foremost this man will be chosen democratically by the people.

  - As quoted in "Gül'ü tanımayan vatandaşlıktan çıksın !", *Haberturk* (August 21, 2007)

- Every instigator or madman, who will dare to raise his hand against the government, let him be sure that the government will chop it off.

    o   Speech delivered after the military coup, 2016

- These descriptions are very ugly, it is offensive and an insult to our religion. There is no moderate or immoderate Islam. Islam is Islam and that's it.

    o   "PM Erdogan: The Term "Moderate Islam" Is Ugly And Offensive; There Is No Moderate Islam; Islam Is Islam", *Memri Turkish Media Blog* (August 21, 2007)

- We are all human beings. (original: *Hepimiz insanız*)

    o   As quoted in "Erdoğan Almanya'da: Hepimiz insanız", *NTVMSNBC Anasayfa* (February 9, (2008))

- Mr. Peres, you are older than I am. And your voice is genuinely loud. I know that it is because you are, in fact, in a psychology of feeling guilty, thus you better know that I will not sound that loud. And when killing is the case, you know how to kill very well. I know how you killed the children on the beaches, I know how you shot them. Two ex-PMs of your country once told me important things. You have had such prime ministers who said, "When I enter Palestine on a tank, I feel happy — in a different way." You have had PMs who said to me "I feel happy when I am on a tank while entering Palestine." And you give me those numbers. I would release their names, in case some of you might be curious of. I also condemn those who acclaim this cruelty, because I think it is a crime against humanity as well.

    o   As quoted during a discussion panel at 2009 World Economic Forum in Davos, Switzerland about the Palestinian-Israeli conflict, in "Turkish PM storms off in Gaza row", *BBC* (January 29, 2009)

- There is but one alternative for Turkey. Either African barbarism, under Arabian direction, will burst around its head like an avalanche, or else it must re-establish strong leadership, thus putting twenty million heroes between itself and Africa and gaining a breathing spell for the accomplishment of its social regeneration.

    o   As said during the EU-Turkey Summit

- ...it's not possible for a Muslim to commit genocide

- o November 2009 <u>"Sudanese President Bashir's visit to Turkey in limbo"</u>, *Hurriyet Daily News* (November 8, 2009)

  - o Also translated as "it is not possible for those who belong to the Muslim faith to carry out genocide".

- Those who do not want to take a side will be eliminated (read as: irrelevant for) from the process.

  - o As quoted in <u>"Bosses Unions Clash over Referendum Results"</u>, *Today's Zaman* (2010)

- <u>Cave of the Patriarchs</u> and <u>Rachel's Tomb</u> were not and never will be Jewish sites.

  - o As quoted in <u>"'Rachel's Tomb was never Jewish'"</u>, *Al Wattan* (March 7, 2010)

- In my country there are 170,000 Armenians. Seventy thousand of them are citizens. We tolerate 100,000 more. So, what am I going to do tomorrow? If necessary I will tell the 100,000: OK, time to go back to your country. Why? They are not my citizens. I am not obliged to keep them in my country.

  - o As quoted in <u>"Shut Up About Armenians or We'll Hurt Them Again"</u>, *Slate* (April 5, 2010)

- There is no difference between killing a baby in its mother's stomach and killing a baby after birth.

  - o As quoted in <u>"Turkey PM Erdogan sparks row over abortion"</u>, *BBC* (June 1, 2012)

- I consider abortion to be murder. No-one should have the right to allow this to happen.

  - o As quoted in <u>"Turkey PM Erdogan sparks row over abortion"</u>, *BBC* (June 1, 2012)

- There is a trouble called Twitter, the finest lies are here. Nowadays, social media is actually the headache of societies.

  - o As quoted in <u>"Erdoğan: Twitter denilen bir bela var"</u>, *NTV* (June 2, 2013)

- Our religion [Islam] has defined a position for women: motherhood. Some people can understand this, while others can't. You cannot explain this to feminists because they don't accept the concept of motherhood.

- - As quoted in "Recep Tayyip Erdoğan: 'women not equal to men'", *The Guardian* (November 24, 2014)

- You cannot place a mother breastfeeding her baby on an equal footing with men. You cannot make women work in the same jobs as men do, as in communist regimes. You cannot give them a shovel and tell them to do their work. This is against their delicate nature.

  - As quoted in "Recep Tayyip Erdoğan: 'women not equal to men'", *The Guardian* (November 24, 2014)

- What women need is to be able to be equivalent, rather than equal. Because equality turns the victim into an oppressor and vice versa.

  - As quoted in "Recep Tayyip Erdoğan: 'women not equal to men'", *The Guardian* (November 24, 2014)

- As Muslims, we cannot overcome our difficulties without achieving unity in spite of our differences.

  - As quoted during the 13th Organization of Islamic Cooperation (OIC) Summit in Istanbul, in "Islamic leaders pledge to combat sectarianism", *Al Jazeera* (April 15, 2016)

- A woman who says 'because I am working I will not be a mother' is actually denying her feminity.

  - As quoted in "Turkey's Erdogan says childless women are 'incomplete'", *Al Jazeera* (June 6, 2016)

- A woman who rejects motherhood, who refrains from being around the house, however successful her working life is, is deficient, is incomplete.

  - As quoted in "Turkey's Erdogan says childless women are 'incomplete'", *Al Jazeera* (June 6, 2016)

- Europe, you don't want us because the majority of our population are Muslim ... We knew it but we tried to show our sincerity.

  - As quoted in "In Turkey's tussle with the EU, Erdogan thinks he holds the cards", *Reuters* (June 22, 2016)

- You cried out when 50,000 refugees were at the Kapikule border... You started asking what you would do if Turkey would open the gates. Look at me — if you go further, those border gates will be open. You should know that.

    - As quoted in "Erdogan Threatens to Let Migrant Flood Into Europe Resume", *The New York Times* (November 25, 2016)

- I am calling on my citizens, my brothers and sisters in Europe. Don't have just three children; have five. The place in which you are living and working is now your homeland and new motherland. Stake a claim in it. Open more businesses, enroll your children in better schools, have your families live in better neighborhoods, drive the best cars, live in the most beautiful houses. That's because you are the future of Europe. It will be the best answer to the vulgarism, antagonism and injustices made against you.

    - As quoted in "Erdoğan to Turks in EU: Have 5 children, you are the future of Europe", *TurkishMinute* (March 17 2017)

- If Europe continues this way, no European in any part of the world can walk safely on the streets. We, as Turkey, call on Europe to respect human rights and democracy.

    - As quoted in "Turkey's Erdogan warns Europeans 'will not walk safely on the streets' if diplomatic row continues", *The Independent* (March 22 2017)

13. References

[1] "Recep Tayyip Erdoğan'ın hayatı" (in Turkish). Ensonhaber. 1 July 2014.

[2] "İşte Ahmet Kaptan'ın bilinmeyen hikayesi" (in Turkish). Odatv. 4 December 2016

[3] "Turkey's charismatic pro-Islamic leader". BBC News. 4 November 2002. *Retrieved 23* July 2006

[4] "Profile: Recep Tayyip Erdogan". BBC News. 18 July 2007. Retrieved 29 August 2008.

[5] https://www.tccb.gov.tr/en/receptayyiperdogan/biography/. Presidency of The Repubic of Turkey. Biography. 19 March 2018

[6] https://www.dailysabah.com/football/2017/11/14/erdogan-i-enjoyed-5-titles-in-my-football-career . "Erdoğan: I enjoyed 5 titles in my football career". Daily Sabah Football. 14 November 2017

[7] "Antisemitism in the Turkish Media (Part III): Targeting Turkey's Jewish Citizens". Middle East Media Research Institute. 6 June 2005. Retrieved 5 September 2011

[8] *M*ustafa Akyol. "The making of Turkey's prime minister". Hürriyet Daily News. Retrieved 31 October 2010

[9] "Recep Tayyip Erdogan Biography- Political Beginnings". https://www.biography.com/people/recep-tayyip-erdogan-37630. Access Date 12 April 2018

[10] "1986 Ara Seçimleri Sonuçları". T.C. Resmi Gazete. http://www.resmigazete.gov.tr/arsiv/19247.pdf. 10 October 1986.

[11] "Beyoğlu Belediyesi - 1989 belediye başkanlığı seçimleri sonuçları". http://web.archive.org/web/20160304123307/http://www.yerelnet.org.tr/belediyeler/belediye_bm_secimsonuclari.php?yil=1989&belediyeid=128413. YerelNet. Retrieved 16 August 2016

[12] "Recep Tayyip Erdoğan – Biyografya" . http://www.biyografya.com/biyografi/15508 . Access Date 28 April 2018

[13] "Recep Tayyip Erdoğan participated in the World Leaders Forum event, Turkey's Role in Shaping the Future, in November 2008". Columbia University. 12 November 2008.

[14] "İstanbul 1994 Belediye Seçim Sonuçları". https://www.yerelnet.org.tr/belediyeler/belediye_secimsonuclari.php?yil=1994&belediyeid=128393 Access Date 28 April 2018

[15] "Turkish premier is winner of Rafik Hariri Memorial Award".
https://web.archive.org/web/20100308235302/http://www.unhabitat.org/content.asp?cid=8016&catid
=5&typeid=6&subMenuId=0. Retrieved 1 March 2010.

[16] Quinn Mecham. "Institutional Origins of Islamist Political Mobilization". Pages 145, 146.
Cambridge University Press. 2017

[17] Habervitrini. "Tankların yürümesine neden olan Sincan belediye başkanı'ndan özeleştiriler."
http://www.habervitrini.com/spor/tanklarin-yurumesine-neden-olan-sincan-belediye-baskanindan-
ozelestiriler-164655/. 28 February 2005

[18] Ekrem Buğra Akıncı. "Feb 28: A 'post-modern' coup of religious, political opression". Daily
Sabah Feature. August 25, 2016

[19] Quinn Mecham. "Institutional Origins of Islamist Political Mobilization". Pages 147. Cambridge
University Press. 2017

[20] Freedom House. " Freedom in the World 2006 -Turkey Report"
https://freedomhouse.org/report/freedom-world/2006/turkey . 2006

[21] Walter Mayr (16 July 2007). "Turkey's Powerful Prime Minister: Who Can Challenge Erdogan?".
Der Spiegel. Retrieved 3 December 2014.

[22] Sontag, Deborah (11 May 2003). "The Erdogan Experiment". The New York Times. Retrieved 3
December 2014.

[23] "Erdoğan'a ceza şoku" [Erdoğan's punishment shock]. Zaman (in Turkish). 22 April 1998.
Archived from the original on 31 May 2009. Retrieved 3 February 2007.

[24] Shambayati, Hootan (May 2004). "A Tale of Two Mayors: Courts and Politics in Iran and
Turkey". International Journal of Middle East Studies. Cambridge University Press. 36 (2): 253–275.
Retrieved 3 December 2014

[25] "Profile: Recep Tayyip Erdogan". Al Jazeera. 27 May 2011. Retrieved 3 May 2017

[26] "Erdogan goes to prison". Hurriyet. 27 March 1999. Archived from the original on 20 April
2017. Retrieved 3 May 2017.

[27] France-Presse, Agence (15 January 2016). "The Chief: feature film to trace early life of Turkish
president". The Guardian. ISSN 0261-3077. Retrieved 30 October 2016.

[28] GlobalSecurity.org "Virtue Party (Fazilet Parti FP)".
https://www.globalsecurity.org/military/world/europe/tu-political-party-fp.htm . 11 July 2011

[29] Quinn Mecham. "Institutional Origins of Islamist Political Mobilization". Page 150. Cambridge University Press. 2017

[30] BBC News. "Profile:Abdullah Gul". http://news.bbc.co.uk/2/hi/europe/6595511.stm . 28 August 2007

[31] Quinn Mecham. "Institutional Origins of Islamist Political Mobilization". Page 151. Cambridge University Press. 2017

[32] "Turkish PM quits for Erdogan". CNN. 11 March 2003. Retrieved 28 July 2012.

[33] Soner Cagaptay, Yasemin Çongar. "Local Elections in Turkey: A Landslide Victory for the Incumbent AKP". http://www.washingtoninstitute.org/policy-analysis/view/local-elections-in-turkey-a-landslide-victory-for-the-incumbent-akp .April 1 2004

[34] "New Turkey presidency row looms". BBC News. 14 August 2007.

[35] "Aday Gül" (in Turkish). Hürriyet. 24 April 2007. Retrieved 2007-04-22.

[36] "Genç Parti Gül'le görüşmeyecek!". Haberpan. 28 April 2007. Retrieved 2010-08-15

[37] "'Tek adam' tepkisi" (in Turkish). Milliyet. 22 April 2007. Archived from the original on 2007-04-24. Retrieved 2007-04-22

[38] "Yarbay's withdraw". Turkish Daily News. 28 April 2007. Archived from the original on 2007-09-27. Retrieved 2007-04-28.

[39] "Excerpts of Turkish army statement". BBC News. Saturday, 28 April 2007

[40] "Army 'concerned' by Turkey vote". BBC News. 2007-04-28.

[41]" Turkey's presidency vote annulled". BBC. Tuesday, 1 May 2007, 17:33 GMT

[42] "NTV-Msnbc" 01.05.2007"

[43] "Cumhurbaşkanlığı Seçim Süreci Resmen Sona Erdi". Haberler.com.
https://www.haberler.com/cumhurbaskanligi-secim-sureci-resmen-sona-erdi-2-haberi/ . 9 May 2007

[44] "Turkey lines up presidential poll". BBC News. August 10, 2007.

[45] "People's Daily Online - Turkey to elect new president without crisis: PM". July 24, 2007

[46] "Turkey's Ruling AKP nominates Abdullah Gul for president. More soon". BBC News. August 13, 2007

[47] " DSP'nin cumhurbaşkanı adayı İçli". http://www.hurriyet.com.tr/gundem/dspnin-cumhurbaskani-adayi-icli-7116122 . 19 August 2007

[48] Turkey re-elects governing party BBC News. 22 July 2007

[49] People's Daily Online - Turkey to hold referendum on constitutional amendment package on Oct. 21

[50] "Turkey's ruling party announces FM Gul as presidential candidate". People's Daily Online. 24 April 2007. Retrieved 2007-04-25.

[51] "DYP ve ANAP birleşti" (in Turkish). Retrieved 2007-05-06.

[52] "Turkey court rules reforms valid". BBC News. 2007-07-05. Retrieved 2010-05-26.

[53] "Turkey president vetoes poll plan". BBC News. 2007-06-19. Retrieved 2010-05-26.

[54] "Erdogan: History Will Judge President's Veto". TurkishPress. http://www.turkishpress.com/news.asp?id=178755 May 29, 2007

[55] "Turkish MPs back election reform despite president's opposition" Asharq Alawsat Newspaper (English). https://eng-archive.aawsat.com/author/theaawsat/page/2756 May 29, 2007

[56] Hurriyet Daily News. "Ruling party main loser in local ballot". http://www.hurriyet.com.tr/gundem/ruling-party-main-loser-in-local-ballot-11326291 . 31.03.2009

[57] MSNBC. "Genç Parti yerel seçimlere katılmayacak"

[58] Hurriyet Daily News. "Pro-Kurdish DTP sweeps Diyarbakir" http://www.hurriyet.com.tr/gundem/pro-kurdish-dtp-sweeps-diyarbakir-11318806 . 30.03.2009

[59] Hürriyet Daily News. "Turkey's AKP loses against independent Fakibaba". http://www.hurriyet.com.tr/gundem/turkeys-akp-loses-against-independent-fakibaba-11318022 . 30.03.2009

[60] Al Jazeera English. "AK party fails to sweep Turkey poll". https://www.aljazeera.com/news/europe/2009/03/20093300385479554.html . 30 Mar 2009

[61] Government of Turkey, Supreme Election Board (YSK) (12 September 2010). "Official Results – 12 September 2010 Constitutional Referendum" (Website) (in Turkish).

[62] "Turkey backs constitutional changes" BBC News. 12 September 2010. Retrieved on 12 September 2010.

[63] Head, Jonathan (13 September 2010). "International backing given to Turkish reform vote". Istanbul: British Broadcasting Corporation. Retrieved 13 September 2010

[64] Schedule of referendum to be set after Constitutional amendment published in Official Gazette. The Free Library. 12 May 2010. Retrieved on 12 September 2010.

[65] Government of Turkey, Prime Ministry; translated by Secretariat General for European Union Affairs (19 August 2010). "Law No 5982 Amending Certain Provisions of the Constitution" (pdf). Secretariat General for European Union Affairs. Retrieved 13 September 2010.

[66] Turkish constitutional reform package goes to final round, Hürriyet Daily News. 29 April 2010.

[67] Pro-democracy NGO calls reform package a major step for democracy, Today's Zaman. 25 March 2010.

[68] Opposition vows to challenge reforms after Turkish president signs package, Hürriyet Daily News. 12 May 2010.

[69] Kiliç, Ali Aslan (4 May 2010). "Political party closure article dropped from package". Today's Zaman. Ankara: Feza Gazetecilik. Retrieved 14 September 2010

[70] "Turkey's Constitutional Court does not block referendum", SETimes. 7 August 2010

[71] "Call to try Turkish coup leaders". Al Jazeera English. 2010-09-13. Retrieved 2011-06-13.

[72] "Novelties await voters in June 12 elections with new law". Today's Zaman. February 17, 2008. Retrieved March 27, 2011.

[73] "Turkey's June 12 elections to provide many 'firsts'". Hürriyet Daily News. March 6, 2011. Retrieved March 27, 2011.

[74] "Turkish elections turn deadly in local feuds". Al Jazeera English. 30 March 2014.

[75] Constanze Letsch in Istanbul (30 March 2014). "Turkish local elections: AKP set for victory". Guardian. Retrieved 31 March 2014

[76] "Ak Parti Ankara'da Zaferini İlan Etti, CHP İtiraz Etti !". Gazetebalikesir. Retrieved 31 March 2014

[77] "Yalova mayoralty changes hands after CHP's demand for vote recount – POLITICS". hurriyetdailynews.com. Retrieved 29 October 2015.

[78] Gianluca Mezzofiore. "Turkey's Riot Police Use Water Cannons on Vote Fraud Protesters". International Business Times UK. Retrieved 29 October 2015.

[79] Ayşegül USTA/İSTANBUL (5 June 2015). "Yerel seçimde hile cezası 5 yıl hapis". hurriyet.com.tr. Retrieved 29 October 2015.

[80] "Bunları biliyor musunuz? Bunları biliyormuydunuz?seçimler için aday tanıtım forumu,genel seçimler,yerel seçimler". Kimneredenaday. Retrieved 31 March 2014.

[81] "Türkiye'de kaç muhtar var biliyor musunuz?". İHA. 16 May 2009. Retrieved 31 March 2014.

[82] "SEÇİM SONUÇLARI – 2009 Yerel Seçim Sonuçları". Seçim Haberler. Retrieved 31 March 2014.

[83] "Kapanacak köy ve beldeler listesi". YAYED. 30 March 2014. http://www.yayed.org/id315-incelemeler/kapanacak-koy-ve-beldeler-listesi-buyuksehirler.php#.W26Qc7ihnIU

[84] "Official 2009 metropolitan municipal results" (PDF). Supreme Electoral Council of Turkey. Retrieved 4 August 2014.

[85] "Official 2014 metropolitan municipal results" (PDF). Supreme Electoral Council of Turkey. Retrieved 4 August 2014.

[86] "Turkey sets Aug 10 for presidential election: source". Reuters. 7 March 2014. https://www.reuters.com/article/us-turkey-election/turkey-sets-aug-10-for-presidential-election-source-idUSBREA2610R20140307

[87] "Yüksek Seçim Kurulu." 10 August 2018. http://www.ysk.gov.tr/ysk/content/conn/YSKUCM/path/Contribution%20Folders/HaberDosya/2014CB-Gecici-416_d_Genel.pdf/

[88] "Turkey's Davutoglu expected to be a docile prime minister with Erdogan calling the shots". Fox News World. http://www.foxnews.com/world/2014/08/21/turkey-davutoglu-expected-to-be-docile-prime-minister-with-erdogan-calling.html .21 August 2014.

[89] "OSCE alarmed over Turkish PM's intimidation of female journalist: source=OSCE". Hürriyet Daily News. Retrieved 13 August 2014.

[90] "Seçimlere katılım oranı 12 yılın en düşük oranında kaldı (SEÇİM 2014): source=Bugün". Bugün. Retrieved 13 August 2014.

[91] "CHP olağanüstü kurultaya gidiyor: source=CNN Türk". CNN Türk. Retrieved 17 August 2014.

[92] "OSCE praises election process, says it was well-organized". DailySabah. 8 June 2015.

[93] Hürriyet. "Davutoğlu: Kırmızı çizgimiz yok". 10 June 2015.

[94] "Erdoğan görevi Davutoğlu'na verdi". hurriyet.com.tr. 9 July 2015.

[95] "Cumhuriyet Gazetesi – Bahçeli koalisyona kapıları kapattı 'erken seçim' dedi". cumhuriyet.com.tr. 8 June 2015.

[96] "Kılıçdaroğlu CHP'nin 14 ilkesini sıraladı". Posta.

[97] "Ak Parti kaynakları: CHP'ye 3 aylık seçim hükümeti değil süreli reform hükümeti teklif edildi". Radikal.

[98] "İşte MHP'nin koalisyon için 4 şartı". hurriyet.com.tr. 17 August 2015.

[99] "AKP-MHP görüşmesinden de sonuç çıkmadı, hükümeti kuramayan Davutoğlu, görevi iade edecek mi?". t24.com.tr.

[100] "Alman Basınından Türk Siyasetine Karamsar Bakış". Amerika'nin Sesi – Voice of America – Turkish.

[101] "'Başbakan Davutoğlu, koalisyon istemeyen Ömer Çelik'i, Saray'a yakın diye heyetteki görevinden alamadı'". t24.com.tr.

[102] Umut Uras. "Turkey's AK Party wins back majority in snap election". Al Jazeera. 1 November 2015.

[103] "33 saat çalışan vekiller 25. dönemi böyle kapattı: CHP:1300, MHP:502, HDP: 420, AKP:0". Radikal. 29 October 2015

[104] "Turkey snap election called after coalition talks fail". BBC News. 21 August 2015.

[105] Calderwood, Imogen (2015-11-01). "Turkish election result is hailed a personal victory for President Erdogan | Daily Mail Online". Dailymail.co.uk.

[106] "CHP, MHP and HDP destined to remain in opposition". Daily Sabah. 2 November 2015.

[107] "Turkey election: Ruling AKP regains majority - BBC News". Bbc.co.uk. 2 November 2015

[108] "Turkish parliament nears approval of presidential system sought by Erdoğan". Reuters. 19 January 2017

[109] "Turkey Parliament Triggers Referendum on Presidential System". Bloomberg. 22 January 2017

[110] "Erdoğan claims victory in Turkish referendum but result swiftly challenged by opposition". Telegraph.co.uk. Retrieved 18 April 2017.

[111] "Birçok ilde referandum ve YSK protestosu". Gazeteduvar.com.tr. 2017-04-18.

[112] "AKPM referandum raporunu açıkladı 'YSK kararı yasaya aykırı'". Habererk.com. 2017-09-01.

[113] "Bahçeli: Danışmanı "eyalet sistemi" diyor, Erdoğan ses çıkarmıyorsa, ülkücülerin kararı ne olabilir?". Retrieved 16 April 2017

[114] "Milli Gazete - Almanyadaki referandum sandığında hile". Archived from the original on 11 April 2017.

[115] Inside Turkey's Irregular Referendum, The Wall Street Journal

[116] "Anayasa Mahkemesi". Anayasa.gov.tr. Retrieved 28 February 2017.

[117] "TBB | Anayasa Değişikliği Teklifi'nin Karşılaştırmalı ve Açıklamalı Metni". Anayasadegisikligi.barobirlik.org.tr. Retrieved 28 February 2017.

[118] "21 maddelik anayasa teklifi Meclis'te: Cumhurbaşkanı yürütmenin başı". Diken. Retrieved 28 February 2017.

[119] "Plans to expand the powers of Turkey's Erdoğan have passed the first hurdle". Businessinsider.com. Retrieved 28 February 2017.

[120] "Turkey referendum: Erdoğan wins vote amid dispute over ballots – as it happened | World news". The Guardian. 16 April 2017.

[121] "Erdoğan açıkladı... Erken seçim tarihi belli oldu". Hürriyet. 18 April 2018.

[122] "HDP'nin cumhurbaşkanı adayı Demirtaş". tr.sputniknews.com. 26 April 2018.

[123] "Turkey's main opposition nominates combative former teacher to challenge Erdogan". Reuters. 6 May 2018.

[124] "100 bin imzayla Cumhurbaşkanı adayı olacağım". NTV. 18 April 2018.

[125] "President Erdoğan announces ministers of Turkey's new cabinet". Hürriyet Daily News. 10 July 2018.

[126] "Erdogan announces first cabinet under new presidential system". TRT World (in Turkish). 10 July 2018.

[127] Editorial, Reuters. "Turkey's Erdogan to name cabinet as signals action on economy". U.S. Retrieved 10 July 2018. "...Erdogan will select his own cabinet and regulate ministries and remove civil servants, all without parliamentary approval. ..."

[128] "Turkey: Decree out making first changes in new system". Anadolu Agency. 15 July 2018.

[129] Shaheen, Kareem. "Erdoğan rejoins Turkey's ruling party in wake of referendum on new powers". The Guardian. 2 May 2017.

[130] "Anayasa Mahkemesi seçim kararını verdi". Retrieved 24 June 2018.

[131] "Seçim ittifakı için yarın son gün". Retrieved 24 June 2018.

[132] "Cumhur İttifakı'nın protokolü belli oldu". Retrieved 24 June 2018.

[133] "BBP, AK Parti listesinden seçime girecek". NTV. Retrieved 2018-07-19.

[134] Davutoglu, Ahmet (2010-05-20). "Turkey's Zero-Problems". Foreign Policy. Retrieved 2015-08-12.

[135] Kanbolat, Hasan (July 27, 2010). "Turkish opening for NATO: Ambassador Hüseyin Diriöz". Today's Zaman. Retrieved July 29, 2010.

[136] Villelabeitia, Ibon (June 10, 2010). "Analysis: Turk vote on Iran sanctions suggests shift to East". Reuters. Ankara.

[137] Djavadi, Abbas (October 30, 2009). "'Turkey's Kissinger' Leads Foreign-Policy Balancing Act". Radio Free Europe/Radio Liberty. Retrieved October 30, 2009.

[138] "Turkish MPs back attacks in Iraq". BBC News. 2007-10-18.

[139] "Turkey approves Iraq incursion". CNN.com. 2007-10-17. Archived from the original on 2008-02-09.

[140] "Turkey recalls ambassador over genocide resolution". CNN.com. 2007-10-11.

[141] "Turkey–U.S. Relations: How to Proceed after Obama? | The German Marshall Fund of the United States". www.gmfus.org. Retrieved 2017-02-26.

[142] Aslan, Ali H. (2009-05-02). "Parris: 'Genocide' reference would have frozen Turkey ties". Today's Zaman.

[143] "Turkey and Armenia set 'roadmap'". BBC News. 2009-04-23. Retrieved 2009-04-29.

[144] Paul Richter (2009-04-03). "Turkey, Armenia are likely to ease conflict". L.A. Times. Retrieved 2009-04-03.

[145] "Davutoğlu expects Obama message to Muslims to change 'atmosphere'". Today's Zaman. 2009-06-03.

[146] "Model partnership with US necessity rather than preference". Today's Zaman. 2009-06-04.

[147] "Wexler urges US to positively 'channel' Turkey's value". Sunday's Zaman. 2009-05-16.

[148] "Top US commander discussed Afghanistan, Iraq in Turkey talks". Today's Zaman. 2009-05-01.

[149] "Turkey and Armenia move to ease tensions". Today's Zaman. 2009-04-25.

[150] "Turkey and Armenia expect gradual normalization in ties". Today's Zaman. 2009-04-25.

[151] Dişli, Fatma (2009-04-25). "Turkey makes last-minute move to placate Obama administration". Today's Zaman.

[152] Sami, Kohen (2009-04-25). "Road map is OK, but…". Today's Zaman.

[153] "US says anti-terror cooperation key in partnership with Turkey". Today's Zaman. 2009-05-02.

[154] "Turkey to face pressure over US nukes on its soil". Today's Zaman. 2009-05-04. Archived from the original on 2009-05-06.

[155] "'Religious freedoms in Turkey curbed by hard-line secularism'". Today's Zaman. 2009-05-02.

[156] "Turkey can always count on America, say US senators". Today's Zaman. 2009-06-02.

[157] Despite its views on Israel and Iran, Turkey is trying to prove it's still a friend to the U.S.

[158] "Cable Viewer". Cablegate.wikileaks.org. 25 March 2005. Retrieved 1 December 2010.

[159] "Leaked cables point to vital, volatile U.S. relationship with Turkey". CNN. 30 November 2010. Retrieved 30 November 2010.

[160] "WikiLeaks US embassy cables: live updates". The Guardian. 1 December 2010. Retrieved 2 December 2010.

[161] "Secretary Of Defense Gates's Meetings With Turkish" 16 February 2010.

[162] "US threat on Turkey arms sales." Al Jazeera, 17 August 2010.

[163] Daniel Dombey (2012-02-15). "Turkey-US harmony has its limits". Financial Times. Retrieved 2012-02-16.

[164] Knee, Daryl. "U.S. pilots plant SEAD with Turkish counterparts." USAF. March 9, 2012.

[165] "US-Turkey: The strained alliance". BBC. 29 March 2016.

[166] "Turkey-US relations are strained as Erdogan arrives in Washington". EuroNews. 30 March 2016.

[167] "US support for PKK's Syrian wing risks Turkey-US relations". Daily Sabah. 29 March 2016.

[168] "ISIS In Turkey: US Orders Diplomats, Military Dependents To Leave Over Security, Islamic State Concerns". International Business Times. 29 March 2016.

[169] "Why post-coup Turkey is suspicious of Hillary Clinton". Harvard Journal of Middle Eastern Politics and Policy. 29 October 2016.

[170] "Turkey's Erdoğan to drop lawsuits against people who insulted him". BBC News. 29 July 2016.

[171] Lake, Eli (2016-07-28). "America's Friends Get Arrested in Turkey's Post-Coup Purges". Bloomberg View.

[172] "US Commander Campbell: The man behind the failed coup in Turkey". Yeni Safak. 25 July 2016.

[173] La Porte, Amy. "United States and Turkey mutually suspend visa services". CNN. CNN. Retrieved 2017-10-22.

[174] "US Official Accuses Turkey of Pushing Extreme Islamist Ideology". Voice of America. 13 December 2017.

[175] "US sanctions Turkey over Pastor Brunson detention". The National. 1 August 2018.

[176] "US sanctions Turkish officials over detained pastor". Politico. 1 August 2018.

[177] Trump doubles metal tariffs on Turkey as lira falls by 20%

[178] US changing strategic NATO partner with pastor, Turkish President Erdoğan says

[179] US changing strategic NATO partner with pastor, Turkish President Erdoğan says

[180] Turkish municipality strikes at social media giants as response to US

[181] Turkey to retaliate against Trump's metal tariffs

[182] Turkey vows to defend domestic steel, aluminum exporters against additional US tariffs

[183] Erdoğan says Turkey will boycott US electronic products

[184] Municipality in Turkish capital Ankara stops issuing licenses to major US food brands

[185] Turkey escalates trade dispute with US by raising tariffs

[186] Turkey detains two men over shooting at U.S. embassy in Ankara

[187] "Interview with European Commission President Jose Manuel Barroso on BBC Sunday AM" (PDF). European Commission. 15 October 2006. Archived (PDF) from the original on 21 November 2006. Retrieved 17 December 2006.

[188] Phinnemore and İçener, David and Erhan (14 May 2016). "Never mind Brexit scaremongering – Turkey is a long way from joining the EU". blogs.lse.ac.uk. LSE. Retrieved 14 May 2016.

[189] EU-Turkey refugee deal – Q&A, The Guardian

[190] "Freeze EU accession talks with Turkey until it halts repression, urge MEPs". European Parliament.

[191] "EU parliament votes overwhelmingly in favour of scrapping Turkey accession talks". The Telegraph. Retrieved 8 December 2016.

[192] "EU says won't expand Turkey membership talks". Yahoo. 13 December 2016.

[193] Marc Pierini (12 December 2016). "Turkey's Impending Estrangement From the West". Carnegie Europe.

[194] EU-Turkey Relations Reaching a Crossroads, Carnegie Europe

[195] "Turkey is no longer an EU candidate", MEP says, Euronews

[196] "EU plans to cut financial assistance to Turkey". Ahval. 6 May 2018.

[197] "European Council: EU would open accession negotiations with Turkey" (PDF). Retrieved 5 September 2017.

[198] "Independent Commission on Turkey". Archived from the original on 9 January 2016. Retrieved 7 June 2015.

[199] Today's Zaman: Turkey Starts Full Membership Negotiations with EU[permanent dead link]

[200] Turkey, with eye on EU, says determined to reform Archived 17 April 2009 at the Wayback Machine., EUbusiness, 15 March 2009

[201] "Cyprus threatens to block EU deal on Turkey talks". Retrieved 7 June 2015.

[202] "The ins and outs: The EU's most effective foreign-policy instrument has been enlargement. But how far can it go?". The Economist. 17 March 2007. Retrieved 4 July 2007.

[203] "EU freezes talks on Turkey membership". 12 December 2006. Retrieved 5 September 2017.

[204] "Cyprus won't open EU accession chapters for Turkey". Retrieved 7 June 2015.

[205] "Fule urges Turkey to implement Additional Protocol". Retrieved 7 June 2015.

[206] http://www.epc.eu/documents/uploads/pub_3021_turkey-eu_relations.pdf

[207] "Turkey tells EU it may postpone competition chapter if needed". TodaysZaman. Archived from the original on 15 July 2015. Retrieved 7 June 2015.

[208] "Turkey sees bleak future for EU accession talks in 2012". TodaysZaman. Archived from the original on 15 July 2015. Retrieved 7 June 2015.

[209] "Turkey: EU political benchmarks 'were never given to us'". eurActiv. 7 February 2013. Retrieved 9 February 2013.

[210] "EU Commissioner Fule: Positive Agenda to put EU process back on track". Anadolu Agency. Retrieved 5 September 2017.

[211] "Turkey-EU Relations". Republic of Turkey Ministry of Foreign Affairs. Retrieved 7 June 2015.

[212] "Bağış: 'Dört fasılda kapanış kriterlerini yerine getirdiğimizin teyidini aldık'". Retrieved 7 June 2015.[permanent dead link]

[213] Kubosova, Lucia (30 March 2007). "Turkey targets 2013 for EU legal compliance". EUobserver. Retrieved 26 August 2008.

[214] Kubosova, Lucia (17 April 2007). "Brussels declines to endorse 2013 date for Turkey's EU entry". EUobserver. Retrieved 26 August 2008.

[215] "Interview with European Commission President Jose Manuel Barroso on BBC Sunday AM" (PDF). Retrieved 13 April 2007.

[216] Coskun, Orhan; Hudson, Alexandra (31 October 2012). "Merkel reassures Turkey on EU talks, Erdogan raps Cyprus". Reuters. Retrieved 4 November 2012.

[217] "Gül: 'Biz de AB üyeliğini referanduma götüreceğiz'". Archived from the original on 15 July 2015. Retrieved 7 June 2015.

[218] Dombey, Daniel, James Fontanella-Khan, and Quentin Peel (21 June 2013). "Germany blocks Turkey's bid to join EU". Financial Times. Retrieved 21 June 2013.

[219] "New Eurobarometer poll results show a drop in Turkish support for the EU". Hürriyet. Retrieved 23 September 2013.

[220] "Turkey welcomes new chapter in EU talks, wants more progress". Today's Zaman. 5 November 2011. Archived from the original on 9 November 2013. Retrieved 10 November 2013.

[221] "Turkey could put EU talks to a referendum next year: Erdogan". Reuters. 14 November 2016. Retrieved 22 November 2016.

[222] "Euro MPs vote to freeze Turkey EU membership talks". BBC. 24 November 2016. Retrieved 24 November 2016.

[223] "Turkey's EU bid in jeopardy after Council of Europe vote". Euractiv. 25 April 2017.

[224] "Turkey-Russia relations". euractiv.com. November 17, 2005.

[225] "Turkey, Russia eye strategic partnership in Medvedev visit". Today's Zaman. May 11, 2010.

[226] "Russia and Turkey agree on visa-free travel". Russia Today. May 12, 2010.

[227] "Erdoğan to visit Russia next month, report says". Today's Zaman. 2009-04-25.

[228] "Erdoğan seeks Russian backing in Karabakh peace effort". Today's Zaman. 2009-05-16.

[229] "Putin to visit Turkey next month". Today's Zaman. 2009-05-20.

[230] 2013 World Service Poll BBC

[231] "Turkey shoots down Russian warplane on Syria border". 2015-11-24. Retrieved 2015-11-24.

[232] Turkey-Russia jet downing: Moscow announces sanctions, BBC News, 28 November 2015

[233] Russian clubs banned from signing Turkish players, BBC News, 29 November 2015

[234] "Russian deputies seek accountability for Armenia genocide denial". Reuters. 2015-11-25. Retrieved 2015-12-07.

[235] "Greece: Third Country to Criminalize Denial of the Armenian Genocide". Asbarez.com. Retrieved 2015-12-07.

[236] "Orthodox Council moved from Turkey to Greece over Russia crisis". Hürriyet Daily News. 19 April 2016.

[237] Last-minute politics overshadow historic pan-Orthodox council. The Washington Post, 18 December 2015.

[238] Patriarch of Moscow: pan-Orthodox Synod to be held in Crete

[239] Собрание Патриархов в Стамбуле Nezavisimaya Gazeta, 30 December 2014.

[240] "Erdoğan has apologised for downing of Russian jet, Kremlin says". The Guardian. 2016-06-27. Retrieved 2016-07-14.

[241] "Russia closes 'crisis chapter' with Turkey". Al Jazeera. 2016-06-29. Retrieved 2016-07-14.

[242] "Erdoğan and Putin discuss closer ties in first meeting since jet downing: Turkish president holds talks in St Petersburg with Russian counterpart, thanking him for support in wake of last month's coup attempt". The Guardian. 9 August 2016.

[243] Turkey's Erdogan unnerves West with Putin visit BBC, 9 August 2016.

[244] "Why killing of Russian diplomat may well bring Turkey and Russia closer: Putin and Erdoğan are likely to find common ground in their desire to blame third parties for death of Andrei Karlov". The Guardian. 19 December 2016.

[245] "Russian president guarantees envoy's murder won't damage Russia-Turkey ties". Hürriyet Daily News. 23 December 2016.

[246] Переговоры в Астане по урегулированию конфликта в Сирии RIA Novosti, 3 May 2017.

[247] "Совместное заявление министров иностранных дел Исламской Республики Иран, Российской Федерации, Турецкой Республики по согласованным мерам, направленным на оживление политического процесса с целью прекращения сирийского конфликта, Москва, 20 декабря 2016 года". www.mid.ru. Retrieved 11 July 2017.

[248] "Russia, Turkey and Iran continue cooperation on de-escalation zones in Syria". TASS. 23 June 2017.

[249] Putin, Erdogan Pledge To Closely Cooperate On Syria, Increase Trade Radio Liberty, 29 September 2017.

[250] Putin, Erdogan meet for third time in less than a month

[251] Russian-Turkish talks kremlin.ru, 11 December 2017.

[252] Turkey Signs Russian Missile Deal, Pivoting From NATO. The New York Times (Europe), 12 September 2017.

[253] Turkey will reportedly start getting Russia's advanced missile defense system in 2019, despite US efforts to block it Business Insider, 21 August 2018.

[254] Russian Sputnik shuts down Kurdish website at Turkey's request

[255] https://www.reuters.com/article/russia-turkey-us-sanctions/russias-lavrov-in-turkey-calls-us-sanctions-policy-illegitimate-idUSR4N1V0039

[256] Russia's Lavrov, in Turkey, calls U.S. sanctions policy illegitimate Reuters, 14 August 2018.

[257] Turkey never supported anti-Russian sanctions — top diplomat TASS, 14 August 2018.

[258] Turkey Shifts Toward Russia as Sanctions Sour U.S. Relations: Foreign ministers slam Western sanctions, as Erdogan plans boycott of U.S. electronic goods WSJ, 14 August 2018.

[259] Greg Myre, New York Times (2 May 2005). "Turkish leader visits Israel, offers to help with peace process". SFGate. Retrieved 17 April 2016.

[260] "Turkish Leader Visits Israel, Restoring Friendly Ties". The New York Times. 2 May 2005. Archived from the original on 20 August 2014. Retrieved 17 April 2016.

[261] "Erdogan's travels". The Economist. Archived from the original on 25 April 2016. Retrieved 17 April 2016.

[262] "News". Radikal. 1 July 2005. Archived from the original on 21 October 2012. Retrieved 23 March 2013.

[263] Yaakov Katz (12 November 2007). "Israel may sell Arrow and Ofek to Turkey". The Jerusalem Post. Archived from the original on 8 December 2017. Retrieved 12 November 2007.

[264] "Damascus confirms channel with Israel". The Jerusalem Post. 30 March 2008. Archived from the original on 8 December 2017. Retrieved 30 March 2008.

[265] Yaakov Katz (13 November 2007). "Peres, Gul at odds over Iran nuke threat". The Jerusalem Post. Archived from the original on 8 December 2017. Retrieved 12 November 2007.

[266] Stormy debate in Davos over Gaza Archived 30 January 2009 at the Wayback Machine. Al Jazeera English (29 January 2009)

[267] Erdogan Clashes With Peres, Storms Out of Davos Panel (Update1) Archived 26 June 2009 at the Wayback Machine. Bloomberg

[268] "Turkey rallies to Gaza's plight" Archived 19 January 2009 at the Wayback Machine. BBC News by Sarah Rainsford (BBC Istanbul), Friday, 16 January 2009

[269] "Turkey's drift away from the West" Archived 8 December 2017 at the Wayback Machine.. Jerusalem Post (14 January 2009). Retrieved on 4 February 2009

[270] Hurriyet DN Online with wires (4 January 2009). "Hundreds of thousands protest in Turkey against Israeli offensive". Archived from the original on 14 February 2009. Retrieved 17 April 2016.

[271] Hurriyet DN Online with wires (2 January 2009). "Thousands protest Israeli attacks on the Gaza Strip in Turkey". Retrieved 17 April 2016.

[272] "Livni, Turkish FM hold secret reconciliation talks" Archived 11 December 2017 at the Wayback Machine., Haaretz, 5 March 2009

[273] "Turkey, Israel in secret talks for swift end to diplomatic crisis - report" Archived 13 January 2015 at the Wayback Machine., Hurriyet Daily News

[274] "Haaretz; Israel and Turkey in quiet talks", Today's Zaman

[275] "Stormy debate in Davos over Gaza". Al Jazeera English. 30 January 2009. Archived from the original on 30 January 2009. Retrieved 1 February 2009.

[276] "Israel hits back at Turkey over scuppered air force drill". Haaretz. 10 November 2009. Archived from the original on 5 November 2012. Retrieved 24 March 2011.

[277] "Netanyahu: Turkey can't be 'honest broker' in Syria talks". Haaretz. 18 October 2009. Archived from the original on 19 October 2009. Retrieved 18 October 2009.

[278] "Turkish PM storms off in Gaza row" Archived 30 June 2009 at the Wayback Machine., BBC News

[279] "Turkish PM storms out of Davos' Gaza session, slams moderator" Archived 22 May 2011 at the Wayback Machine. Hurriyet Daily News

[280] "Stormy debate in Davos over Gaza" Archived 30 January 2009 at the Wayback Machine. Al Jazeera English (Thursday, 29 January 2009)

[281] "Lay off Iran's nukes, Turkish leader says." Archived 30 October 2009 at the Wayback Machine. JTA. 28 October 2009

[282] "Turkish TV show has IDF soldiers 'killing' Palestinian kids". Ynetnews. Archived from the original on 5 January 2010. Retrieved 5 June 2010.

[283] Renaudie, Jean-Luc (14 January 2010). "Israeli media slam govt handling of row with Turkey". AFP. Archived from the original on 21 January 2010. Retrieved 21 January 2010.

[284] "Turkey, Israel and the US". Thenation.com. Retrieved 2010-06-05.

[285] "Ayalon to 'behave diplomatically' in future" Archived 16 January 2010 at the Wayback Machine., Ynetnews, 13 January 2010

[286] "Israel-Turkey tensions high over TV series". CNN. 12 January 2010. Archived from the original on 14 August 2011. Retrieved 5 June 2010.

[287] "Shin Bet: Hamas operating in Turkey, China". The Jerusalem Post - JPost.com. Archived from the original on 24 October 2012. Retrieved 17 April 2016.

[288] Ignatius, David (16 October 2013). "Turkey blows Israel's cover for Iranian spy ring". www.washingtonpost.com. The Washington Post. Archived from the original on 17 October 2013. Retrieved 16 October 2013.

[289] Black, Ian; Haroon Siddique (31 May 2010). "Q&A: The Gaza Freedom flotilla". The Guardian. London: Guardian News and Media. Archived from the original on 3 June 2010. Retrieved 2 June 2010.

[290] Tia Goldenberg (31 May 2010). "Pro-Palestinian aid flotilla sets sail for Gaza". The San Diego Union-Tribune. Associated Press. Archived from the original on 10 December 2017. Retrieved 4 June 2010.

[291] Noah Kosharek; Liel Kyzer; Barak Ravid (2 June 2010). "Israel transfers hundreds of Gaza flotilla activists to airport for deportation". Haaretz. The Associated Press and DPA. Retrieved 2 June 2010.

[292] "Turkey condemns Israel over deadly attack on Gaza aid flotilla". London: Telegraph. 31 May 2010. Archived from the original on 3 June 2010. Retrieved 5 June 2010.

[293] "Archived copy". Archived from the original on 8 October 2011. Retrieved 6 February 2016., "Turkey downgrades ties with Israel"

[294] Arsu, Sebnem; Cowell, Alan (2 September 2011). "Turkey Expels Israeli Envoy in Dispute Over Raid". The New York Times. Archived from the original on 19 February 2016. Retrieved 4 September 2011.

[295] ""Israel refuses to apologize or pay compensation regarding the 2009 Gaza flotilla raid"".

[296] Maayan Lubell (2 September 2011). "Israel hopes to mend ties with Turkey-govt official". Reuters. Archived from the original on 12 June 2012. Retrieved 3 September 2011.

[297] Darren Mara; Chuck Penfold (3 September 2011). "UN chief tells Turkey, Israel to improve ties for sake of Middle East". Deutsche Welle. Archived from the original on 3 September 2011. Retrieved 3 September 2011.

[298] "Hamas welcomes Turkey move to expel Israeli envoy". The Egyptian Gazette. 2 September 2011. Archived from the original on 27 March 2012. Retrieved 3 September 2011.

[299] "'Erdogan painted himself into a corner' - Israel News, Ynetnews". Ynetnews.com. 20 June 1995. Archived from the original on 27 March 2013. Retrieved 23 March 2013.

[300] Turkey: Israel possibly target of more sanctions Archived 8 September 2011 at the Wayback Machine. by Selcan Hacaoglu and Aron Heller, Huffington Post, 6 September 2011.

[301] "Barak on Turkey: This wave will pass." Archived 9 October 2011 at the Wayback Machine. Ynetnews. 8 September 2011. 8 September 2011.

[302] Keinon, Herb. "Erdogan threatens to send gunboats with next flotilla". JPost. Archived from the original on 24 October 2012. Retrieved 23 March 2013.

[303] Benhorin, Yitzhak. "Obama urges Erdogan to resolve crisis with Israel." Archived 23 September 2011 at the Wayback Machine. Ynetnews. 21 September 2011. 21 September 2011.

[304] "Foreign Ministry: Turkey condemns Israeli military operation in Gaza Strip". En.trend.az. 15 November 2012. Archived from the original on 17 November 2012. Retrieved 23 March 2013.

[305] "APA - Turkey condemns Israeli attack on Gaza, demands halt". apa.az. Archived from the original on 19 April 2016. Retrieved 17 April 2016.

[306] "PM: Turkey does not intend to negotiate with Israel on Gaza situation". En.trend.az. 16 November 2012. Archived from the original on 19 November 2012. Retrieved 23 March 2013.

[307] "Turkish FM defines Israeli attack on Gaza as a crime of humanity". Turkish Weekly. Archived from the original on 18 November 2012. Retrieved 23 March 2013.

[308] Peker, Emre (19 November 2012). "Turkey's Erdogan Labels Israel a 'Terrorist State'". Wall Street Journal. Archived from the original on 18 July 2015. Retrieved 23 March 2013.

[309] "Kerry calls Turkish prime minister's remark about Zionism 'objectionable'". CNN. 1 March 2013. Archived from the original on 20 October 2013.

[310] "US rebukes Erdogan for comments on Zionism". South China Morning Post. 13 March 2013. Archived from the original on 4 March 2013. Retrieved 23 March 2013.

[311] Nathaniel Botwinick (28 February 2013). "Turkish PM Erdogan: Zionism Is 'a Crime Against Humanity' Like 'Anti-Semitism or Fascism'". National Review Online. Archived from the original on 4 March 2013. Retrieved 23 March 2013.

[312] "Erdogan says Zionism crime against humanity". Jerusalem Post. 28 February 2013. Archived from the original on 23 March 2013. Retrieved 23 March 2013.

[313] "Israel: Turk's Remarks Criticized". The New York Times. 28 February 2013. Archived from the original on 22 July 2016.

[314] "EJP". Archived from the original on 20 October 2013.

[315] "Turkish PM says Zionism comments misinterpreted". The Times of Israel. Archived from the original on 3 March 2016. Retrieved 17 April 2016.

[316] Israel behind coup to oust Morsi, Turkish PM Erdoğan says Archived 4 November 2014 at the Wayback Machine., Hürriyet

[317] Turkey's Erdogan claims Israel responsible for Egypt coup Archived 24 August 2013 at the Wayback Machine., Jewish Telegraphic Agency (JTA), August 20, 2013.

[318] Turkey has evidence that Israel was behind Egypt coup: Erdoğan Archived 21 October 2013 at the Wayback Machine., Journal of Turkish Weekly, August 20, 2013.

[319] 'Israel behind Egypt coup' – Turkish PM Archived 23 February 2015 at the Wayback Machine., Russia Today, August 20, 2013.

[320] US, Egypt pan Turkish PM for saying Israel ousted Morsi Archived 20 August 2013 at the Wayback Machine. by Gavriel Fiske and Stuart Winer, Times of Israel, August 20, 2013.

[321] Ravid, Barak (29 June 2016). "Israeli security cabinet approves Turkey reconciliation agreement". Haaretz. Archived from the original on 16 August 2016. Retrieved 30 June 2016.

[322] Humeyra Pamuk and Dasha Afanasieva (20 August 2016). "Turkish parliament approves deal ending rift with Israel". Reuters. Archived from the original on 23 September 2016. Retrieved 21 September 2016.

[323] DPA (31 August 2016). "Erdogan signs deal to repair Turkey's broken ties with Israel". EBL News. Archived from the original on 8 November 2016. Retrieved 21 September 2016.

[324] "Turkey chooses envoy to Israel, in final stage of reconciliation deal". Archived from the original on 12 October 2016.

[325] "Israel postpones choosing new ambassador to Turkey". Archived from the original on 27 October 2016.

[326] "Ties on the mend, Israel names new ambassador to Turkey". Archived from the original on 17 November 2016.

[327] "Turkey appoints PM advisor as ambassador to Israel: Erdogan". Archived from the original on 16 November 2016.

[328] "New Israeli envoy arrives in Turkey after rapprochement". Archived from the original on 4 December 2016.

[329] "Turkey drops court case against Israeli raid on Gaza flotilla". Archived from the original on 12 December 2016.

[330] Ravid, Barak (12 December 2016). "New Turkish Ambassador to Israel Hopes Reconciliation Will Also Benefit Palestinian Lives". Archived from the original on 13 December 2016 – via Haaretz.

[331] Turkish President accuses Israel of 'genocide' after Palestinian deaths on Gaza border

[332] Israeli reporters 'shoved' in Istanbul amid diplomatic rift

[333] Turkey temporarily expels Israeli ambassador

[334] Israel expels Turkish consul

[335] Agricultural imports from Turkey frozen

[336] Israel expels Turkish consul

[337] Turkey 'will never accept' Jerusalem as Israel's capital: Erdoğan

[338] Erdogan: Hamas is not a terrorist organization

[339] Erdogan slams world's 'silence' on 'Israel's tyranny'

[340] Israel should be taken to international criminal court over recent massacre: Turkish foreign minister

[341] Muslim leaders gather in Istanbul at OIC summit for Palestine

[342] Thousands gather in Istanbul's Yenikapı district to support Palestine

[343] Israeli reporters 'shoved' in Istanbul amid diplomatic rift

[344] 'Gov't must take solid steps if sincere on Israel,' says CHP's presidential runner İnce

[345] Turkey launches major aid campaign for Palestinians

[346] "Turkey, Israel: Potential for a fresh start?". Archived from the original on 27 April 2016. Retrieved 17 April 2016.

[347] "Israel's trade with Turkey worth $2b in first half - Globes English". Archived from the original on 8 January 2013.

[348] Uri Friedman. "The Tie That Still Binds Israel and Turkey: Trade". The Wire. Archived from the original on 19 March 2012. Retrieved 17 April 2016.

[349] "ECONOMY - Business as usual between Turkey, Israel". Archived from the original on 13 April 2016. Retrieved 17 April 2016.

[350] Morris, Chris (2005). "Introduction". The New Turkey. London: Granta Books. pp. 1–10. ISBN 1-86207-865-3.

[351] Morris, Chris (2005). "Chapter 9: Crossroads". The New Turkey. London: Granta Books. pp. 203–227. ISBN 1-86207-865-3.

[352] Morris, Chris (2005). "Chapter 8: Euro-Turks and Europeans". The New Turkey. London: Granta Books. pp. 186–202. ISBN 1-86207-865-3.

[353] "Turkey, Syria to forge defense industry cooperation". Today's Zaman. 2009-04-27.

[354] "Turkey, Syria conduct military drill, Israel disturbed". Today's Zaman. 2009-04-28.

[355] "Turkish PM Erdoğan slams Israel". Hürriyet.

[356] "Gül to urge Syria to contribute to Palestinian unity in visit". Today's Zaman. 2009-05-12.

[357] "Gül begins three-day visit to Syria, Israel talks on the agenda". Today's Zaman. 2009-05-15.

[358] "Syria says ready to resume talks with Israel". Today's Zaman. 2009-05-13.

[359] "Turkey urges Israel to accept Syria's overtures". Today's Zaman. 2009-05-17.

[360] "Assad: Syria has total confidence in Turkish mediation". Today's Zaman. 2009-05-18.

[361] "Peres urges Syria to join direct peace talks". Today's Zaman. 2009-05-19.

[362] Chulov, Martin; Hassan, Nidaa (7 June 2011). "Syrian town empties as government tanks mass outside". The Guardian. Retrieved 7 June 2011.

[363] "Turkish PM warns Syria against second Hama massacre". Dünya Bülteni. 2 May 2011.

[364] SEVİL KÜÇÜKKOŞUM (10 June 2011). "Turkey slams Damascus, refrains from calling fleeing Syrians 'refugees'". Hurriyet Daily News.

[365] BBC News - Syria unrest: Turkey presses Assad to end crackdown. Bbc.in (9 August 2011). Retrieved 23 June 2012.

[366] Turkish pilgrims attacked as four die in Syria, thenews.com, 22 November 2011.

[367] Turkish Muslim pilgrims' bus 'shot at in Syria', BBC, 21 November 2011.

[368] Muir, Jim. "Turkey Protests as Syrians Open Fire at Border". BBC News. BBC. Retrieved 9 April 2012.

[369] Reuters. "Syrian military says it downed Turkish fighter jet". BBC News. BBC. Retrieved 23 June 2012.

[370] Stack, Liam. "Turkey Vows to Take Action After Downing of Jet by Syria". The New York Times. New York Times Company. Retrieved 23 June 2012.

[371] Jonathon Burch & Erika Solomon (23 June 2012). "Turkish, Syrian forces seek downed Turkish jet". Reuters. Retrieved 24 June 2012.

[372] "Turkey, U.S. Officials Hold First Operational Meeting On Syria." AFP, 23 August 2012.

[373] Turkey-Syria border tension, Guardian, 4 October 2012

[374] "Turkey, Seeking Weapons, Forces Syrian Jet to Land". New York Times. 10 October 2012.

[375] "Turkey: Syrian plane was carrying ammunition". San Francisco Chronicle. 11 October 2012.

[376] "Turkey: Syrian plane was carrying ammunition". The Associated Press. 12 October 2012.

[377] "After civilian plane grounded, Syrian minister bashes Turkey's 'air piracy'". The Times of Israel. 11 October 2012.

[378] "'Turkey violated Convention on International Civil Aviation' – airline chief to RT'". Russia Today. 11 October 2012. Archived from the original on 12 October 2012.

[379] "Syria bans Turkey civilian flights over its territory". BBC News. 14 October 2012.

[380] "UPDATE 1-Shell from Syria hits Turkish health center - CNN Turk". Reuters. 23 October 2012.

[381] "Death toll rises to 42 as explosions hit Turkish town on border with Syria". Hurriyet Daily News. 11 May 2013. Retrieved 11 May 2013.

[382] "Blasts kill dozens in Turkish town Reyhanli on Syria border". BBC News. 11 May 2013. Retrieved 11 May 2013.

[383] "Deadliest Terror Attack in Turkey's History Might Be Another Attempt to Derail Peace Talks? But Which One? Syria or PKK?". The Istanbulian. 11 May 2013. Retrieved 11 May 2013.

[384] "Turkey Blames Syria's Assad for Its Deadliest Terror Attack". Bloomberg News. 11 May 2013. Retrieved 11 May 2013.

[385] "Turkish Armed Forces shot down Syrian jet". BBCTurkish. 23 March 2014. Retrieved 23 March 2014.

[386] "Turkish Armed Forces shot down Syrian jet". CNNTurk. 23 March 2014. Retrieved 23 March 2014.

www.ingramcontent.com/pod-product-compliance
Lightning Source LLC
LaVergne TN
LVHW080509200726
843507LV00008B/1058